The Capitalist Manifesto

Also by Johan Norberg

Open

Progress

The Capitalist Manifesto

Why the Global Free Market
Will Save the World

Johan Norberg

Atlantic Books
London

First published in hardback and trade paperback in Great Britain in 2023 by
Atlantic Books, an imprint of Atlantic Books Ltd.

3 5 7 9 10 8 6 4

A CIP catalogue record for this book is available from the British Library.

Hardback ISBN: 978 1 83895 789 6
Trade paperback ISBN: 978 1 83895 790 2
E-book ISBN: 978 1 83895 791 9

Printed in Great Britain by CPI Group (UK) Ltd, Croydon CR0 4YY

Atlantic Books
An imprint of Atlantic Books Ltd
Ormond House
26–27 Boswell Street
London
WC1N 3JZ

www.atlantic-books.co.uk

MIX
Paper | Supporting
responsible forestry
FSC
www.fsc.org   FSC® C171272

To classical liberals of all parties

CONTENTS

Preface

WHAT HAPPENED TO REAGAN AND THATCHER?

'No one is particularly keen on globalization now, except possibly Johan Norberg.'

PO TIDHOLM, SWEDISH PUBLIC RADIO, 29 MAY 2020

Twenty years ago I wrote a book in defence of global capitalism. I never thought I would do that. Capitalism, I had thought, was all about greedy monopolists and mighty landlords. But then I began to study the world and realized that it was in the least market-based societies that such elites were protected from the free choice of citizens and therefore had the greatest power. Paradoxically, it was capitalism – in the form of free markets and voluntary agreements based on private ownership – that threatened the powerful. The argument for capitalism is not that capitalists always behave well – if that were the case, we could safely give them monopoly power – but that they often *do not* behave well unless they have to. And it is freedom of choice and competition that force their hands.

In fact, Marx and Engels were right when they observed in that other manifesto, the communist one of 1848, that free markets had in a short time created greater prosperity and more technological innovation than all previous generations combined and, with infinitely improved communications and accessible goods, free markets had torn down feudal structures and national narrow-mindedness. Marx and Engels realized much better than socialists today that the free market is a formidable progressive force. (Unfortunately, they were not sufficiently dialectically minded to understand that communism was a reactionary counterforce that would bring societies back to a kind of electrified feudalism.)

A century and a half later, global capitalism made it possible for ever more people to free themselves from lords and monopolies. The growth of markets gave them the opportunity to choose, to bargain and to say no for the first time. Free trade gave them cheaper goods, new technologies and access to consumers in other countries. It lifted millions and millions from hunger and poverty.

However, at the turn of the millennium capitalism was under fierce attack. An international anti-capitalist movement wanted the government to take more control of the economy with a barrage of tariffs, regulations and taxes. Huge demonstrations took place against the World Trade Organization's negotiations for more open markets. Free trade, foreign investment and multinational corporations were accused of making the poor poorer. Attac, a French left-wing protectionist movement, spread rapidly throughout Europe. I saw them as a reactionary counterforce that would deprive poor societies of the freedoms they had just begun to take.

I compiled my arguments against them in the book *In Defence of Global Capitalism*, published in 2001. It was a classical liberal manifesto about why global justice takes more capitalism, not less. Timing is everything and the book became an international bestseller, translated into more than twenty-five languages, including Arabic, Persian, Turkish, Chinese and Mongolian.

And eventually, the globalization debate began to change. Supporters of open economies started fighting back. The critics were often driven by sincere anger about global poverty and injustice. We free traders could start from this common ground and show – with realistic explanations and clear statistics – that we needed freer markets to fight poverty and hunger. The more we discussed, the more it felt as if the opponents realized that it was not as simple as they had assumed, and parts of the audience began to change their mind. They had associated globalization with the status quo, the EU, the World Bank and the IMF, and were taken aback when challenged by opponents who were equally dissatisfied with today's injustices and offered radical solutions. Soon, the most common position in the debate was that poor countries need *more* trade, investment and entrepreneurship to develop economically and socially. As UN General Secretary Kofi Annan stated, the problem was too little globalization, not too much.

Soon, Attac lost its popular appeal and faded away. The British anti-capitalist George Monbiot apologized for his protectionism with an article in the *Guardian*: 'I was wrong about trade'. There he explained that a world without the WTO would probably be more unfair. And soon, a major campaign against the EU's agricultural protectionism was launched by the British charity Oxfam, which usually leans left and has been a critic of free markets.

'I've had an epiphany in recent years about commerce. It has upended everything for me,' declared Bono, the Irish rock musician and activist against global inequality. 'In dealing with poverty here and around the world, welfare and foreign aid are a Band-Aid. Free enterprise is a cure. Entrepreneurship is the most sure way of development.' It was a conversion that surprised not just his fans but himself too: 'Rock star preaches capitalism. Sometimes I hear myself and I just can't believe it.'[1]

It goes without saying that this was not just my doing. There were many others who fought day and night and there were many other factors that came into play, especially the simple fact that globalization delivered. Poverty declined in countries that integrated themselves into the global economy, faster than ever before. Oxfam even publicly denied that their new stance was a result of having been converted by me. And Bono has surely listened to me less than I have listened to U2.

The end of globalization was called off, but there was to be no happy-ever-after ending. The twenty years since I wrote my book have been a rough ride for the planet. We experienced the greatest financial crisis of modern times in 2008–9, a major pandemic that shut down the world and killed millions, chaos in the Middle East, terrorist attacks, the migration crisis, geopolitical tensions and the return of large-scale wars of aggression, as Putin invaded Ukraine. During the same period, global warming's calamitous effects on the planet began to make themselves felt for real.

This has all contributed to a new sense of vulnerability and a renewed suspicion of an open world economy. It inspired a longing for strong men and big governments to protect us from a dangerous world. WTO negotiations stalled completely, its dispute settlement mechanism was undermined by the US and, after the financial crisis, trade's share of GDP stopped increasing for the first time since World War II. Global economic freedom stagnated and the wave of democratization was ended by an authoritarian backlash.

In China, a thirty-year reform process was reversed, and the state began to regain lost ground. In the Western world, once again it was said that globalization has gone too far and that businesses must be controlled. Where international summits previously talked about opening up, deregulating and liberalizing (even though it was not always translated into action), language was suddenly blurred and fuzzy code words such as inclusivity, sustainability, strategic autonomy and 'partnership' between this and that pushed out concrete reform agendas.

Shortly afterwards, a peculiar intellectual swap took place. After the leftist offensive against globalization stumbled, the opposition suddenly migrated to the right. Fighting protectionism is like fighting a skin disease, as the US economist Paul Samuelson once said: no sooner do you cure it in one place than it appears somewhere else. A new generation of conservative politicians now sound very much like Attac did in 2001: the world is dangerous, there is no longer anyone in charge and free trade is destroying local traditions and good jobs. A 'globalist', US president Donald Trump explained, is a person 'frankly not caring about our country so much'.

The rapid progress in poor countries may have shown the West that those countries could benefit from globalization, but since the myth persists that the economy is a zero-sum game that assumes that someone's gain is always another one's loss, many have concluded that we in the rich world must be the losers. The worldview is the same, the roles are just reversed – twenty years ago free trade was considered bad because *we* exploited *them*, now it is considered bad because *they* exploit *us*. Twenty years ago, capitalism was wrong because supposedly it made the world's poor poorer. Now it is wrong because it makes the poor richer.

When I originally presented my pro-market, pro-trade and pro-immigration arguments I was often attacked for being on the 'crazy right'. When I express the same arguments today, I am sometimes accused of being 'woke left'. I'm not the one who's changed. But since right-wing nationalists do not have much more of an economic agenda than the urge to stop the world so that they can get off (and to throw out immigrants), their rage against globalization has created a new front for what used to be a classic left-wing programme of government intervention. To provide us with a false sense of security, governments have made trade, migration and construction more difficult, all but ensuring slower growth, hurting the very people politicians claim to be protecting.

Today's dominant narrative about global capitalism – shared by right-wing and left-wing populists but now also, in a milder form, by large sections of the political and economic establishment – does not deny that prosperity has been created during these twenty years, but it says it did end up in far too few hands and that those hands belong to the wrong people. The big global winner is China, they argue, which took our factories and our jobs – and it is a dangerous winner, stealing our technology and undermining our national security. This in turn has made it popular to talk about the global economy as a geopolitical winner-takes-all game, where we have to introduce trade barriers and renationalize value chains.

According to this narrative, growth in the West benefited mainly the rich, while the wages of the general public have stagnated for decades. Inequality has skyrocketed and employees have become a new precariat that has to drag itself along, insecure and stressed out. The factories have closed and the working class has been wiped out, sometimes even physically, by 'deaths of despair' (a term we'll look at in chapter 3) . In the market, monopolies have returned, predominantly in the form of a small circle of untouchable tech giants that have entered more and more areas and crushed the sympathetic mom-and-pop stores.

Apparently, it's that bad. And that is before we factor in global warming's effects on the planet. To counteract all this, we are told that big government must now return, to regain control, redistribute resources and, with enlightened industrial policy, steer resources to particular national industries and green technology.

This is what the debate looked like even before the pandemic. When the new coronavirus ravaged the planet, suspicion of the outside world and free trade exploded. Governments began to close their borders and demand that supply chains be repatriated. 'I don't want to talk about a victory lap,' Trump's rather enthusiastic business secretary said about the ravages of the virus, but 'I think it will help to accelerate the return of jobs to North America.' *Financial Times*' global business columnist Rana Foroohar declared that 'Globalisation as we've known it for the last forty years, has failed.'

Governments, meanwhile, decided that the way to protect the economy was bailouts for everyone – first for the financial sector, then for everybody else. People got used to the idea that gains are to be privatized but a growing share of losses are to be covered by taxpayers or central banks. When they run out of money, they just print more and when this creates inflation, people need another round of bailouts to compensate for higher prices. And so on. The pandemic, explained the Swedish Prime Minister Magdalena Andersson, was the definitive 'end of the neoliberal era inaugurated by Thatcher and Reagan'.

We don't just hear that from Social Democrats these days. Now right-wing populists, journalists and economists also claim that 'the Reagan/Thatcher era is over'. These two leaders are often used as symbols of the era of economic liberalization in the early 1980s, and I agree that it feels an awful lot like that era has come to an end.

Donald Trump's advisor Stephen Moore declared that the Republicans are no longer Reagan's party but Trump's, and that's exactly how the party comes across in their recent agitation against free trade, immigration and tech companies, not to mention lies about election fraud. (Reagan once called the peaceful transfer of power the 'magic' of the free world.) Thatcher's Tories have abandoned the European single market she was once instrumental in developing, and have simultaneously abandoned many other economic orthodoxies, toying with more active industrial policies and 'Buy British' slogans – a new attitude that Boris Johnson in an unguarded moment happened to summarize as 'fuck business'.

His short-lived successor, Liz Truss, who famously declared that large-scale imports of cheese were 'a disgrace', tried to invoke the Iron Lady, albeit through her boldness rather than her policies. Instead, Truss railed against the 'consensus of the Treasury, of economists, with the *Financial Times*' that budgets should be balanced and went on to doom her premiership with a massive, unfunded package of energy subsidies and tax cuts, which markets refused to finance.

Reagan and Thatcher are not usually declared dead as part of an objective assumption about which way the winds are blowing. These declarations are formulated as if their era was some kind of ideological deviation, when wild theorists and radicals dragged politics in a dogmatic neoliberal direction, and as if now we can finally return to common, interventionist sense. That is not what the reform era was about. Although liberal economists inspired many of the changes associated with Reagan and Thatcher, their era was never an ideological experiment but a pragmatic attempt to deal with the fact that an earlier model of inflation and regulation, along with a constantly expanding government, was in free fall.

One sign of this is that the 'Reagan/Thatcher era' started *before* Reagan and Thatcher. It was actually initiated by their political opponents. It was Reagan's Democratic representative, Jimmy Carter, who in his first State of the Union speech in 1978 declared: 'bit by bit we are chopping down the thicket of unnecessary federal regulations by which the government too often interferes in our personal lives and personal business.'[2] It was the Carter administration that deregulated aviation, railways, trucking and energy (and craft beer! Before him you would not have been allowed to drink a Samuel Adams). It was Carter who appointed Federal Reserve chairman Paul Volcker, who declared war on inflation in October 1979.

In Britain, Thatcher's predecessor, Labour's James Callaghan, explained to party members in 1976 that they used to believe recessions could be ended through higher spending and more inflation: 'I tell you now, in all candour, that that option no longer exists,' and in so far as it ever did exist, it was only by 'injecting a bigger dose of inflation into the economy, followed by a higher level of unemployment as the next step.'[3] Thatcher's fight against the unions to close 115 loss-making and environmentally damaging coal mines made her admired and hated, but did you know that the two previous Labour prime ministers, Callaghan and Harold Wilson, closed no less than 257 coal mines in total?[4]

It was not libertarian ideologues that carried out the great liberalizations of the 1970s, 80s and 90s. Socialist parties began to de-socialize India, Australia and New Zealand. Protectionist parties opened the economies of Brazil and Mexico. In China, Vietnam and Chile, economic liberalization was carried out by dictators, whose hearts did not in any way beat for liberal values. In most cases, these were parties and leaders who would have loved to be able to continue to control their people and the economy. But the idea of big government had an annoying problem that they could not escape – a problem that the Swedish Social Democratic Minister of Finance Kjell-Olof Feldt once summed up when speaking of the dreams of democratic socialism in his country: 'To put it simply, it just turned out to be impossible.'

And that's the point. It may sound irresistibly appealing. It is always popular when someone promises us the world, bailouts and free stuff. But it just does not work. Still doesn't. There are no free lunches, and wealth has to be created before it can be distributed. Sooner or later you always run out of other people's money, as Thatcher put it, and if you print more then sooner or later you'll ruin its value. And, as Liz Truss learned, sooner or later you'll run out of Thatcher quotes to defend everything-to-everyone budgets that just don't add up. Debts pile up and inflation rises, and you are going to have to start thinking instead about how wealth is created.

That will not stop new generations of politicians from repeating these mistakes. As memories of previous failures fade, the temptation to try again is often overwhelming. And with the simmering hostility towards foreigners and businesses, it might come in the form of outright irrational attempts at protectionism, top-down industrial policy, clumsy regulations and confiscatory taxes. It would squeeze growth out of the economy and hurt the most vulnerable. It would sabotage a global economy that has turned out to be the best hope for human progress.

Yes, we have had twenty terrible years, full of shocks, pandemics and war. And yet, in terms of human well-being, they have been the best twenty years in human history. Extreme poverty has been reduced by 70 per cent. This means that we got more than 138,000 new arguments for global capitalism every day since I wrote my first defence of it. That's how many people have risen out of poverty every day during these two decades: 138,000 men, women and children. Every day. Despite all these shocks and obstacles and despite the increase during the pandemic. That's progress worth fighting for, and encouraging in more places.

That is why these lessons have to be relearned, and the arguments against a reversal have to be restated. At least every twenty years we need a capitalist manifesto that makes the case for economic freedom, applied to the problems and conflicts of the present era. That's why I wrote this book. For all these reasons – and one more: some time in the last decade, economic issues stopped being a priority. Obviously, the debate continued, but it became a sideshow. Something else has captured hearts and minds and tweets. When the Cold War conflict between capitalism and communism was over, many felt that economic policy could disregard ideas and be reduced to a question of which party has the right set of skills and administrative dexterity. Instead of the struggle for freedom or class war, we got culture wars.

Where we once discussed where we were going, everyone suddenly started asking themselves who we are – and who does not fit in. Both the statist left and the nationalist right started engaging in some sort of purge of everything that does not fit into their pure, safe world. Borders would be closed, statues toppled, dissenters cancelled, 'woke' businesses threatened into silence.

The culture war is a zero-sum game about what kind of homogeneous identity should be imposed on everybody else. Capitalism, on the contrary, is a positive-sum game that creates growing, dynamic societies and so gives greater opportunities for all groups to live according to their identity and realize their visions and projects. Instead of 'victory or death' or 'silence is violence', the liberal capitalist puts 'live and let live – as long as you do not pick my pocket or break my leg'.

This book is an attempt to distract you from the culture war and get you back to the issues that are decisive for our future.

Why 'capitalism'? Words have an unfortunate tendency to confuse. Free market capitalism is not really about capital, it is about handing control of the economy from the top to billions of independent consumers, entrepreneurs and workers, and allowing them to make their own decisions about what they think will improve their lives. So careless talk about 'taking control of capitalism' actually means that governments take control of citizens.

But it doesn't sound like it, does it? One of my intellectual heroes, Deirdre McCloskey, complains that the word capitalism gives the misleading impression that it is about the rule of capital, rather than liberating people to make their own economic decisions, which is really what the free market is about: "'Capitalism' is a scientific mistake compressed into a single word, a dramatically misleading coinage by our enemies, and still used by the sadly misled among our friends.'[5] So why do I use it? Because, no matter what we think of it, and no matter which word we would prefer for a system of private property and free markets, this is the word that has become inextricably linked to it, and if its supporters don't fill that word with meaning, its opponents will.

It will become clear in the following pages that the market economy is not primarily about competition and rivalry but about cooperation and exchange. It's about being able to do something with others that you would not be able to do on your own. Similarly, neither did this book emerge from my brain as Athena out of Zeus's head, fully grown, in shining armour. It is the result of people I have met and books I have read, of researchers who have broadened my knowledge and opponents who have helped to correct my mistakes. This book is the product of the efforts of an incredible number of people, just like every product and service on the market, even if any mistakes are of course mine.

In that spirit of cooperation and solidarity, I would like to thank Mattias Bengtsson, Andreas Birro, Christian Sandström, Fredrik Segerfeldt, Patrik Strömer, Mattias Svensson and Daniel Waldenström for ideas, inspiration and data. I am deeply grateful to Caspian Rehbinder for useful comments and suggestions, in both form and substance. Thanks also to Benjamin Dousa and Andreas

Johansson Heinö for their role in bringing this book about, to my literary agent, Andrew Gordon, for being such a reliable champion for my work, to my editor at Atlantic, James Nightingale, for careful editing and valuable comments, and my copyeditor, Charlotte Atyeo, for her attention to detail.

I am especially grateful to you, Frida, for your love, patience and courage. I love capitalism, but I love you even more.

May the market force be with you – always.

Johan Norberg

1

LIFE UNDER
SAVAGE CAPITALISM

*'[After 1990] capitalism was suddenly free to lapse into
its most savage form.'*

NAOMI KLEIN[1]

Twenty years ago, I began *In Defence of Global
Capitalism* with a chapter about how the world was
improving faster than ever. I attacked the popular
perception that the world was getting worse, more dangerous and unfair, and that the poor were getting poorer.
In 1999, the World Bank claimed that 'world poverty has
increased and growth prospects have dimmed for developing countries'. The famous American activist Ralph Nader
declared: 'The essence of globalization is a subordination
of human rights, environmental rights, democracy rights
to the imperatives of global trade and investment.' Or as
Sweden's archbishop summarized the state of the world:
'our journey leads straight to hell'.[2] In contrast, I talked
about the strangely unheralded progress that I saw in poor
countries that had begun to liberalize their economies,

which now had better incomes, agricultural production, nutrition, health, vaccination and education.

It was not easy to get such information back then. For some strange reason, tax-funded international organizations still preferred to keep secret the data they had collected. It was four years before Gapminder was founded and Hans Rosling began to fill the gaps in our knowledge about world progress in a fun and easily accessible way, and ten years before Max Roser started Our World in Data, which compiles an incredible amount of user-friendly statistics.[3] But what I did find was enough to impress me and completely change the worldview I grew up with.

I was especially fascinated by the fact that global extreme poverty, contrary to the World Bank's claims but according to its own data, seemed to have decreased from 38 to 29 per cent in the 1990s.[4] I explained that poverty continued to decline rapidly and presented an extremely optimistic forecast that this could be halved by 2015. It was far exceeded. In 2015, extreme poverty was around 10 per cent.

Between 2000 and 2022, extreme poverty decreased in a way we have never seen before – from 29.1 per cent of the world's population to 8.4 per cent. (As recently as 1981, the figure stood at more than 40 per cent.) For the first time in history, fewer than one in ten people were poor. Despite the fact that the world population increased by more than 1.5 billion people during this period, the number of poor decreased by more than 1.1 billion. That is the greatest thing that has ever happened to mankind. The relentless hardship that most of humanity has suffered throughout its existence has been pushed back faster than ever in more places than ever. It is such a remarkable development that I must admit that I find it difficult to take writers and pundits seriously who do not take it as a central point of departure when analysing our time.

A common objection is that this poverty reduction is not real because it 'is just China'. It is a little strange to dismiss a country that holds one in five of the world's inhabitants when talking about global development. Furthermore, it's wrong. Even if China is removed from the 1990–2019 dataset, global poverty has been reduced by almost two-thirds, from 28.5 to around 10 per cent.

During the era of globalization, the development of the world's poorest countries has been so strong that extreme poverty in East Asia, South Asia, Latin America and the Middle East today is actually lower than it was in Western Europe in 1960, a time we remember today as the post-war boom. Only in sub-Saharan Africa is poverty higher than it was in Western Europe in 1960.[5]

The economist and Nobel laureate Angus Deaton has written: 'Some argue that globalization is a neoliberal conspiracy designed to enrich a very few at the expense of the many. If so, that conspiracy was a disastrous failure – or helped more than a billion people as an unintended consequence. If only unintended consequences were worked so favorably.'[6]

Other indicators that I looked at have continued to show very rapid improvements, partly because technology has become cheaper and because local purchasing power has increased.[7] Between 1990 and 2020, the proportion of children who die before the age of five decreased from 9.3 per cent to 3.7 per cent. Despite a significantly larger population today, this means that almost 7.5 million fewer children die annually compared with the early 1990s.[8] During the same period, maternal mortality decreased by more than 55 per cent.

Global life expectancy increased from 64 years to almost 73 years between 1990 and 2019. The proportion of the world population receiving basic education has skyrocketed and the illiteracy rates have almost halved: from 25.7 per cent to 13.5 per cent. In the age group 15–24, illiteracy is now just over 8 per cent. Between 2000 and 2020, child labour in the age group 5–17 decreased globally from 16 to just under 10 per cent.[9]

Global Progress: 1990–2020[10]

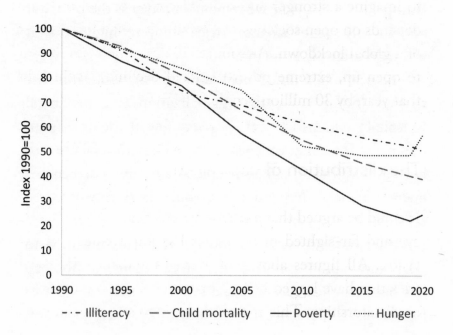

The three decades after 1990 – when capitalism, according to Naomi Klein, enveloped the planet in its 'most savage form' – have seen greater improvements in human living conditions than the three millennia before that combined. It has also been three difficult decades, full of wars, crises and injustices. I am not saying that the era has been unequivocally good, only that it has been better than any other era humanity has experienced.

The pandemic reversed some gains – when the world was closed and trade, migration and education were blocked. It seems like life expectancy was pushed back to seventy-one in 2021, and the number of people in extreme poverty probably increased by almost 70 million during the first year of the pandemic. Based on various estimates of income, poverty and health, the world was thrown back in time by two to three years as a result of the pandemic. It is difficult to imagine a stronger and more tragic proof that progress depends on open societies and economies than the disaster of a global lockdown. As soon as 2021, as the world began to open up, extreme poverty started declining again – in that year, by 30 million people.

The distribution of capitalism

It could be argued that a person who is near-sighted in one eye and far-sighted in the other has, on average, perfect vision. All figures above are averages and include countries that have lagged behind or even collapsed due to war or dictatorships. This means that progress has been even higher elsewhere. These successful countries are found on all continents and in all cultural spheres. The only common denominator is that, for one reason or another, they have given their citizens a little more freedom to innovate, create, work, buy and sell.[11]

We can see this by looking at when and where economies took off historically. During the first 1,800 years of the Common Era, global average income barely budged. But 200 years ago, something suddenly happened in Britain, which was then the world's freest economy. The Industrial Revolution began to create rapid growth and Britain's extreme poverty rate was halved between 1820 and 1850, which was something completely unprecedented. Then Britain was followed by Western Europe and the United States, which began to take over the position as the freest economy. The Scandinavian economies started to be liberalized in the middle of the nineteenth century and then had a hundred years of faster economic development than any other country, with the exception of Japan, which opened its economy after the Meiji Restoration of 1868 and reduced poverty from 80 to just over 20 per cent in half a century.[12]

But most of the south and east, which were subjected to authoritarian leaders and colonial masters with command economies, stagnated. The famous sociologist Max Weber felt compelled to write books on why Confucianism and Hinduism make it difficult to modernize societies and economies. We got used to dividing the world into industrialized countries and developing countries – rich and poor.

Global GDP per capita between the years 1–2020[13]

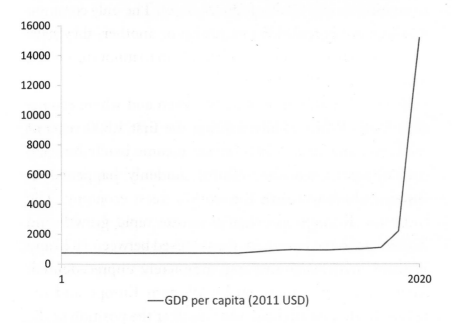

—GDP per capita (2011 USD)

However, four East Asian tigers would soon disrupt our worldview. The British colony of Hong Kong and the city-state of Singapore did the opposite of all other countries, and opened their economies wide, without trade barriers. The experts claimed that free trade would knock out the small manufacturing sectors they had, but, on the contrary, they industrialized at a record pace and shocked the outside world by becoming even richer than the old colonial master, Britain.

Taiwan and South Korea learned from this and began to liberalize their economies with amazing results.[14] Their rapid growth took them from being some of the poorest countries in the world to some of the richest in a few generations. It was a global wake-up call because it was so easy to compare what the Chinese in Taiwan achieved compared to the Chinese in Mao's China, and what the Koreans in the capitalist south created compared to the Koreans in the communist north. In the mid-1950s, Taiwan was only marginally richer than China. In 1980, it was four times richer. In 1955, North Korea was richer than South Korea. (The north was, after all, where mineral resources and power generation were located when the country was partitioned.) Today, South Korea is twenty times richer than North Korea.

It was no longer possible to say that only the Western world could become rich through capitalism, so a new narrative took hold: although a few developing countries might be able to enter global markets from the periphery, it is only because they are very small, almost insignificant. Strangely enough, today you sometimes hear the opposite: that developing countries might make it, but only if they are very large.

This is due to the transformation of two giants, China and India, which for decades were held back by, in one case, a communist despot, and in the other a democratic but strictly protectionist command economy. Therefore, people said that Chinese and Indians will be successful all over the world – except in China and India. But then, in 1976, China's dictator Mao Zedong, as the US economist Steven Radelet put it, 'single-handedly and dramatically changed the direction of global poverty with one single act: he died'.

His successor, Deng Xiaoping, began to accept the private enterprise that peasants and villagers secretly engaged in and extended it to the entire economy. All the restrained creativity and ambition was finally let loose and China grew at record speed. Ironically, intellectuals around the world – modern-day Max Webers – soon explained that this is itself not that strange, as Confucianism made it easy to modernize the economy.

India held back a little longer, but an Indian economist, Parth Shah, tells me that the country started looking at what was happening around them, in Taiwan, South Korea and now also China: 'We saw that they actually changed their model and they did succeed in what they had done, and it was time for India to learn the lesson.'[15]

That was decisive in 1991, when a debt-financed boom crashed and the foreign exchange reserve had shrunk to such a level that India was three weeks from running out of money. The crisis prompted the Minister of Finance Manmohan Singh to quote the nineteenth-century romantic Victor Hugo in parliament: 'No power on earth can resist an idea whose time has come.' The idea was to dismantle trade barriers and stifling regulations that held India back and kept half the population in extreme poverty.

In the past, economists spoke condescendingly of the 'Hindu growth rate' as if there was some kind of complacency built into the country's tradition that stopped the economy from growing faster than the population. After the reforms of 1991 and those that followed, this culture changed as if by magic and growth took off. Today, average income is three times greater than before reform and extreme poverty is only one-fifth of previous levels.

Around the same time, communism in Central and Eastern Europe finally fell, but its economic rivalry with capitalism had, of course, long since been decided. It's easy to think that these countries were never close to the market economies, but in 1950 countries such as the Soviet Union, Poland, Czechoslovakia and Hungary had a GDP per capita about a quarter higher than poor Western countries such as Spain, Portugal and Greece. In 1989, the eastern states were nowhere close. The eastern part of Germany was richer than West Germany before World War II. When the Berlin Wall fell on 9 November 1989, East Germany's GDP per capita was not even half that of West Germany's.[16]

Of these countries, those that liberalized the most have on average developed the fastest and established the strongest democracies. An analysis of twenty-six post-communist countries showed that a 10 per cent increase in economic freedom was associated with a 2.7 per cent faster annual growth.[17] Political and economic institutions have improved the most in the Central and Eastern European countries that are now members of the EU, not least the Baltic countries, Estonia, Latvia and Lithuania. Today, they are some of the freest countries in the world and have more than tripled average incomes since independence. But one can also observe a recent reformer like Georgia. It was seen as an economic basket case, but after the Rose Revolution in 2003 it increased per capita incomes almost threefold and cut extreme poverty rates by almost two-thirds.

All over the world this connection is discernible. Economic and social progress does not happen because a country is small or because it is big, and it has much less to do with religion and tradition than we think. (Religions and traditions are complex things and societies constantly reinterpret them in order to fit into the prevailing culture and economy.) It has to do with freedom. Where people are given a little bit of freedom, they begin to develop their countries and make great progress. The unequal distribution in the world is due to the uneven distribution of capitalism: people who have it become rich; those who do not have it stay poor.

Why not Latin America?

Latin America has long suffered from a phenomenon that can be called growth without development – when the economy and export revenues grow without the population as a whole getting better off. This was the result of a colonial legacy that was not uprooted but in many ways deepened by domestic elites after the independence of Spain and Portugal. The economies were semi-feudal with a small, protected landowner class with colossal lands and a huge class of poor and uneducated farm workers.

Landowners were able to expand their production by taking more land from the indigenous population and exploiting the abundance of labour. Therefore, there were never any incentives to invest the proceeds in better technology and more highly productive agriculture. At the same time, discrimination, business regulations and a lack of education stopped entrepreneurship in other sectors. Latin American intellectuals of the 1950s and 1960s who were rightly appalled by this hacienda economy based on raw materials and agricultural products developed the 'dependency theory', which declared that the way out was to invest in 'import substitution', where the state kept imported goods out with high tariffs and instead supported domestic industrialization with subsidies and regulations. The cruel irony is that this policy reinforced every problem these intellectuals had warned about.

Inefficient, protected industrial companies could now enrich themselves at the expense of poor consumers and small businesses, so inequality increased even further. In the early 1960s, average tariffs could reach a few hundred per cent and were supplemented by quotas and other trade barriers. An Argentine truck, which in fact was mostly an imported truck disassembled at the border and then reassembled, cost almost one and a half times more than the world market price. A Chilean car could cost three times as much. Instead of focusing on specialization and economies of scale, companies began to do just about any product in small series at a very high cost per item.[18]

As companies became politicized, those who wanted to thrive had to get involved in politics, with even more corruption as a result. Since domestic businesses were not pressured by competition to modernize technology and knowledge, governments had to attract multinational corporations that could do so, lured there by promises of new protections and privileges. And absurdly, these economies became even more dependent on the export of raw materials and agricultural goods since it was the only way to finance the import of machinery and inputs for closed economies with small domestic markets.

Industries could still expand, but it was a growth of inefficient and expensive production, increasingly funded with loans from global financial markets. That road closed when international interest rates rose sharply and Mexico declared bankruptcy in August 1982. The whole region suffered a devastating economic collapse that has been summarized as 'the lost decade'. Almost in a state of panic, country after country had to abandon its economic models, clean up inefficient structures and open up to the outside world. As a final, spectacular irony, it was one of the pioneers of dependency theory, the sociologist Fernando Henrique Cardoso, who began liberalizing Brazil in the role of president between 1995 and 2002. 'To fight hunger effectively, aid is necessary – especially in famine-ridden countries. But the fact remains that international trade, as defined by a fair, rules-based system in the WTO, is much more important, not only to fight hunger, but also to foster development worldwide', the old protectionist eventually explained.[19]

Since 1990, Latin America's economies have begun to grow again, albeit with a legacy of commodity dependence and political instability that creates vulnerabilities and volatility. The region's inequality has finally begun to diminish. In countries such as Brazil, Chile and Peru, income inequality has decreased by around 10 per cent. Extreme poverty has decreased by three-quarters.[20]

Latin America's freest economies are Chile and Peru, which have also been the most successful ones in recent decades. In the mid-1970s, Chile was poorer than the Latin American average, but after market reforms – first under the brutal dictator Pinochet, but then under democratic left- and right-wing governments – the country grew so fast that it is now almost twice as rich as the average.

Peru's policies are chronically chaotic and the country has had eleven presidents since the turn of the millennium, but since economic liberalization in the 1990s, the economy has grown 150 per cent under nationalists and populists, technocrats and left-wing radicals. Extreme poverty has decreased by 85 per cent. Such progress creates new forms of discontents, as those who have been left behind want to join in, and those who get ahead raise their expectations. Riding this wave, left-wing radicals were recently elected presidents in both Chile and Peru. But the most fascinating aspect of the leftist populist Pedro Castillo winning Peru's presidential election in 2021 was his campaign message: 'No poor people in a rich country.' No one would ever have thought of describing Peru as a 'rich country' in 1990, when it was as poor as Congo-Brazzaville.

Why not Africa?

Speaking of Congo-Brazzaville, in most discussions of global development, sub-Saharan Africa is mentioned as some kind of a synonym for hopelessness. That was not always the case. In the 1960s, most African countries were richer and had higher growth than Asian countries, and were blessed with more natural resources. Economists such as Gunnar Myrdal believed more in Africa than Asia, where they worried that governments were not strong enough to push industrialization and Confucian attitudes were thought to block innovation and development. In 1967, the World Bank's chief economist listed seven African economies that he thought could grow by more than 7 per cent annually. Thirty years later, two other World Bank economists concluded that these seven countries had since registered *negative* growth.[21]

Sub-Saharan Africa is not the poorest part of the world because the region lacks the economic conditions needed for growth but because it has lacked freedom. Its economy is based on a centuries-old development. Long before colonialism, many Africans suffered from despotism and conflict, and before the transatlantic slave trade, they suffered from the indigenous slave trade and the trans-Saharan one. But as Ghanaian economist George Ayittey has shown, there is also a strong African tradition of private property and markets with free pricing. Most parts of the continent were integrated into vast trade networks where merchants, goods and currencies moved about freely.[22]

European colonizers undermined these markets in two ways: partly by dividing the continent and isolating the populations from each other, partly by creating centralized structures in each colony, where farmers and workers were plundered to enrich robber barons thousands of miles away. The next tragedy was that when African countries gained their independence after World War II, domestic elites did not dismantle colonial structures but took them over. Whether the new leaders called themselves liberation heroes, Marxists, nationalists or anti-communists, they became occupiers who continued to plunder their people. They seized natural resources to enrich themselves and forced the rural population to produce food at prices far below the market rate.

What Western economists thought of as strongmen who would enforce stability and development were, in fact, looters who vacuumed their lands for assets. In almost every country, strict government control, planned economies and import substitution were applied in weak domestic markets, isolated from neighbours through arbitrary borders. Often, even domestic tariffs were introduced to stifle spontaneous trade. Africa's dictators had many conflicting aims, but the president of the Club du Sahel, Anne de Lattre, once summed up their common denominator: 'Well, there is one thing we all agree on: that private traders should be shot.'[23]

Western countries made the situation worse by sending development aid to undemocratic, closed economies just because they were former colonies, which enriched the despots and prolonged the oppression. By handing over huge amounts of capital to the leaders of desperately poor countries, the West intensified a tragedy created by the nationalization of natural resources: the path to wealth for disadvantaged groups was to take up arms and invade the capital.

It became an orgy of corruption, aid dependence and underdevelopment. Major food exporters soon became dependent on imports for survival. State-owned companies that were supposed to bring glory and prosperity instead destroyed wealth as they turned every valuable resource into expensive, worthless products. The only thing that saved factories from destroying even more value was that mismanaged electricity companies caused constant power outages. Like Latin America, African states extended this death march by borrowing, and just like in Latin America, the debt crisis of the 1980s became devastating. Machines ground to a halt, the trucks stopped and deliveries of food and medicine failed to appear. In the mid-1980s, many of the countries with the richest lands and the greatest natural resources were poorer than they had been at independence – except, of course, the leaders whose ideology has sometimes been called Swiss bank socialism. A generation of children became shorter due to malnutrition, but the leaders' cars and yachts only got longer.

In an attempt to get out of the quicksand, many African countries implemented reforms in the 1990s that made me write in *In Defence of Global Capitalism* that it was not impossible for the 2000s to become 'Africa's century'. The reforms have not continued in a way that makes this probable, but median growth per capita on the continent still increased from 0.2 per cent in 1980–99 to 1.6 per cent in 2000–19. Throughout this period, the African countries that opened their economies to the outside world grew three times as fast as those that did not. As a whole, Africa's GDP per capita grew by 35 per cent between 2000 and 2019, faster than the world as a whole. Extreme poverty decreased from almost 60 per cent to just over 40 per cent. Industrial production nearly doubled and the share of the population working in manufacturing has increased.[24]

It is often said that Africa is doomed to underdevelopment due to history, geography, ethnicity, culture, climate, disease, drought or any other factor. But how do we know that it is not rather a matter of corrupt leaders destroying the possibilities of Africans with control, corruption and confiscation? Imagine that an African country had taken a different path after independence, had developed democracy, independent courts and freedom of the press, and had applied free enterprise, low taxes and free trade? Could it not have worked even there, even though the country may have lacked a coastline, mostly consists of desert and was hit harder than others by HIV/AIDS?

In fact, there is one such country: Botswana in southern Africa. How did it work? Very well, thank you. In fact, better than in any other country in the world. During the forty years after 1960, the Asian tigers and China grew annually between 5.2 and 5.8 per cent per capita. Botswana, on the other hand, grew by an incredible 6.4 per cent on average – more than ten times faster than the world average.[25] Since 1985, extreme poverty has declined from 42 to 15 per cent, compared with 40 per cent in Africa as a whole.

Some would object that this is only because Botswana has diamonds. But valuable natural resources are more the rule than the exception in Africa, and are often something that creates conflict and stagnation. What distinguishes Botswana in the region is not the resources but the fact that it did not nationalize them. Instead it privatized them, and after independence from Britain in 1966 it created a stable regulatory framework that attracted foreign investment.[26]

There is another African country that has had a high degree of economic liberalism for a long time: Mauritius. In 1961, the Nobel laureate James Meade predicted that in such a small country, with ethnic divisions, without natural resources and dependent on a single commodity (sugar), the 'outlook for peaceful development is weak'. But precisely because Mauritius was so small, it realized early on that it could not do without world trade, and import substitution was abolished as early as the 1970s. The country introduced export-processing zones where a deregulated textile industry could grow, and the economy has continued to diversify with a modern service sector. After uninterrupted high growth, Mauritius was classified by the World Bank as a high-income country in 2019. Even though it slipped back because of Covid-19, it will probably soon rise again. Today, Mauritius and Botswana have GDP per capita similar to a EU country like Bulgaria.

In recent years, countries such as Uganda and Rwanda have tried to imitate such policies after brutal episodes of conflict and massacre. Although they have had authoritarian leaders, they have liberalized their economies more than their neighbours and also grown faster. While Africa's GDP per capita grew by 35 per cent after 2000, Uganda did so by 75 per cent and Rwanda by 157 per cent. As Africa's population continues to grow rapidly, it is crucial for the future of the continent and for hundreds of millions of young people that such liberalization deepens and spreads, and that hopeful ideas about African free trade unions do not remain on the drawing board.

Meeting your grandkids

The broadest and most systematic measure of free markets is the Economic Freedom of the World, conducted by the Canadian Fraser Institute in conjunction with partners around the world. Each year 165 countries are assessed on the basis of five broad categories that consists of forty-two different components – the size and tax burden of the state, legal system and property rights, the monetary system, free trade, and regulations. Its data reveal that nothing improves people's lives as much as the freedom to look for better jobs, find new markets and invest in the future.[27]

When you compare the economically freest quarter of countries with the least-free quarter, you see that GDP per capita is more than seven times higher in the free countries, while extreme poverty is as much as sixteen times greater in the least-free countries. In addition, this difference is reflected in better access to nutrition, healthcare and security. For example, the average life expectancy in the most

Economic freedom and income per capita[28]

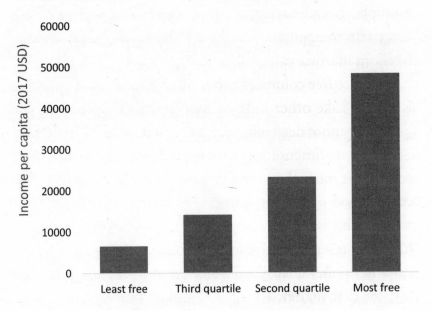

The world's countries by level of economic freedom

economically free countries is almost fifteen years longer. As Robert Lawson, one of the scholars behind the index, told me, the difference between living to the age of sixty-five or to eighty is the chance to see potential grandchildren grow up. Capitalism is sometimes characterized by expensive watches and fast cars, but what gets overlooked is the fact that it enables us to get to know our grandkids.

A review of 1,303 academic articles that explored the index showed that the correlation between economic freedom and societal outcomes was overwhelmingly positive: countries with freer markets have faster growth, better wages, greater poverty reduction, more investment, less corruption, higher subjective well-being and are more democratic, with greater respect for human rights.[29] At the same time, the data show that you do not have to get high grades in each individual category to perform well overall. For example, Scandinavian countries have comparatively high taxes but compensate for this by having higher economic freedom in other categories.

Why are free countries better off? What is cause and what is effect? Like other indexes that provide snapshots of the world, it cannot determine the issue on its own. What if rich, happy, well-functioning democracies decide to liberalize economies more than others? Then it is not capitalism that causes good outcomes but good outcomes that cause capitalism. This is a complex issue that must be combined with historical research and studies of individual countries before and after policy changes. The Western world and East Asia (or, for that matter, China and India) were not rich when they liberalized their economies, but they liberalized because they *were not*. As they became richer, they continued to increase freedom in certain areas but also expanded public spending simply because growth made it possible for them to do so. (Despite all the casual talk about a dismantling of the welfare state since the Reagan/Thatcher era, social spending as a share of GDP grew by about half in the United States and the United Kingdom in 1980–2010.)[30]

Sometimes a snapshot can actually give the appearance that economic freedom creates social problems, since many countries abolish controls and open markets because the previous model had created a catastrophic situation. Many critics of *In Defence of Global Capitalism* made a point of this. When I wrote that liberalization lifted countries, they argued that many countries that had just liberated their markets were at the absolute bottom. Sometimes they had a point. During the 1980s and 90s, it was often countries in disintegration that began to open their economies in desperation, and it was often a painful process. Countries that have spent money they did not have on things they didn't need will obviously have to implement tough austerity measures that suppress the economy for several years. When they ran out of money, many leaders sacrificed resources for education and healthcare rather than on industrial subsidies and the military, and then blamed everything on 'neoliberalism'.

Furthermore, many mistakes were made during the reform processes, because of bad luck, ignorance or plain corruption. If you privatize companies without first having competitive markets, you only create new, private monopolies. And markets without rule of law and protected property rights often hand control to states, oligarchs and criminals.

It took a long time for some countries to get this right. Some, like Russia, have still not done so. In the 1990s the Russian government sold powerful natural resource monopolies to cronies for a song. When Putin got into power, he just took the monopolies from the oligarchs and handed them over to his own friends instead.

For all these reasons, this made it difficult to perceive much of a growth spurt in emerging markets in the 1980s and 90s, even after reforms. One of the critics was the economist William Easterly, who was particularly influential because he worked at the World Bank, which had finally begun to recommend liberalization. In a 2001 study, Easterly pointed to the minimal growth in poor countries as a 'major disappointment' for those with great expectations of reform. Some who made a big deal out of Easterly's conclusion have missed that he repeated his effort in 2019 and this time he observed a different result. He now says that he underestimated how few reforms had actually been undertaken in many countries at the time of the previous survey, and now finds that growth has been rapid in countries where they have begun to be introduced. Easterly states: 'the previous disappointment now needs an update'.[31]

This suggests that we cannot just look at lots of countries as a group, but must examine more closely what policies they actually pursued. For that reason, one study distinguished between countries that implemented substantial economic liberalization and those that did not, from 1970 to 2015. In a database of 141 countries, they found forty-nine countries that had reformed their economy. Over a five-year period, annual growth in those countries was on average about 2.5

percentage points higher than in similar countries that did not liberalize. This means that those countries were 13 per cent richer after five years. Another study with a narrower definition of reformed countries showed that for the first two years they grew more slowly than other countries – which is often the result of changing policies in times of crisis – but then they began to beat them, and after a decade were more than 6 per cent richer.[32]

Reforms made in low- and middle-income countries, combined with greater free trade, cheaper transport and better communication technology, led to a historic shift some time in the 1990s: poor countries began to grow faster than rich ones. Economists have always believed that they would do so, as they can use technologies and solutions that have already been developed at great cost in the leading countries. But this convergence did not take place before the 1990s, since global markets were not very open until then and protected companies had not been pressured to upgrade methods and technologies by the competition.

In addition, the poor faced an ancient problem. Their fastest way to development would be to gain access to the technology that meant no longer having to dig with a shovel, spin by hand or use scythes to cut grains, crops and grass. But who has an interest in disseminating such technology and, above all, who wants to invest resources in developing it in a form that suits their particular level of technical infrastructure and local conditions? Leading economies have no interest in creating technology that would make it much more efficient to manufacture, say, industrial goods manually instead of with robots. So if poorer countries wanted to take the first steps towards industrialization, they would have to settle for much older technology.

Then there was a revolution, thanks to the emergence of international supply chains. Foreign investors and global companies now consider suppliers in a poor country an integral part of their own business and it is in their own commercial interest to invest massively in their productivity. This is one reason why many countries that have been integrated into global supply chains – not least through much-maligned low-wage factories and 'sweatshops' – have been able to skip several stages of development and grow at a record pace. Once you have built factories, roads and ports to manufacture and transport clothes and toys, you can then also use them to produce and export high-tech components.[33]

Surprisingly, this spread of technology has gone hand in hand with stronger local protection for intellectual property. In many ways it is a prerequisite: companies would not be interested in investing so much technology in other parts of the world if everything could be instantly copied by the factory on the other side of the road.

This technological advance – combined with the fact that low- and middle-income countries had stronger macroeconomic stability and experienced fewer crises – helped them to grow. In 1960–99, high-income countries grew 1.4 percentage points faster than low- and middle-income countries per capita annually, thus contributing to global inequality. In 2000–19, low- and middle-income countries grew 2 per cent faster than rich countries and thus got a little closer to them with each passing year. It is an unweighted average for all countries, so it is not a matter of a few big shots raising the average. Vanuatu and China weigh equally heavily.[34]

There is no guarantee that this convergence will continue. It depends on local politics and the openness of the world economy. If rich countries go further to repatriate supply chains, this will deprive the world's poor of many opportunities.

It is also probable that not every country that grew faster did so because they had managed to create a growth model that will keep on delivering every year. Instead, in some countries the growth spurt came from getting rid of witless leaders and insanely ineffective policies. We have yet to see if those countries can move from avoiding an outright destruction of wealth to policies that create much more of it in the long run. But as this seems to be the first time since the Industrial Revolution – researchers speculate that it may be the first time since the sixteenth century – that global inequality has declined, it may be worth stopping and reflecting on its importance.

Strong men make weak nations

Just as there are success stories on all continents, there are also governments that engage in self-harm on all continents. In *In Defence of Global Capitalism* I warned against Zimbabwe, where dictator Robert Mugabe declared that he would show the world that the 'neoliberal model' and its wild market forces could be dismantled.[35] He nationalized agriculture, financed the state through the printing press and handled the subsequent hyperinflation with price controls. The result was a historic collapse. Between 2000 and 2008, GDP per capita collapsed by about half.

At the same time, on the other side of the Atlantic, in Venezuela, the authoritarian populist Hugo Chávez and his disciple Nicolás Maduro initiated a similar policy of massive spending, corruption and nationalization. The difference was that Chávez had control over the world's largest oil reserves at a time when oil prices were soaring, so he received almost $1,000 billion that could keep that policy afloat for a little longer. That was enough for Chávez to be the left's favourite demagogue for a while. Bernie Sanders said that the American dream was more alive in Venezuela than in the US. Labour's Jeremy Corbyn praised Chávez for showing that 'the poor matter and wealth can be shared'. Oxfam called Venezuela 'Latin America's inequality success story'. In an open letter to 'Dear President Chávez', luminaries of the Left such as Jesse Jackson, Naomi Klein, Howard Zinn and others state that they 'see Venezuela not only as a model democracy but also as a model of how a country's oil wealth can be used to benefit all of its people.'[36]

On paper, that $1,000 billion was enough to make every extremely poor individual in Venezuela a millionaire. But still, it is not much money if you do not invest it productively and if you destroy the ability to create new wealth with nationalization and price controls. When the price of oil began to fall only slightly, it became obvious that the business sector was in a shambles and the oil industry had been demolished by corrupt mismanagement and underinvestment. The result was one of the worst economic disasters to have occurred anywhere in the world in peacetime. Between 2010 and 2020, Venezuela's average income plummeted by an incomprehensible 75 per cent. South America's richest country suddenly turned into South America's poorest country with breadlines and a mass exodus from an increasingly tyrannical state. Around seven million Venezuelans have fled the crumbling country, an unbelievable 25 per cent of the country's population.

Since then, Venezuela has been less frequently mentioned as the hope of the international working class. This is because the country followed the three steps of socialism, which were identified by the British economics writer Kristian Niemietz when he studied how an admiring outside world viewed countries such as the Soviet Union, China, Cuba and Venezuela:[37]

Step 1: *The honeymoon.* The strongman distributes the country's resources and Western supporters declare triumphantly that he has shown that socialism is superior to capitalism and should be introduced everywhere, instantly.

Step 2: *The excuses.* The honeymoon does not last for ever. Soon, the outside world receives information about how the economy doesn't work, resources run out and problems pile up. Now the admirers become defensive and explain that the difficulties are due to bad luck, the wrong administrators ending up in the wrong places, falling commodity prices, bad weather that destroyed the crops, or sabotage from the elites or the outside world. If not for that, you would all have seen how well socialism works.

(In Venezuela, for example: 'They were unlucky with the oil price' – despite the fact that the price in 2010 was still around six times higher than when Chávez took office. 'It is because of US sanctions' – even though sanctions against the oil industry were not introduced until 2019, when the collapse was already a fact.)

Step 3: *'It was not real socialism.'* In the end, it's impossible to deny that the economy is not working, hunger is rising and people are fleeing for their lives. No one wants to be associated with the experiment any more. Now instead it is said that the country never introduced real socialism but some form of corrupt state capitalism that only appropriated the socialist brand, and it is intellectually dishonest to use that failure as evidence that socialism is not working, especially as real socialism right now is being developed elsewhere, in the hopeful country X, which you should look at instead. (At which point the foreign admirers move on to the next experiment and the process begins again from step 1.)

To witness the damage a single person can inflict on a country, one can head to South Africa. Following the liberation from apartheid, Nelson Mandela, as president from 1994, created a climate of reconciliation while democratizing the country and liberalizing the economy. Under Mandela and his successor, Thabo Mbeki, inflation was tamed, government debt was halved and the growth rate reached 5 per cent. The outside world thought South Africa could be the next economic miracle. But the leader of the ANC's left wing, Jacob Zuma, agitated against this 'neoliberal' model and gained power in 2009–18 on a programme promising that state control of the economy would create fair distribution.

He really did change things – for the worse. Zuma jacked up public spending, but for consumption and corruption, not investment. State-owned companies were drained by Zuma and his lackeys, who are suspected of having looted about the equivalent of 20 per cent of GDP. Constant power outages and collapsing infrastructure contributed to growth collapsing and soon becoming negative. After being halved under the predecessors, public debt doubled under Zuma. Extreme poverty had also halved under the previous administration; under Zuma it not only stopped declining but even began to increase.[38]

That's the way it usually goes. Strongmen who complain that growth takes too long to provide results are like the farmer who has no patience with the harvest and quickly makes himself popular by letting everyone gorge on the seed. Fewer seeds means you will have less to eat next season. Sooner or later, you'll run out of other people's harvests, as Thatcher would have said.

Some long for a dictator like Chile's Pinochet or China's Deng Xiaoping who they assume will establish order and create economic development in a poor country. However, they are rare exceptions, not the rule. It is far more likely that an authoritarian will destroy the economy than save it. Contrary to popular myth, low-income democracies have had higher growth than low-income dictatorships since 1960.[39] It is just that the more capricious policies of dictators create a wider variety of outcomes, so at each given moment there is always a couple of despots who can report superior growth and can be applauded at Davos. But on average, dictatorships perform worse and are more prone to sudden, sharp dips – often the same countries that grew faster the previous decade. Investors, captivated by the strongman's ability to get things done, soon realize that this ability extends to seizing their business or blocking the ports if he suddenly fancies doing that instead.

Yet this fact is often obscured for a long time, since dictatorships lie about their economic performance. By comparing a country's reported growth rate with its night-time light, which is strongly correlated with growth but cannot be manipulated as easily, US economist Luis Martínez has shown that autocracies exaggerate their annual growth numbers by around 35 per cent.[40] Revealingly, this mismatch between growth and light did not appear until after the dictatorships were too rich to receive foreign aid, and it appeared in areas that are highly reliant on information provided by the state, like investment and government spending.

One study showed that anti-capitalist populists in Latin American countries such as Venezuela, Nicaragua and Bolivia on average make their countries 20 per cent poorer than comparable countries.[41] A more comprehensive database of fifty populist leaders on both the right and the left (sometimes democratically elected), between 1900 and 2018, reveals that in the long run it is almost impossible to find someone who creates the thriving economy they all promise. With populists in power, the economy fares worse both in relation to the country's previous trend and the global average. Fifteen years after they take control, their economies are, on average, more than a tenth smaller than comparable economies. The database shows that the economy does just as badly under right-wing and left-wing populists; the difference is that right-wing populists also tend to increase income inequality.[42]

When people finally see that the harvest is withering away, the populists have already changed the rules of the game so that they can cling to power despite popular dissatisfaction. On average, press freedom decreased by 7 per cent during their reign, civil rights by 8 per cent and political freedom by 13 per cent.[43]

What populists fail to see is that there are no perfect solutions, just trade-offs. When I hear populists on the right and left say that there are no such difficult trade-offs and that they can solve our problems here and now, quickly and easily (Trump: 'I will give you everything') if they just get the treacherous elites out of the way, I think of the story of the man who comes to the job interview:

'It says in your CV that you are quick at mathematics. What is seventeen times nineteen?'

'Sixty-three.'

'Sixty-three? That's not even close!'

'No, but it was quick.'

2

AT EACH OTHER'S SERVICE

'In the pre-capitalist world, everyone had a place. It might not have been a very nice place, even maybe a horrible place, but at least they had some place in the spectrum of the society.'

NOAM CHOMSKY[1]

At an event in Newcastle during the Brexit campaign, a professor discussed the possible effects on Britain's gross domestic product of different outcomes. One heckler instantly shouted back: 'That's your bloody GDP, not ours.'

Why did I just spend the first chapter of this book on statistics and GDP growth rates? Why am I so obsessed with growth? Whose GDP is it anyway? Would a country with a few percentage points more growth be better than another? No, of course that's not a given. But think about it this way: in the late nineteenth century, Sweden's journey of prosperity began, thanks to free enterprise and international trade. What if Sweden had since then had an annual per capita growth rate a single percentage point lower than it actually had? That doesn't sound that dramatic, does it?

But in this case, Sweden would today have been as poor as Albania.

Think of the difference between Sweden and Albania, where per capita incomes are just a quarter as high, and the difference that prosperity makes in people's daily lives, consumption choices, the opportunity for leisure and holidays, the resources that can be invested in care, education, culture and working conditions or to solve environmental problems and reduce child mortality (about four times higher in Albania than in Sweden). Well, then it suddenly becomes obvious that growth is not something to be sniffed at.

In a recent TV debate on growth, Sweden's most prominent leftist intellectual, Göran Greider, recently explained that in 1970 the country had reached a standard that 'filled our basic needs', and that the growth since then is mainly 'completely unnecessary gadget production'. Really? If Sweden had not become richer since 1970, how would it have financed the big government of which Greider always speaks so warmly?

If you look at the public spending of today, you realize that Greider has a point about the most basic needs: with the prosperity of the 1970s, Sweden would actually be able to afford what it spends today on public administration, the nightwatchman state, healthcare, education and social protection (although he probably thinks it is too little) – but only on the condition that it simultaneously ended all investments in roads, railways, public transportation, development aid, basic research, culture, leisure activities, waste and sewage management, water supply and environmental protection. Nor would its citizens be able to spend a single penny on frivolous private interests, such as eating, buying clothes, having a home or transporting themselves. Obviously they would not be able to afford newspapers, books and TV programmes where one can complain about the banalities of growth. If there were unforeseen expenses, such as a need to develop green technology or a vaccine against a new virus, then that money would have to come from healthcare, education or policing.[2]

Even judging by prosperity levels as far back as 1950, the country would still be able to afford today's investments in education, healthcare and social support for children, the sick and disabled, but then it would also have to abolish all pensions, unemployment benefits and social assistance, public administration, the judiciary, police, defence – and of course, again, have to do without food, clothes, transport and housing. It's not just mobile phones that would be lost.

The value of all the goods and services a country produces is called gross domestic product (GDP). To find out how much is created per person, we divide it by the number of inhabitants in a country (per capita). Growth is what it's called when we raise this level – when we create more or better goods and services tomorrow. It is an embarrassingly deficient measure of a society's prosperity. It does not include unpaid work in the home and it does not include natural resources. Therefore, it is important to combine it with other measures of what we value. GDP is the worst way to quantify wealth – except all the other ways that have been tried from time to time.

Growth is not a value in itself either. When European colonizers or Marxist dictators forced farmers into modern production methods, it was also growth. But growth that does not take place on people's own terms – because they have chosen new methods and innovations themselves – is not the kind of growth I want. Of course, if some prefer to devote more time to leisure than productivity, then they should do that. If people are willing to work for lower wages in less productive businesses in quieter areas, one should not sabotage those opportunities. The growth I care about is the one in which people generate more value tomorrow by deciding to create something that is in demand. If we choose to do that, we will also accomplish many other great things.

I have lost count of the number of various UN agencies' international studies on poverty, health and education that repeat the message that growth is not enough to guarantee good development. But then, as I flip through the statistical compilations – those gathered at the end, where few readers reach – I notice an almost unambiguous connection between growth and progress. It is not completely unambiguous as there is always a country that deviates: a rich country that has an unusually short life expectancy or a poor state in India that has unexpectedly good health indicators. However, the overall connection is usually striking and, if we are to use data to learn how to improve the world, the general rule is more interesting than the exceptions: the richer a country is, the longer and healthier people live, with improved outcomes on almost all indicators of well-being. Unfortunately, growth has also been an effective way of exploiting nature but, as we will see in chapter 8, richer countries are also better at reducing and repairing environmental damage once they decide that is a priority.

This means that, almost no matter which values we want to maximize, we should prefer a society with a faster-growing economy, and no matter which threats and disasters we risk in the future, it is better that we face them with greater prosperity, more knowledge and greater technological capacity than with less. We must move forward, and one reason is that our previous solutions have unforeseen consequences that we must also solve. We save lives with antibiotics, but some bacteria become resistant and then we have to work with that problem. More people live longer and then we have to develop hip replacements and bypass surgery. We reduce hunger with fertilizers, and poverty with industry, but that causes large carbon emissions and so we need to develop technical solutions to that problem. There is never a point where all problems are solved and we can live happily ever after.

If a country can achieve a growth rate of 2 per cent per capita, its average income will double in about thirty-five years. If we could increase it to 3 per cent, it would double in just twenty-three years. In a hundred years, that 1 per cent means the difference between becoming seven times as rich or nineteen. It is such a huge improvement of all our opportunities and assets that everything else pales in comparison.

It is growth that ends global poverty. If a country that belongs to the poorest fifth of countries manages to maintain an annual per capita growth of 2 per cent for twenty years, extreme poverty is halved on average. If the country succeeds in increasing growth to 4 per cent over twenty years, poverty will decrease on average by more than 80 per cent.[3]

Again and again, economic institutions and well-meaning intellectuals ask the question of how to make growth 'pro-poor' – how growth can become 'inclusive' and benefit the poorest? But a survey of 118 countries over forty years shows that we already have the answer: the best way to create inclusive growth is to increase growth for everyone and to keep it up. The study shows that more than three-quarters of the differences in the income the poorest 40 per cent have in different countries can be explained by the growth in average income. The size of the cake is more important than its distribution.

'The bad news,' the researchers write, is that 'we do not find robust evidence that certain policies are particularly "pro-poor" or conducive to promoting "shared prosperity" other than through their direct effects on overall economic growth.'[4]

This is why redistributive policies are so terribly over-rated. If Sweden had distributed its total GDP equally in 1900, everyone would have been as poor as the average person in Kenya. Sweden's GDP, evenly distributed in 1950, would have been enough to correspond to today's average Tunisians. What lifted the country from that level is not that the seeds were distributed in a new pattern, but that they were constantly planted and the harvests grew. The political debate surrounding inequality is mostly about who should receive limited financial assistance from somebody else, whereas the question should really be, which institutions will help us create more for everyone? The problem is that evolution has made us prioritize a small instant reward over a big possible reward some time in the future, so we become obsessed with who gets what today. But today we live in the future that seemed so distant a few decades ago. So if we care about more people than ourselves right now, right here, we should strive for economic growth.

A Swede today who lives at the income level that was the median in 1995 would now be considered poor (with the relative poverty measure defined as 60 per cent of the median income). Those who fall below the poverty line in the United States own more amenities such as dishwashers, washing machines, dryers, air conditioners and televisions (and of course computers and mobile phones) than the average American did in 1970, as productivity has made all these things much cheaper.[5]

Let's say that you are a median person with a median income and that your income grows in line with the economy. If you only care about your personal finances, do you think you should vote for the party that promises to give you a brand-new government benefit of $100 a month or the party that says they do not intend to give you anything but will implement reforms that raise the country's growth per capita from 1 to 2 per cent? If you were to vote for the benefit party, you would make a loss after as little as three years. After ten years, you would lose more than $4,000 a year.

In addition, the growth created by the second party would have been a gain that benefited the majority of the population, while the benefit would be taken from that population. This means that government redistribution is not only paltry but also perilous, because higher taxation of labour, entrepreneurship and investment will reduce labour, entrepreneurship and investment and thus growth. After all, it is because we want less smoking and pollution that we tax cigarettes and pollution. As the English social liberal John Stuart Mill put it: 'To tax the larger incomes at a higher percentage than the smaller is to lay a tax on industry and economy; to impose a penalty on people for having worked harder and saved more than their neighbours.'[6]

However, a government also has to tax people for the services it provides. Borrowing to pay for public expenses is just a way of delaying taxation, which also adds uncertainty for everyone involved, including for lenders. If lenders begin to doubt that a government will be able to repay them – as they did after Liz Truss's UK budget in November 2022 – they run for the doors, interest rates surge and shock waves go through the economy.

Economists Andreas Bergh and Magnus Henrekson conclude that the research points to a negative correlation between the size of government and growth. An increase in the size of the public sector by 10 percentage points is associated with a reduction in the annual growth rate by between 0.5 and 1 per cent.[7] That growth means the most for those who have the least. The share of a country's income that goes to the poorest tenth does not differ much depending on how free the economy of a country is: in the least-free quarter of countries, the poor get 2.7 per cent; in the freest quarter they get 2.9 per cent. The big difference comes from the fact that the free countries are so much wealthier, so even if the poor's share of the cake is not that much larger, they have a share of a much larger cake. In the freest quarter of the countries, the income of the poorest is more than eight times greater than in the least-free quarter.[8]

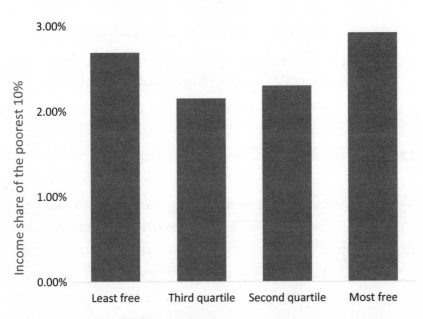

Economic freedom and the income share of the poorest 10%[9]

Income share of the poorest 10%

3.00%

2.00%

1.00%

0.00%

Least free   Third quartile   Second quartile   Most free

The world's countries by level of economic freedom

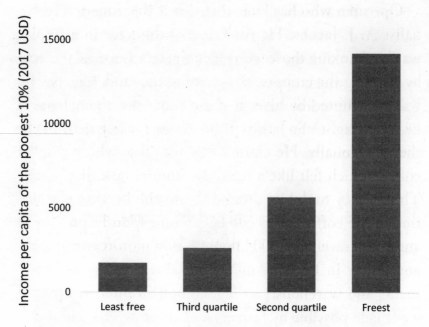

Economic freedom and the income earned by the poorest 10%[10]

Income per capita of the poorest 10% (2017 USD)

The world's countries by level of economic freedom

Least free — Third quartile — Second quartile — Freest

Let's break for coffee

Why do people create so much more in free economies? To sharpen the senses before I answer that question, I just made a cup of coffee.

But that is not quite true. I can't make a cup of coffee; neither can you. In fact, no one can make a cup of coffee. Those invigorating drops are the result of lots of people's knowledge, skill and hard work that no single person can undertake. I am not just thinking of those who cultivate, pick and roast the beans, but also of everyone else who makes it possible. There are so many people involved that the thought is dizzying.

One man who has looked at this is the American journalist A. J. Jacobs. He sometimes says grace in a secular way by thanking those who made the family's meal possible by growing the crops or transporting the food. One day he was interrupted by his son: 'You know these people can't hear you, right?' So Jacobs decided to actually go and thank them personally. He chose to thank those who made his coffee, which felt like a relatively limited task. It was not. The journey took him around the world, because production of the coffee in his cup began nine months previously and then travelled 4,000 kilometres on motorcycles, trucks and ships, in buckets, metal containers as big as apartments and warehouses as big as football pitches. His cup was made possible by farmers and truck drivers and warehouse workers, but also by those who manufactured the pallets, ships and buildings, and those who produced and processed the raw materials. And don't forget the engineer who designed the process for the production of steel, the designer who developed the special plastic bag that keeps the beans fresh and the cleaner of the stockroom. From the small (like the entrepreneur who created the device to measure the density of beans) to the big (like those responsible for the water that fills 99 per cent of the cup and the treatment plants and the chemicals that make it safe) to the absurd (like the team behind the special pheromones that are spread in the warehouse so that the moths stop being interested in the opposite sex and refrain from procreating and eating all the beans).

Jacobs tried to thank them all but was quickly over-whelmed. He realized that he really should also thank those who make the plastic for the helmets that the miners wear to dig iron ore that is made into steel, which is turned into saws that the forest workers use to cut down trees to be made into pallets on which coffee beans are transported. He also had to think about the software, the hardware, the internet, the energy sources and the fuel that keeps everything going – and the financial system that makes sure that everyone involved gets paid before he had even promised to pay for the coffee. Jacobs had to make do with a thousand thanks, all of which are listed in his book *Thanks a Thousand*, but behind each of them we can easily find at least ten people who have in a very direct way made that person's job possible.[11]

The point is, your simple cup of coffee is magical. Tens of thousands of people have collaborated to pour coffee into your cup, not because they are forced to do so, not even because they have been organized for the purpose. They do not know who you are or who the others in the supply chain are, and most of them do not even know that they are involved in making coffee, but all of them have chosen to make an effort for your mental peace. They started making your cup of coffee nine months ago (iron, wood and chemi-cals much earlier, of course) in a world-spanning network. And yet there is a cup of coffee at the cafe or at work or at home at the exact moment you want one, which you might not have even known you wanted ten minutes ago. This is true for your cup and for the two billion other cups served every day worldwide.

Your coffee cup is magical. So is the food on your table. And the table. And the house it is in, and the vehicle you drove to make it there. Your shirt too, your mobile phone, books and wallpaper. That and almost everything else you use daily has been created by complex networks of tens of thousands of people who have voluntarily moved to the place where their labour is paid better than in other jobs.

Free enterprise is not primarily about efficiency or optimal use of resources. It is about opening the dams for human creativity – to let everyone participate and test their ideas and see if they work. But this is precisely why it guarantees a decent use of resources. We test more solutions and we get immediate feedback from consumers that is honest because their response is not about which project they think has the best intentions, think sounds convincing or has passed some sort of bureaucratic test, but about what they are actually willing to buy with their own money.

People from all over the world work together for your sake, individuals with every conceivable colour on their skin and beliefs in their hearts, people who are attracted to the opposite sex or their own, both or none. These are individuals living in urban and rural areas, vegetarians and carnivores, rightists and leftists, synth-kids or heavy metal fans. Most of them have never met and do not know of each other's existence. Many would not like each other if they actually met. Some of them may be mortal enemies on Twitter. Still, they cooperate, and the prejudiced person who suddenly refused to finance, work for, hire, buy or sell to a person who belongs to the 'wrong' group, even though it would have been the financially smart choice to do so, would lose out. Of course, there are always idiots, but in a free market they have to pay dearly to be idiotic.

There's a reason why it's so pathetic when some on the left claim that capitalism is racist and racism is capitalist. On the contrary, the market economy is the first economic system that makes it profitable to be colour-blind and look for the best supply and the best demand, regardless of who is responsible for it. Of course, it will not make everyone colour-blind, but it does so more than otherwise would have been the case (especially in combination with the liberal values on which capitalism is based). Attitude surveys show that Western market economies are the world's *least* racist societies. In an empirical study of seventy countries, economists Niclas Berggren and Therese Nilsson document that economic freedom is positively correlated with tolerance of other ethnic groups and gay people and with the belief that it is important to teach children to be tolerant.[12]

Everyone knows about the segregation on buses, trams and trains in the American South, until Rosa Parks and the civil rights movement aroused public anger about it in the 1950s, and I thought it had always been so until I read the African-American economist Thomas Sowell. He has showed that railroads, streetcars and buses in the South did not engage in systematic race discrimination until the end of the nineteenth century. The reason was that they were mostly privately owned and treated customers equally – not because the owners were less racist than other white Southerners but because they were for-profit and recognized that black Southerners were also paying customers. Segregation would alienate consumers, demand larger wagons and force the staff to conduct an unpleasant policing task. The Southern states introduced racist Jim Crow laws because they were outraged that greedy capitalists only thought of money and refused to discriminate against black people. In Montgomery, Alabama, where Rosa Parks boarded the bus, segregation was first enacted in 1900. Companies lobbied against the racist laws, challenged them in court and often delayed them by refusing to enforce them. Alabama and other Southern states responded by arresting and fining employees who did not uphold discrimination and by threatening the directors with imprisonment.[13]

I have myself witnessed how market forces are breaking down the caste system in India. When companies began to face competition in the early 1990s, it suddenly became costly to favour the upper castes and discriminate against good workers just because they were Dalits – the quarter of the population denied education, given the dirtiest jobs, called 'untouchables' and isolated from the rest. A Dalit I met, Madhusudan Rao, moved from his village to Hyderabad in search of a better life. There he happened to hear a building contractor scolding an employee for not being able to get enough workers who could dig trenches for the laying of cables. Madhusudan stepped forward and offered to provide him with twenty-five workers as soon as that evening. The contractor had a pressing economic need for a trench, but not a pressing economic need to get one dug by people from a particular caste. So he gladly accepted. Madhusudan rented a truck, gathered willing men outside the city and made more money that day than he had seen all his life. He then created his own construction company with 350 workers: 'When I'm hiring employees, I am not seeing any caste. I'm seeing if they're talented.'

In the two decades after 1993, poverty in India fell by about 25 per cent faster among Dalits than for Indians in general. At the same time, other forms of discrimination began to break down. A survey in India's largest state showed that the custom of separating seats at weddings, so that higher castes are not 'polluted', decreased by more than 80 per cent during that period and the proportion of non-Dalits who would accept food and water in Dalit households increased from 3 to 60 per cent. Chandra Bhan Prasad, a mentor and advisor to Dalit companies, once joined Maoist rebels to fight the caste system; now he says that 'capitalism is changing caste much faster'.[14]

The economy's GPS

Ten thousand people do not serve you coffee because they are part of a Big Coffee Plan where a coffee tsar decides who will make what, when, how and at what price. In fact, it can only happen because there is no such coffee plan. The process works because each of these ten thousand people uses their individual knowledge of what they can do and how they can do it better. A centrally placed coffee tsar would never be able to centralize all this complex knowledge. Even if he had been able to do so, the interests, skills, supplies and circumstances would have changed before he had time to send out detailed orders about who should do what.

The free market is first and foremost a cooperation machine, and it works better than all forms of centralized systems because it utilizes the knowledge, talent and imagination of far more people. Free trade allows the farmer to grow a new mobile phone in his wheat field, the textile worker can sew a new motorbike and the author can (if lucky) write a holiday trip to Tuscany. The free trade alchemy constantly turns our particular work into the goods and services we need but cannot produce as well ourselves.

The ten thousand people increase growth because they have an individual motive to think about how they can work a little smarter, and to come up with ideas for which technologies and which methods could make their process faster, cheaper or better – or if they could create greater value by doing something completely different. They think so much about your coffee that you don't have to.

No one in central authority can know whether it is better to direct a little more steel to containers or to refrigerators, or whether the salary for chemists who develop pheromones is reasonably high, or whether it is better to manufacture more powerful tractors at a higher price, or smaller, cheaper models. No bureaucrat can know if it's worth experimenting with a lid on the cardboard mug that lets through a little more aroma, or how much the lifting of bags of beans should be automated. We can only test different solutions, observe the results, learn from them and adapt.

The free market is based on Socratic wisdom – that the most important thing is to be aware of what we do not know. We do not know which ideas offer the most productive innovations or are the best solutions to our problems. We know that we have not yet come up with the best ways to teach students, cure illnesses, organize family life, insure against risk, produce food, or make a cappuccino. We only know that the chance of finding ever better methods is greater if everyone is allowed to join in the search. An underestimated consequence of this (which the Austrian thinker Friedrich Hayek devoted several books to explaining[15]) is that whenever we make today's best solution mandatory, we stop further development – whether it's one form of education or a particular mobile phone charger. It would hamper the experiments and the competition that can teach us more and take us further.

This is the main reason why it is so important to have private alternatives and freedom of choice in the welfare sector, which Sweden has experimented with more than others. It is not primarily a matter of believing that a private school or caregiver will make the services cheaper and the users more satisfied (although, according to research, they tend to do that).[16] The most important role of the alternatives is to try to compensate for the fact that the public sector by its nature has to go for a one-size-fits-all approach and therefore blocks innovation in some of the areas that are most important to us. This freedom of choice is a way to see if the welfare state can be open to alternative ideas and be more experimental, which is necessary precisely because it is in the surprise results that we find development.

One day in the middle of the nineteenth century, a young Frenchman from the countryside visited Paris. It fascinated him that millions of people there slept peacefully even though they would die within a few days if transports from all over the country did not continue to flow to the big city. The thought was dizzying. How could it be that this huge marketplace was filled every morning with almost exactly the number of goods that the inhabitants needed, neither more nor less? And how could it be that the Parisians could suddenly feel an urge for something new they had never thought of before and go to a store and just expect it to be there?[17] What, then, is the secret and ingenious power that governs this complicated system that everybody seems to have such trust in even if they barely give a thought to its existence (except for that one time when what they are looking for is not on the shelf)? That power is nothing but prices and the profit motive.

All information is local and it is not even always available to ourselves. I do not know how much coffee I want next week, or how important it is for me to drink the coffee from a cardboard cup that allows the drink's aroma to float out while I drink. The steel industry does not know if their products are currently best needed for frames for glasses, refrigerators or cars. But what we want can be revealed by our actions, and they are visible because we constantly send signals of supply and demand that are visible in the prices. If we are heading for autumn darkness and we suddenly drink more coffee, the income of those selling it increases, and if there is a shortage of coffee beans or specially designed plastic bags, the prices rise. Prices act as information disseminators because they reduce the information to the absolute simplest and most important signals: what works and what does not work? What do we want more of and what do we want less of? It does not matter who wants more roasted beans or why they want them; the important thing is that the signal is being sent to start roasting. If the demand for lumber increases because we need more pallets for coffee bags or because everyone suddenly decided to build a porch does not matter to the forestry companies; the important thing is that they suddenly benefit from hiring more forest workers. Prices constantly convey changing information about what we want, but they also encourage us to react to that information and adapt to what others want. Free pricing and profit opportunities act as the economy's GPS, describing the landscape and showing you how to navigate to the place you want to be.

This is one reason why regulations are always problematic – even those that are necessary, for example, to maintain safety or environmental protection. Every ban or requirement placed on the ten thousand people from the outside makes it a little harder, more expensive and slower for them to adapt, adjust and do something else a little better.

That pricing is unregulated, and determined by nothing else but the voluntary actions of all market participants, is crucial if the economy's GPS is to show us right. Politicians do not have much ability to control the economy, but they know how to create surpluses and deficits. If they want a surplus, they can just pay the producer more for a certain item than people want to pay for it. Then we will have overproduction, as when the EU's fixed, high agricultural prices in the 1980s created milk lakes and meat mountains that were dumped in poor countries. Or they can force everyone to pay more for something than they would otherwise, such as with high minimum wages that mean that job opportunities disappear for those with poorer qualifications and less experience.[18] If politicians want a deficit instead, they can just force producers to sell at a price that is clearly lower than what consumers are willing to pay. Regardless of whether it is rent control or the Venezuelan price controls on food, the result is the same: supply decreases, waiting times increase and an informal market emerges. The only way to make sure one can get the coveted product is to have contacts with power and influence.

Another way to undermine the price system is inflation. Inflation is often described as something outside of our control, but every rapid and general increase in prices is a monetary phenomenon: when central banks create more money (for example, to deal with funding problems during a financial crisis or a pandemic) we get more liquidity but no more wealth, so more money chases the same number of goods. Prices increase and our purchasing power is undermined. It is a way of taxing people without them understanding what happened. But it's worse than taxation because it also distorts the price system. It makes it impossible to distinguish a real price signal from inflation noise.

The economist John Maynard Keynes, who has often been used by politicians to play down the risks of inflation, understood that it was in fact one of the great dangers to an economy. High inflation, he wrote, makes economic relationships 'so utterly disordered as to be almost meaningless; and the process of wealth-getting degenerates into a gamble and a lottery.'[19]

The voluntary economy

According to Karl Marx, we have capitalism when the economy is based on privately owned means of production, with workers who voluntarily sell their labour, and when coordination is market-based. He put it in a slightly depressing way, setting up a false dichotomy between classes (he had a hard time imagining a thriving capitalism where capitalists are also wage earners, workers own companies through pension funds and there are a multitude of partnerships, cooperatives and companies owned by workers), but in essence it is a decent working definition.[20]

Property rights are the foundation, so that we make a distinction between yours and mine, defining who has the right to decide how property is to be used, divided, transferred or sold. It is basically an institution for social peace that ensures property can be transferred and distributed in any way as long as it is done through voluntary agreements not force. And when something is yours, it creates an incentive to manage it well, as Aristotle stated 2,300 years ago.

Property rights have often been described as a form of protection for the rich and powerful but, in fact, if we do not have legal protection for private property, it is only the rich and powerful who will rule. They will dictate how resources are to be used. In both India and Africa, I have met people who have been denied formal ownership of land that they have used for generations and they always say the same things: that they feel powerless; that someone else controls their lives; that it does not pay off to invest long-term, to renovate their home, dig wells or buy tractors.

For example, the Ministry of Forestry's officials regularly demand money under the table in order not to raze people's plantations with a bulldozer. And if a brother-in-law of a government minister suddenly comes up with something he wants to use the land for, one day he will just step in and take it, meaning all their hard work has been in vain.

It is not always the case that the ten thousand people who make your cup of coffee participate in the process voluntarily. It is not uncommon for the land of the coffee plantations to have been stolen and for those who lived there to be displaced or forced into the local industry. In some cases, there is direct slave labour in coffee production. These are primarily legal issues, and the government's most basic role is to uphold people's right to their freedom and their property. But it is also a reason why the commercial economy has to expand, so that landowners lose their complete control and people have an alternative to staying and obeying.

Many countries that have moved from rags to riches have begun with land reforms, which break down feudal structures, take land from the land-owning aristocracy and give individual property rights to the people. This may sound like a form of government redistribution, but it is not a recurring arrangement, it is a one-time correction for a history of looting, often centuries-old with racist overtones, where a small elite has seized huge areas without working for it or receiving it through voluntary transactions (see Nozick's rectification principle).[21] In many cases, land reforms are about legally recognizing what people already possess but are denied by the elite. An innovative research project came to a rough estimate around the turn of the millennium: people in low- and middle-income countries hold informal land and buildings worth about $10,000 billion – almost as much as the total value of all companies on the rich countries' stock exchanges at the time. Because governments do not recognize these holdings as property rights, the owners can't use them to take loans, do not dare to expand and can't transfer the property. It remains dead capital, controlled by the powerful rather than the real owners.[22]

Property rights are not just about sound incentives but also human dignity. I have, on a very modest scale, been involved in sponsoring a project that helps black South Africans formally register their property, in a country whose official policy has long been to deny it to them. One of the first women to receive a document confirming her ownership was ninety-nine-year-old Maria Mathupe, who cried with happiness when she got it. 'Why?' someone wondered. 'After all, you are ninety-nine years old, and it is not certain that you will be able to use the property for that long, or get so much pleasure from investing in the future.' Mary replied, 'I cry, for now I can die with dignity.'

All the ten thousand people you can thank for your cup of coffee certainly do not go to work with joy. Some do it just to survive; others do it because the alternatives are terrible. Many probably hate their jobs. Wherever we work, we also have Monday mornings when we curse the toil and think we have 'bullshit jobs'. Work is not always fun – that's why we pay each other to do it! In free capitalism we go to work not because someone has forced us there but because we need the money and have decided that this is a better way of getting it than the alternatives. And that's a pretty new phenomenon in history.

Life is a struggle to create or make available the resources that enable us to survive and thrive. The utopians who have dreamed about avoiding this struggle always land in some variant where they force others to perform it for them, just like in Aristophanes' play *Ecclesiazusae* from 391 BC:

> **Proxagoras:** I shall begin by making land, money, everything that is private property, common to all. Then we shall live on this common wealth.
>
> **Blepyrus:** But who will till the soil?
>
> **Proxagoras:** The slaves.[23]

Throughout history, the powerful have always come up with new ways to force someone else to struggle so that they themselves can escape. Most societies have applied slavery, where people have been reduced to the property of others. Feudal systems have imprisoned the peasants on the land, where they were whipped to work for their lords. In modern times, communism and fascism have sought to drag humanity back to its dark past. The Soviet communist Trotsky described 'a country where the sole employer is the state' as being one in which 'The old principle: who does not work shall not eat, has been replaced by a new one: who does not obey shall not eat.'[24] The radical break with this dark history came with Enlightenment ideas that started to emerge in the seventeenth century along with classical liberalism and the notion that man owns himself: he is not just a means to others' ends but has the right to pursue his own happiness in the way he thinks best.

The free market was the sort of economy that followed when people were given the right to shape their relationships and collaborations, and to exit them if they became exploitative. It was the only system that meant that, if you were to earn anything, you had to serve others and give them the goods, services and rewards they wanted. It therefore creates the impetus to come up with even better ways to do it tomorrow, enabling the immense supply of hard work and ingenuity that makes all the difference between poverty and prosperity.

The uniqueness of the free market is revealed every time you arrive at the counter and pay for your coffee. You say thank you, and the cashier answers with a thank-you. We hear such strange double thank-yous in all marketplaces, from the square where we buy vegetables and the restaurant when we pay the bill, to the meeting room where a contract is written with a supplier. It is not a thank-you followed by a 'you are welcome' or a 'yes, sir'. It is a thank-you that is answered with a thank-you, for each party has done the other a favour. This mutual gratitude is the sign that you have created value for someone else. And the potential profit you make is proof that you have produced goods or services that people are willing to pay more than is required for just the raw materials, technology and working time required to create it. Profit is the reward for those who create a whole that others find more valuable than its constituent parts. All other economic systems have also created winners, but the winners were those who took what others created. In a free market you can also get rich, but only by enriching others.

Slavery, feudalism, socialism and fascism were based on some issuing commands and others obeying. The market economy is instead based on doing your best for others, and getting their best in return. The pyramids, the cotton fields of the American South and the Soviet steelworks were built with beatings and floggings. The coffee cup in front of you was created by a thousand handshakes and double thank-yous (and surely some examples of abuse and oppression as well – there is still work to be done).

The ten thousand people organize their work in different ways, often depending on local circumstances. Some work on their own, others as family households, still others in private or public companies. Maybe they are financed through savings, bank loans or venture capitalists – or they work in consumer cooperatives, kibbutzim or worker-owned companies. Anything that is voluntary. One reason why capitalism is morally superior to socialism is that you are free to live as a socialist in a free market economy, as long as you do not force anyone else to do so.

The free society is based on the fact that, in as many areas as possible, we replace the logic of the chop and the blow with the logic of the voluntary handshake. That we do not compel and command but ask, offer and negotiate. We do not dictate who should do what but let everyone test their ideas and keep the fruits of their labour if there are any. And we say no when something does not add anything to us. As I write this, Starbucks is closing most of its stores in Sweden. It did not help that it is the world's largest cafe chain with huge financial muscle; we Swedes had better coffee here already.

When the crisis comes

You might think yes, yes, all that sounds nice, as long as everything goes smoothly, but then there are pandemics, natural disasters or wars and then we need the government. In desperate times, politicians need exceptional powers to get us to behave properly and produce what is needed. A common interpretation is that the pandemic showed that we can't rely on global supply chains where tens of thousands of people across the globe manufacture our face masks, protective equipment and medical technology. Like China, many countries now think they should have had large domestic production, or at least have large stockpiles full of protective equipment like Finland did. We must 'limit our dependence on other countries,' said EU Health Commissioner Stella Kyriakides. 'We need to invest in making more of our products right here in the United States,' said President Biden.[25]

But knowledge about the economy, about ever-changing possibilities, availability and demand is local and only exists in decentralized form: in the minds of millions of actors on the market. This means that the freedom to act on this information is even more important in times of crisis. We all have a small piece of a great social jigsaw puzzle whose motive continuously changes, especially in times of rapid transformation. Then it is even more difficult for authorities to get an overview of what is needed and who can do it, which then makes it more important than ever that people are allowed to act locally, based on their information about who needs what, when and how, and that all those tens of thousands of producers are free to improvise based on the latest price signals that our new behaviour transmits. Research on the Spanish flu in 1918 shows that the more economically free a country was, the less it was damaged by the economic shock of the pandemic.[26]

A review of all 389 economic crises in the world since 1993 shows that economically free countries (defined as ten units above the average on a hundred-point scale) are 30 per cent less likely to be hit by a crisis in a given year and that the crisis will not be as deep as in other countries. In countries with low economic freedom (ten units below the average), the average GDP decrease is 12 per cent when crises strike, while the decrease in economically free countries is 8 per cent.[27] To a large extent, this can be explained by the fact that less regulated economies give people the opportunity to quickly adapt to new knowledge and move capital and labour to the areas where they are needed instead of keeping them in the wrong place.

It is easy after each crisis to point out exactly what could have been done to deal with it, but the problem is that we do not know what will be the next crisis. In the summer of 2018, Swedes were angry that more had not been invested in firefighting because then the problem was not a pandemic but forest fires. In 2019, Swedes believed more land should have been set aside for animal feed when there was a sudden shortage. In 2020, it was a pandemic and Swedes thought they should have had factories that manufactured protective equipment. Yet the next crisis may not be a pandemic but a flood, a cyber-attack or something completely different. After Putin's attack on Ukraine, most Swedes concluded that it was weapons and ammunition that we lacked.

Even those countries who were well prepared to handle a full-blown pandemic had to react when the need for medical supplies increased twentyfold. Despite all the local factories, China needed to import about two billion face masks and 400 million other forms of protective equipment to meet the outbreak in Wuhan. Finland's famous emergency stockpile contained about 4.5 million face masks, which sounds impressive until you get a pandemic where you need 3.5 million *a day*: if the Finns opened the warehouses on Monday morning, they would have emptied them before lunch on Tuesday.[28]

Therefore, the best defence is not to build a static public health Maginot Line to protect us from the next threat we assume will arrive, but a mobile defence that can quickly react to unforeseen events. That is exactly what free enterprise and international trade help us to do. Concentrating production in order to manufacture all the things we need ourselves sounds safe but – regardless of whether it is war, natural disasters or epidemics – catastrophes usually affect a certain geographical area at a particular time. If we have concentrated production to a certain region, it is also threatened when we are hit and need it most. Protectionism makes us vulnerable. If you think resilience is created by concentrating production, I have some infant baby formula to sell you. No, actually, I don't, since there is a severe shortage in the US as I write this, precisely because regulations and tariff barriers had concentrated the production to a few US factories, and then it didn't take more than problems in one factory to create a devastating national shortage. Resilience is not created by concentrating production but by diversifying it.

Even when a crisis is global, like the pandemic, it strikes different regions at different times. China was hit first and was able to import protective equipment from other countries. When those countries were hit, Asia's factories had started to reopen and could instead export to them. In a study by the European Centre for International Political Economy, I looked at how EU trade was affected during the crisis, and it showed that free trade came to the rescue. In March 2020, EU countries' imports of protective clothing from other EU countries fell by 25 per cent – for a period, all European states wanted to seize everything they came across themselves. What saved hospitals from even worse shortages of protective clothing was that imports from countries outside the EU increased by as much as 44 per cent in one month. During the same month, EU imports of hand sanitizer from the outside world increased by 278 per cent and of gas masks by 430 per cent.[29]

This exposes the danger of the popular idea of 'friend-shoring' – trading more with close geopolitical partners while avoiding rivals. In March 2020, France didn't just impose an export ban on protective equipment, it even confiscated such goods sent through the country by third parties. While France was trying to stop vulnerable neighbours like Italy and Spain from getting hold of the equipment their healthcare systems needed, Italy and Spain could buy it from Asian exporters like China. This is not because China is a better friend and a closer geopolitical ally than France, but for the simple reason that China is far away and so is less likely to suffer from the same shortage at the same time. Putting all your eggs in the same friendly, geographical basket is dangerous.

As globalization came to our rescue, it gave us respite to rearrange our own production. Entrepreneurs across Europe asked themselves how they could contribute based on their local situation, skills and equipment. Vodka distilleries and perfume manufacturers began producing hand sanitizer and disinfectants. Hygiene companies switched to the production of disposable gloves and surgical masks. In less than two months, the number of European companies that made face masks increased from twelve to 500. In the United States, 95 per cent of textile companies switched to making protective clothing for the first time.[30]

If you doubt the ability of people to adapt in times of crisis, take a look at the shelves of your local shop. Do you remember when you stockpiled cans, coffee and toilet paper when the world was closing during the first weeks of the pandemic? The food industry in particular was shaken by a perfect storm. New trade barriers were created, a large part of the workforce stayed at home while others were forbidden to cross national borders, and deliveries to the restaurant industry collapsed at the same time as demand for other food supplies soared when shoppers became preppers. The incredible thing about your shop shelves was that almost nothing happened. Through round-the-clock work to change suppliers, reallocate labour, adjust production methods and redirect transportation, the food industry managed to rebuild global supply chains in just a few weeks. It is an absolutely amazing achievement and we consumers noticed almost none of it. It was not done by any food tsar who dictated what everyone should do. It worked because it was *not* a centralized process. Each adjustment of the processes was based on local knowledge of what could be done in a particular place with the available raw materials and the workforce present – and what they could stop doing without creating catastrophic shortages elsewhere.

It is impossible to centralize all this constantly changing knowledge. It is only found on the ground and on the factory floor and can only be seen in prices that change with our millions of individual acts. Freedom to improvise based on this local information is never as important as when the world is changing rapidly in an unpredictable way.

Now that we are getting out of the pandemic, we have experienced extended waiting times for deliveries and large numbers of container ships lining up outside ports, waiting for access. It is not strange that supply chains are strained in times of random acts of lockdowns, curfews, new quarantine rules and trade restrictions, when ships are suddenly banned from entering a port and the Chinese dictatorship locks down entire cities without warning. The remarkable thing is that heroic entrepreneurs are constantly meeting these obstacles by rebuilding and rerouting supply chains and continuing to deliver. Right now, more goods cross the world's oceans than before the pandemic, despite much tougher restrictions. Free markets faced the most difficult stress test possible, and they passed with flying colours.

One cannot help but think of the great American poet and transcendentalist Henry David Thoreau, who wrote in 1849 that trade and commerce seem to be made of rubber, because they always 'manage to bounce over the obstacles which legislators are continually putting in their way'.[31]

3

THE SILENCE OF THE FACTORY WHISTLE

'This is not a rising tide that lifts all boats. This is a wave of globalization that wipes out our middle class and our jobs.'

DONALD TRUMP, SPEECH IN NEW YORK, 22 JUNE 2016

When I defended free markets twenty years ago, it was often against a leftist afraid that it would make rich countries richer and poor countries poorer. History has already settled that debate. Never before have poor countries grown so fast and never before have so many people been lifted out of poverty.

When I argue for free markets nowadays, I am often rebuked by right-wing nationalists in the West who fear that it will make poor countries richer but rich countries poorer. There is a widespread feeling that the economies of Western Europe and North America have been deindustrialized due to cheap imports from China, especially during the first years of the twenty-first century. That we produce nothing any more, and the old decent, well-paid manufacturing jobs – such as the 1950s car industry in

Detroit – have disappeared and, at best, we can aspire to low-paid jobs at an Amazon warehouse. That wages are stagnating, rural areas are dying and the traditional working class is being wiped out, in some cases physically. That suicide, overdoses and alcohol-related injuries have increased rapidly in vulnerable groups.

In a sense, they are right. Fewer and fewer people work in the manufacturing industry. The factory whistles that sounded through industrial towns to signal when muscular men would put down their tools have long since fallen silent. But if this is a sign of societal decay, one must ask why that process has been the same in all other industrialized countries, even those that are export powerhouses with chronic trade surpluses. Japan and Germany began to 'deindustrialize' in this sense in the 1970s; Singapore did so in the 1980s and South Korea in the 1990s. There is a simple way to disprove the notion that these jobs would have remained if China had not taken them with low wages and massive industrial subsidies: *China is also being deindustrialized.*[1]

The proportion of Chinese workers with factory jobs peaked in 2013 and since then the country has lost some five million jobs in manufacturing a year. Chinese companies are currently reducing their share of the world market for clothing, shoes and furniture. So if even the country that has taken all our manufacturing jobs loses manufacturing jobs, where have all those jobs gone? That would be sub-Saharan Africa, the only continent where the share of manufacturing jobs is currently increasing.

We must abandon the old notion that deindustrialization is a sign of weakness. In fact, it is a sign of strength,

provided it occurs at the right stage. It is a phase all countries go through as they get richer. And in a real sense,
of course, this is not about deindustrialization; on the
contrary, the conveyor belts roll faster than ever. Since
1980, industrial production in the United States has more
than doubled, it's just that we do not need as many workers
to sustain that production.[2]

If you zoom in on the American manufacturing world
during the first ten years of the millennium, you see that
it lost 5.6 million jobs. But that was not because they
produced less. In fact, Americans produced more during
this time – so much more that, if they had produced as much
per worker in 2010 as in 2000, they would have had to hire
three million more people. The loss of jobs was therefore
not due to the fact that the factories were outcompeted, but
to the fact that they became much more productive.[3] About
87 per cent of the lost industrial jobs were due to improved
production, while only 13 per cent were due to trade. This
means that even if strategic industrial policy were to bring
the factories home, it would not bring the factory jobs home
because they were not taken by the Chinese and Mexicans
but by R2-D2 and C-3PO. The Chinese and Mexicans are
also acquiring more and more robots. Since 2010, Chinese
companies have increased the number of industrial robots
from 50,000 to 800,000.[4] That's why they can be more
productive and competitive.

This does not mean that we will run out of jobs – just
like the spinning machine, mechanical looms, the steam
engine, the car, the computer, the ATM and other innovations didn't kill all jobs. Instead, automation creates

complementary industries and frees up purchasing power to hire more people. Current research shows that an increase in automation in a factory by 1 per cent actually *increases* the workforce there by 0.25 per cent after two years and 0.4 per cent after ten years.[5] But it's not the same job. The manual jobs that compete directly with the machine are replaced by other jobs that complement the machine.

In addition, rising prosperity means that an ever smaller part of our consumption is devoted to material objects, and increasingly to services, such as care, nursing, entertainment, design, research, development and education. We can only afford this because the automation of manufacturing means that we can devote a shrinking share of our purchasing power to its products.

This feels wrong because our social psychology and our economic debate is often characterized by a picture-book nostalgia. It seems that we have lost 'real jobs' where 'real men' produced things you could drop on your foot – the kind of jobs that are in children's picture books. In exchange we get a lot of unsatisfactory bullshit jobs (as David Graeber called them in a popular book of the same name) with temporary contracts where it's unclear what is actually produced. Which children's books are really about art directors, personal trainers, PR consultants, content managers, food couriers or biotechnological analysts?

The picture books should be supplemented with the views of people who have actually worked in those fabled factories. If the 1950s and 60s were the golden age of the Western labour market, why is it that those who worked there, with few exceptions, emphasize the dirt, weariness and boredom, worn-out bodies and exhausted minds? The reason why workers in these factories fought so hard to give their children a good upbringing and education was so that their children could get other jobs. As a steel-worker in Pennsylvania warned his children: 'Come in this place, you don't know if you're coming out. And if you do, you might be missing an arm, or eye, or leg. Do something for yourself.'[6] Even in the acclaimed depiction of life in the Rust Belt *Hillbilly Elegy*, author and now Senator J. D. Vance writes that there was one thing he and all his schoolmates agreed on when they were growing up: 'no one wanted to have a blue-collar career'.[7]

Of course, there are exceptions. It must have been a dream to be a worker in Detroit's automotive sector in the 1950s, given how that example always reappears in today's labour market nostalgia. Or was it? Historian Daniel Clark has conducted a major interview project with such workers and expected stories of a lost Eden. What he heard was something completely different. 'Hardly anyone, male or female, white or African American, recalled the 1950s as a time of secure employment, rising wages, and improved benefits.'[8] Instead, he heard about rapid restructuring, economic volatility, precarious employment and recurring unemployment. For a time, one-tenth of all US unemployment was concentrated in the city of Detroit. High hourly wages did not say much about the annual income if you were only called in temporarily and were quickly out the door again. Most car workers Clark spoke to needed to take second jobs – such as movers, cleaners, garbage collectors, waiters, cotton pickers – to pay the bills: 'Autoworkers fell behind on installment plans, resulting in repossessions of their purchases, and they found it impossible to keep up with mortgages and rents. Most autoworkers, and especially those with families, were priced out of the market for the new cars that they built – even though they were ostensibly among the highest paid industrial workers in the country."[9]

The Golden Age myth of Detroit is based on the fact that those who managed to hold on to a long-term, full-time job in these industries had significantly better wages than Americans in general at the time because the general level was so low, and this was especially true of the group employed in Detroit in 1953. So, in other words, the whole narrative of the lost golden age of factories is based on a single American city in a single year during the very peculiar time after World War II, when Europe's industry lay in ruins. And how much did these lucky ones get paid? Well, the strong autoworkers' union managed to push the hourly wage up to about $1.3 – equivalent to around $14.5. It happens to be a little bit below the typical entry-level salary Amazon pays its warehouse workers.

Does work pay?

Anyone can look at the segment of the labour market that is having the toughest time at the moment and conclude that we are living in the age of the precariat. Some write whole books about it. But if we want to know how things are going for the population as a whole, individual stories are not enough. We need to see how things are going for employees in general: have wages stagnated, jobs become more precarious and wage earners been thrown into insecurity?

The story of wage stagnation is just like the nostalgia for factories: imported from America, where wage growth, especially for low-skilled occupations, was slow for many decades. But the story is easily misunderstood as if it were about the fact that wages have not increased. This is not even what the advocates of this position claim; instead they mean that people who have a certain type of work at a certain age today do not have a much better salary than a person in a similar situation and in a similar position in 1980. Whoever has an American minimum wage today is no better than the person who had the minimum wage in 1980. Yet it's not the same person on that wage, then and now. The Austrian economist Joseph Schumpeter pointed out that we often look at distribution issues as if we were looking at a hotel where the rooms are nicer the higher up you get. When we just take a snapshot of national income distribution today and compare it to what it looked like a few decades ago, we will not see much change except that the large suites at the top have become even more luxurious with espresso machines and silk sheets. But Schumpeter's point is that people rarely live on the same floor all their lives. On the contrary, it is common for them to move to higher floors. Those who lived in the luxury suites eventually check out and the hotel is filled with new immigrants and students who get their first room on the ground floor and begin their own journey upwards.

Most of those who lived on the minimum wage in 1980 have during their working life received wage increases, changed jobs, been promoted and received even higher wages, and so on. Those who start working for the minimum wage today will also experience this. As soon as after one year, about 70 per cent who live on the minimum wage in the United States have moved on to a position with a higher wage. In addition, the proportion of American workers living at or below the minimum wage decreased from 15 per cent in 1980 to 1.5 per cent by 2020.[10]

Of Americans born in the poorest fifth (quintile), almost 37 per cent eventually end up in one of the three highest quintiles and almost half of those born in the second-lowest quintile move there.[11] One of the largest recent studies shows that almost one-tenth of all American children born in 1986 in a family in the poorest quintile have a salary that takes them to the richest quintile by the age of twenty-six. It is a measure of social mobility that has been stable since the 1971 generation when the data series began and 'if anything intergenerational mobility may have increased slightly in recent cohorts'.[12] This surprises many who have just assumed that increased inequality would reduce mobility, including several of the researchers themselves. They conclude their report by stating that more research is needed on why mobility has *not* decreased as everyone expected.

Since the differences between the quintiles have increased, this says something very interesting about social mobility in the United States. The steps have become steeper, but the chance of climbing these steps has not decreased. In other words, it has actually become easier for the average person to improve their life in dollars and cents. (This is an important distinction when comparing America with, for example, Sweden and Denmark. It is more difficult for poor Americans to change income category than for Swedes and Danes due to more compressed wages in Scandinavian countries. A few hundred dollars in wage increase is enough to climb to a higher quintile in the Nordic countries, while it requires thousands of dollars in the United States.)

The fact that wages are not much higher for a low-skilled entry-level job today than forty years ago can, in this perspective, be seen as an opportunity for new groups of young people and immigrants to be allowed to enter Schumpeter's hotels, after which most of them can move to higher floors. If they could only enter at a higher wage level, many would not be allowed to check in at all.

The truth of the history of wage stagnation in the United States is that Americans have experienced slower wage increases since the mid-1970s than in previous decades. This is partly because they increased so fast before that – faster than productivity. The United States had a unique position after World War II while Europe was being rebuilt. It was unsustainable for US industry to dominate the globe once Europe's own economies got back on their feet. More jobs were lost in the Rust Belt in the north-eastern United States between 1950 and 1980 – that is, before globalization reached the United States – than in the decades that followed.[13] Lower wage increases there-after were a correction of the cost level, which was required so that the country's business sector would not collapse entirely. When the difficult structural transformation was completed, US wages began to rise again. Since 1990, the average wage adjusted for inflation has increased by about 34 per cent.[14] This means that the debate about wage stagnation is primarily a bad legacy of the 1970s and 80s. Three decades later, this narrative began to take over the political debate completely, which says something about the stagnation of external analysis in that sector.

Of course, an average says nothing about how things have gone for low-income earners, so we should also divide the data into different groups. Then we see that wages for those who are in the lowest-paid tenth actually increased slightly more, by 36 per cent. If you also look at income after taxes and transfers, the advantage of low-income earners increases even more. Income for the poorest fifth of households increased by 66 per cent, compared with the median household's 44 per cent from 1990 to 2016.[15] There are many ways to describe a 66 per cent increase in a quarter of a century, but stagnation is not one of them.

If the stagnation debate is to be taken seriously, one must also keep in mind that the figures we use disregard the fact that an increasing proportion of salaries are paid in various fringe benefits for tax purposes, such as health insurance, pensions or paid holidays that are not visible in the statistics or salary account. If such benefits are taken into account, the average US hourly wage has increased by about 60 per cent since 1980.[16]

For the vast majority, today's service jobs pay much better than industrial jobs did. Even in the group that has been at the forefront of the debate about the unequivocal losers of globalization – American men raised in working-class homes – 72 per cent have higher wages than their fathers had when they were the same age. On average, they earn almost a third more.[17] It can still be described as a deterioration compared to their parents' generation, where probably close to 100 per cent had higher wages than their fathers had, but that was because their fathers had in most cases grown up in severe poverty in agriculture and during the Great Depression. It's easier to do better than that.

However, there is something to the story that the middle class has eroded, since certain types of routine jobs that provided average incomes have disappeared since World War II. This applies to many forms of manufacturing work but also to clerks responsible for registers and warehouses or bank and postal tellers who handled invoices or received, counted and handed over banknotes. These were jobs that required precision and accuracy but not improvisation and social intelligence – just the kind of work industrial robots, computers and ATMs are good at. Yet this does not mean the total number of jobs declines. The money we previously spent on this type of work remains and is now used to buy other types of work in what is sometimes called 'the new middle-class jobs', such as in transport, healthcare, education, entertainment and culture. We have fewer manufacturing workers and bank cashiers but more technical support, package deliverers, truck drivers, installers of broadband, solar cells and air conditioning, family counsellors, legal assistants, masseurs, event organizers, art directors, sound engineers, chefs and lecturers. Still, from this list you can also tell how the labour market has become tougher: most of these jobs require increased problem-solving, improvisation and communication skills. Even the introverted IT support worker must be able to talk to me without revealing how incompetent he thinks I am. Educational requirements have increased for almost all tasks as a consequence. This means that it is increasingly difficult to get a good middle-class job for those with little education – for example, Americans without a high school education. (Even though that proportion has decreased from 40 per cent in the early 1950s to about 10 per cent.)

What once distinguished middle-class jobs was that they gave an average salary. Economist Michael Strain decided to see what has happened to those who used to have it. He defined the American middle class as households that have an inflation-adjusted average salary between approximately $35,000 and $100,000 a year, which is slightly arbitrary but corresponds with many people's assumption about middle-class jobs. The numbers did show that the middle class has eroded, which everyone is worried about (between 1967 and 2018, the proportion with that average salary decreased from 54 to 42 per cent), but they don't ask the relevant question: where did the middle class go? Not down, because the proportion earning less than $35,000 a month has also decreased, from 36 to 28 per cent. The missing middle class has moved upwards. The proportion who earn more than $100,000 a month has more than tripled since 1967, from 10 to 30 per cent. It is not the bottom that has slipped, but the ceiling that has been raised.[18]

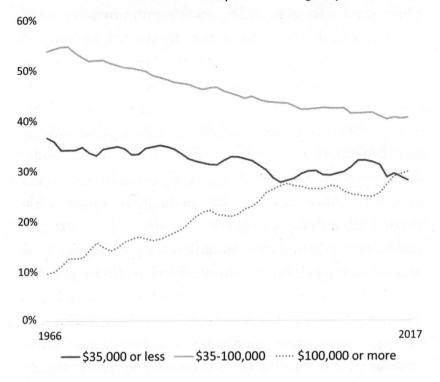

Share of households per income group[19]

— $35,000 or less   —— $35-100,000   ⋯⋯ $100,000 or more

I know, it's easy to get the feeling that 'when my grandfather was my age, he could support his wife and three children and have a house built without borrowing a penny, while I have to take out a payday loan to afford a PlayStation', but it ignores the fact that your grandfather only had to pay a tenth of his income to the government, and that in his time it was actually legal to build a new house somewhere (and as late as 1950, the chance was more than even that his home would lack a bathroom).[20] In addition, the generally low wages made labour-intensive projects such as building a house cheap. Instead, ask Grandpa what he did if he wanted meat for dinner or

needed a new jacket or a book, phone or radio, or transportation somewhere or for that matter a new hip joint,
and you will be treated to a story that is less reminiscent
of the good old days and more of Monty Python's *Four
Yorkshiremen* sketch ('Of course, we had it tough.')

Is it bullshit?

If it feels like work life is becoming more stressful, like
there is more churn and we have to switch jobs all the time
and work harder and more intensely, then we have to think
about where that feeling comes from because right now
we are actually experiencing a very calm period after 150
years of large-scale industrialization and urbanization. An
American study of the years between 1850 and 2015 shows
that the period with the largest churn in the labour market
– the most jobs destroyed and created – was the earliest,
while the one with the least churn was the most recent.
The 1950s and 60s are remembered as boom years, but back
then structural transformation was about five times greater
than today.[21] Then it was also less often about changing jobs
to another company in the same city and more often about
uprooting your whole family and moving to a different part
of the country. During the 1950s and early 1960s, about
20 per cent of the US population moved each year. Since
then, the proportion has decreased continuously. In 2017–
18, it fell to less than 10 per cent for the first time since
1947, when the US Bureau of Statistics started registering
domestic mobility, and has since continued to decline.[22]

The problem today is rather too little churn than too much, because a large part of our growth comes from old jobs and companies disappearing and being replaced by new and more productive ones. When this is not done to a sufficient extent, we do not get the rapid improvement in job quality and wages that we expect. That is an important reason to make it easier to build where the jobs are.

We do not work more than ever, but less than ever. Since the breakthrough of industrialism, working hours have halved in the Western world and have continued to decline in recent decades, albeit at a slower pace. Between 1960 and 2017, annual working hours in Sweden, the United Kingdom, the United States, Germany, France, Spain and Italy decreased by an average of about one-fifth.[23] In addition, we start working later in life and live longer after retirement than ever before.

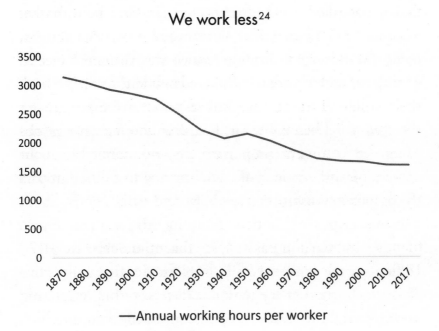

We work less[24]

—Annual working hours per worker

Workplaces have also become much safer. In the 1950s and 1960s, there were around twenty to twenty-five workplace fatalities per 100,000 workers, and that figure has declined continuously – it is now around 3.4 per 100,000 workers according to the Occupational Safety and Health Administration. Worker injuries and illnesses have declined from 10.9 incidents per 100 workers in 1972 to 2.8 per 100 in 2019. Incidentally, the biggest safety gain comes when going from manufacturing work to the service sector.

But even if objective factors do not indicate deterioration or instability, then tougher competition, higher pace of work and more flexible contracts can still create feelings of anxiety and insecurity. If the proportion who claim to be satisfied with their salary, security, career opportunities and boss are all in drastic decline, it would be a sign that we do after all get worse jobs. But it is the other way around on all these points. Gallup has asked Americans how satisfied they are with their job since 1993. During this quarter of a century, when tougher competition and globalization are said to have undermined all good jobs, the proportion who are completely satisfied with their work increased from 35 to 56 per cent. (Together with those who are reasonably satisfied, it is now almost nine out of ten workers.) The proportion who are satisfied with the amount of work required of them has increased by a third and the proportion dissatisfied has halved.[25]

Some critics of modern working life, such as David Graeber and Roland Paulsen, say that all the time we spend talking on the phone, emailing, playing and wasting time at work shows that we may not have very important and meaningful jobs.[26] Of course, this can be the case, although it may be more about our need for micro-breaks and distractions even when doing something urgent. In the same way that you regularly have to stretch and move your body in a different way when you have a demanding physical job, you may need to stretch intellectually with a round of Desktop Tower Defense or YouTube when working with your head. (If only you knew how many Nick Cave videos I have watched while working on this book.) But the interesting thing is this: if you have time to play and email during working hours, or can surf porn 75 per cent of the time without it being noticed on your performance like a particular Aviation Authority employee (one of Paulsen's favourite examples), at least it is an indication that the demands and pace of working life generally can't have been pushed up to inhuman levels.

In his book on 'bullshit jobs', Graeber makes much of the fact that 37 per cent of Britons say no when asked whether their work 'makes a meaningful contribution to humanity'. By equating this with the claim that these 37 per cent are 'convinced their jobs are meaningless', he concludes that the thesis that there are more and more bullshit jobs has 'been overwhelmingly confirmed by statistical research'.[27] Yet the question he asked presents a pretty high threshold for not getting your job declared idiotic. I can come up with a lot of meaningful tasks I perform that do not concern much of humanity in the slightest. (By the way, can one really rule out a certain modesty among Britons when asked if they see themselves as benefactors of humanity?) If instead we ask the question whether you have the feeling that you are doing 'useful work', only 4.8 per cent in the EU answered 'never' or 'rarely' in 2015, and that proportion also decreased from 7.8 per cent in 2005.[28]

If we do not trust what people say about how stressed they are at work, we can swipe the inside of their cheeks to look for stress hormones. Three researchers asked 122 people in a medium-sized American city to do this six times a day. It turned out that most of them were really stressed – in their spare time. The majority of workers experienced more stress at home, surrounded by family and household chores, than they did in the workplace. (Could this mean that shorter working hours have actually made us more stressed?) It could, of course, reflect an unequal labour market, where highly educated workers with high wages and excellent benefits are living an increasingly comfortable life, while low-income earners are working harder. This is why this study was so surprising, as it indicated the opposite: the socio-economically weak, who had lower wages and poorer working conditions, stated that they felt greater satisfaction and less stress in the workplace than the socio-economically strong did.[29]

We must not draw too far-reaching conclusions from a single study, and more research is required (as scholars usually say when they want more bullshit jobs), but it is in any case difficult to confirm the darkest theories about the modern labour market based purely on this. On the other hand, it fits the theory that work can function as a safe place for people with a difficult home environment, such as those with broken families or those who suffer violence or abuse in the home.

Research shows that there are economic cycles in the feeling of insecurity on the labour market – it increases in a recession and decreases in a boom – so those who want to argue about how bad everything has become use a simple trick: they use surveys done in the middle of recessions and compare them with how people responded during a previous boom. If you instead measure over a longer period of time, over several business cycles, the pattern is one of stability and a small improvement. In the United States, United Kingdom and Germany, the experience of labour market insecurity has not increased in the last forty years, despite the major financial crisis towards the end of the period. When researchers try to explain subjectively perceived insecurity, they can't find that it correlates with technological change or labour market legislation. The only long-term and unambiguous correlation is that insecurity rises with the level of unemployment.[30]

There is a new and fast-growing part of the labour market that has much less security than the traditional one: the gig economy, where – rather than a permanent job – you have temporary, insecure assignments to drive taxis or deliver food. I must admit that when I see a food courier cycling fast in rain and headwind to deliver pizza for a few bucks, I also doubt if this is really a step forward for humanity. Even though this is a new sector and research is in its infancy, an interesting survey result is that, on average, gig workers seem to be roughly as satisfied with wages and working hours as permanent employees, even though the spread is large.[31] It has to do with the fact that the absolute majority of gig workers state that they actively sought such jobs, not just because they have no alternatives. For most people, it is a temporary job on the way to or in addition to something else. It is often a matter of complementing another job or earning an income while studying, starting a business or looking for a job that really matches one's skills. And in that case, the opportunity to choose when and how much you work is a feature and not a bug, even if the salary might look dismally low when compared to a full-time salary.[32]

Of course, there is a substantial minority who take these jobs because they don't have anything else, and then the pressure to accept even lousy job opportunities can be great and satisfaction with the job will be low. But if all other opportunities are worse, it means that this job is the least bad. Another word for 'least bad' is 'best'. Studies of Uber and Lyft drivers in the United States consistently show that between 60 and 70 per cent prefer to have the job as a gig over a permanent job. And this is also the wrong question, since the real choice is between being a gig worker and having a smaller chance of permanent employment, because if companies have to pay fixed salaries and benefits, they will not be able to accept anyone, especially not someone who does not pull in a sufficient number of assignments or is not efficient. When Canada banned Foodora from treating food couriers as independent contractors in 2020, the company left the market.

Many dislike the fact that gig workers are only considered to work when they perform a certain task and many platforms have been pressured by trade unions or the law to treat the workers as employees. But if you are to have permanent employment with a fixed salary in an industry with low margins, it presupposes that you give up on the idea of working when it fits your schedule, and instead drivers are directed to the times of day and areas that provide the greatest income. In New York, this has led to gig drivers no longer being able to check in at the moment they want a job and instead having to work shifts. They are no longer allowed to take breaks or holidays when they want, which was one of the points of having a gig job.

When it comes to food deliveries, permanent employment means that workers must be very productive. They must, for example, cycle fast uphill in the rain, and the company must monitor them so that they know they are doing so. If you get the same salary no matter how fast you pedal, the slow cyclists will be thrown out. It thus turns out that some of the worst aspects of the gig economy are paradoxically the result of not having respected the flexible nature of the profession and wanting to regulate them as ordinary jobs. 'And just like that, a simple bywork for anyone who can ride a bike, has turned into a qualified job for the strong, fast and physically fit,' as economist Andreas Bergh puts it.[33]

The wave power of globalization

Nothing I have written here is meant to imply that stories of abandoned industrial landscapes and decaying rust belts are fantasies. Communities grow up around thriving companies that offer attractive jobs. When those business models no longer hold, communities begin to erode. Stores and subcontractors that were created by that purchasing power are shut down and the young start to move out. This is particularly conspicuous in a young country like the United States, where the factories were not built in organic urban environments with long traditions but in places where new communities grew around them. When you travel in some parts of the American Rust Belt today, sometimes you get the gloomy feeling of being in ghost towns without life and hope. The feeling is similar in some old European industrial towns. How can anyone who sees this defend the wave of globalization that is drowning the middle class and all the good jobs?

But wait a minute, with what evidence is globalization named the villain of this drama? Let us look at the most widely used example: China's entry into the global economy after WTO membership in 2001. Between 2001 and 2021, the share of manufacturing jobs in the United States fell by 0.2 percentage points annually, which is obviously painful for those concerned. However, it happens to be a *smaller* decrease than in previous decades. Between 1960 and 2001, the share of manufacturing jobs decreased by almost 0.4 percentage points annually. So this is not a sudden new development, just the continuation of a long trend – at a slower pace.[34]

Critics say that competition from Chinese imports knocked out about 130,000 American jobs annually in 2000–15. That sounds like a big number until you compare it to the approximately 60 million jobs that disappeared in the US economy each year during the same period. About 20 million of those job losses are involuntary, resulting from companies closing down, moving or needing a different composition of staff. This means that for every job that disappeared due to Chinese imports, 150 workers lost their jobs due to a completely different cause.[35] But for some reason we think more about that individual job than about the other 150, perhaps because that one job fits into the picture of predatory global capitalism?

But that bigger number – 150 – reveals that we will always lose jobs. Technology changes, some tasks are automated while others require different skills. People move and the purchasing power moves with it. Consumers constantly change their demand. Suddenly, we would rather order our trip online ourselves than by stepping into a travel agency, and our film consumption no longer requires the production of video tapes. One day we realize that we do not need so many paper mills to read the news in the morning. Jobs will always disappear. All we have to decide is whether we should lose jobs from a position of weakness, where we have tried to conserve all the old, disappearing sectors and so have less productivity and wealth, or from a position of strength, where we have the resources and the expanding industries that help us to restructure and hire people in new, competitive companies. If we choose the latter, it is difficult to imagine a better ally than international trade. It allows us to constantly upgrade our methods and specialize in what we do best, so that we constantly create better jobs than the ones we lost.

Sixty million jobs are lost in the United States every year and more than that number of new jobs are created every year. And who are the ones creating these new jobs? The answer is a bit unexpected: the companies that are most exposed to Chinese imports. They lose some jobs, but in response to competition, they specialize in areas where they can create greater value.

A recent study showed that companies exposed to Chinese imports expanded employment 2 per cent more per year than other companies.[36] Critics say it is not the same job, which is true. They are better jobs: manufacturing jobs with higher wages, because they are in the stages of production where they can add more value, and in complementary service jobs, such as engineering, design, research and development, and marketing. So if it is true that 'China took our jobs' then it is also true that they gave us better jobs in exchange.

You can climb the value chain in different ways. Research on half a million European companies around the turn of the millennium showed that those exposed to Chinese competition responded by investing more in research and development and they accounted for more patent applications. One result was that European employment shifted to more innovative companies. The researchers concluded that Chinese competition was behind 14 per cent of the technological upgrades in the European economy between 2000 and 2007.[37]

In addition, domestic companies can expand production by using cheaper, imported intermediate goods. Studies showing that imports destroy local jobs usually just look at direct competition: if the Smith family buys a refrigerator from a Chinese company, they don't buy it from an American company. But that's just one aspect of trade and it's not the biggest. Most things that cross our borders are inputs, materials and components that companies need to be able to manufacture goods. Sometimes we buy a refrigerator from China, but it is more common for an American refrigerator manufacturer to buy doors, cables or lamps from China, to make a better and cheaper refrigerator. A recent study showed that if you look at the entire value chain from 2000 to 2007, the net effect of trade with China is *more* American jobs. The average US region increased employment 1.3 per cent more annually than a hypothetical region that had no trade with China. As a result, 75 per cent of American workers got higher real wages.[38]

But why sacrifice any jobs at all? Just look at an iPhone. Donald Trump could not understand why Apple assembles its mobile phones on the other side of the globe. 'China is the biggest beneficiary of Apple – not us,' he complained in January 2019, urging Apple to 'build their damn computers and things in this country instead of in other countries'. But is China really the biggest winner? Some researchers disassembled an iPhone 7 that sold for $649. They observed that the manufacturing cost of just over $237 (which looks like $237 of Chinese imports in the data tables) mostly consists of components that have previously been imported to China, such as American, Japanese, Korean and Taiwanese microprocessors, memory chips and displays. But some are, of course, Chinese labour and parts. How much? Just under $8.5 – not much more than an hourly US minimum wage. The 'biggest winner' thus receives only 1.3 per cent of what you pay for an iPhone.[39]

The remaining 98.7 per cent goes to other manufacturers of components, as well as to Apple and American workers, researchers, designers, programmers, salespeople, marketers, warehouse workers and tax authorities. And that is the answer to the question of whether it would be better to bring those factories home. These are routine assembly jobs that few Americans would be willing to take – and if they were tempted to do so with US wages, iPhones would be so expensive that the company would have difficulty competing (for example, against Chinese mobile phone manufacturers). If the assembly is instead outsourced where it can be done efficiently and cheaply, then Americans are able to retain the skilled jobs – developing the designs, components, software and advertising campaigns – and bring the big bucks home.

Systems of despair

Everyone is not better off, though, and there is one group of losers who have shaken my optimism. These are parts of the old working class in America, especially the middle-aged in the rust belts around the Appalachians. Since 1999, bad health and mortality have increased rapidly in this group as a result of suicide, alcohol-related injuries and, above all, overdoses. Their mortality has increased so much that it is back where it was in the 1980s. The scholars Anne Case Deaton and Angus Deaton have summed it up with the uncomfortable but apt concept 'deaths of despair'.[40]

This is also the group that has performed the worst in the labour market during this time. Wages have not kept pace with the rest of the market and many of them have left the workforce altogether, which in turn has destabilized families and local communities. It is tempting to blame globalization. However, a chart of men between the ages of twenty-five and fifty-four who have left the labour force shows an almost constant increase since 1965, where it is difficult to discern any effect of deregulation, the North American free trade agreement (NAFTA) or China's membership of the WTO, and where neither boom nor bust affect the long-term trend. In fact, the proportion of men who dropped out of the labour force increased more during the good old days 1965–75 than during the entire period 2000–19.

US men not in labour force 1965–2019[41]

— US men aged 25–54 not in the labour force

Anne Case and Angus Deaton agree that globalization cannot be the explanation for deaths from despair: 'As its name tells us, globalization is *global*, as is automation'.[42] The entire Western world has made the same globalization journey, including many countries that are more open to trade than the United States. How come deaths of despair did not occur there? Western Europeans do not seem to have been affected and in the United States we have not seen this increased mortality among Latinos or among black people (at least not in the first stage), or for that matter among white people with a college degree. So there is something else going on in this group that makes their difficult labour market situation particularly serious.

It is not poverty in itself, according to the Deatons. The problems do not correlate with poverty among whites and cannot explain why the risk of mortality in all age groups is lower (and continues to fall) for Latinos than for non-Hispanic whites, even though they are significantly poorer. Nor is it about inequality. The most unequal states, such as New York and California, have lower mortality rates. It has to do with a dysfunctional and increasingly expensive healthcare system. Most people receive health insurance from their employer (for tax reasons), which means that companies have an incentive to get rid of the least productive workers and that the workers lose the insurance if they lose their jobs. Another American peculiarity is a large increase in the proportion of the population who have been convicted of a crime and often suffer from discrimination in the labour market. In healthcare, education and jobs that require a professional licence, discrimination is sometimes imposed by government authorities. A third peculiarity is the large proportion of war veterans in the population, who often suffer from poor physical and mental health.

All these factors have affected ethnic minorities to at least the same extent. According to the Deatons, one reason why it is still white people with little education who have had the worst development in the last twenty years is that the United States has become less racist and that black people and Latinos have made rapid social progress. This is obviously a very positive development but can be perceived as threatening for those who have become accustomed to having a superior status just because they were born into a certain group. When you're accustomed to privilege, equality can feel like oppression, as the saying goes.

Added to the problem is the fact that the US government has often dealt with the loss of jobs by removing those affected from the workforce, much more so than countries with a more active labour market policy. Those who lose their jobs can receive benefits, food stamps, disability benefits, early retirement and healthcare, which cushion the fall, but most of that support is dependent on not retraining, taking another kind of job or moving to regions with stronger economies. They stay in areas that can no longer offer them any jobs. Of every dollar that the United States gives to the unemployed, about 99 cents go to getting the person to stay on the couch and only 1 cent to helping him find a new job.

The American welfare state creates extreme lock-in effects. Of course, we want those who suffer from unemployment or illness to get some sort of financial assistance, but if it means that the support disappears the moment you get a job, you have created a welfare trap. If you take a job, save money or get married, you will be punished financially. The welfare system is absurdly rigged to encourage everything that politicians on both the left and the right say is a destructive lifestyle. It's not just an American phenomenon: almost 40 per cent of the unemployed in OECD countries suffer an 80 per cent marginal tax if they take a job.[43]

A few years ago, I approached Americans living on welfare to study their situation. The common denominator was that they felt trapped and could not understand the system. Chris, a single mother with four children, said she receives five different forms of compensation and that they are incomprehensible: 'All five of those have different rules and regulations and guidelines for what you can earn or not earn or for what's counted and not counted. It's very complicated to figure out what the sweet spot is of what I can earn.' She can lose money by taking a job with a low income, and if the salary goes up to $30,000 a year, so many benefits fall away that it was as if she only earned $15,000.

Keith and Monique said they were punished financially for marrying and moving in together after having children. Overnight, their total benefits decreased by 55 per cent and it was not certain that Monique would be allowed to keep her subsidized apartment. 'A lot of people don't tell public assistance about their children's father,' said Monique. 'Sometimes I wish I would have done the same thing.'

Angel, who has a criminal record and has lived on benefits all his life, noted that any attempt to save something rings up in the authorities' registers and results in less assistance. 'If you don't want to get cut off, you take the money and spend it.' Have you ever wondered how the poor in inner cities can have such large sets of expensive sneakers? I asked the question and got the answer that it is a form of savings. An entire wardrobe of sneakers does not make the authority remove your health insurance or subsidized apartment. If you get an unexpected expense, you sell a pair of shoes or go to a 'sneaker bank' where you can get a loan with the shoes as collateral.

I found out that economically devastated areas can often be close to places where companies are searching for labour. West Virginia was hard hit but borders the more attractive states of Virginia and Maryland. Crisis-hit Maine is next door to fast-growing New Hampshire. In previous generations, the unemployed moved to jobs when an industry closed down, but that has become increasingly difficult. A combination of building restrictions and a NIMBY epidemic[44] means that it is only possible to build without objections in areas where no one wants to live. This leads to an increase in property prices, which means that moving to a new town for work risks costing you money.

Another obstacle to mobility is that professional licences have become a way to protect those who already have a job and keep outsiders away. The proportion of employees covered by laws on licences and credentials has increased from less than 5 per cent in the 1950s to just over 25 per cent today. Over 1,100 different professions are regulated in at least one state, from nurses and opticians to make-up artists and florists. And the requirements are different from state to state. If you lose your job, it is difficult, expensive and time-consuming to obtain a special education and licence to do the exact same thing on the other side of the state border.[45]

Many reforms are needed to deal with the problem of stay-at-home labour, both in the United States and in other parts of the world. However, restricting free trade and competition is not a solution – not only because it would make us all poorer, but also because it would create more losers.

I am sometimes asked to explain to a person who has lost his job because of free trade why he has lost out in the name of restructuring. I frame it like this: perhaps we could save a traditional manufacturing job in, say, steel production with a tariff. But what would have happened if we did? We would have saved a job, at least in the short term. We'd have shown vigour and might be re-elected. That is what you see, as the French nineteenth-century economist Frédéric Bastiat would have said. What you don't see, however, but usually happens afterwards, is something like this: steel becomes more expensive and struggling companies that use it to produce their products get fewer sales, so Person A loses a job in that company. Consumers who face higher prices for everything made of steel now have less money to spend on other goods and services and then Person B loses a job when demand is absent in these sectors. In addition, your tariffs would cause Person C in the exporting country to lose his job and then there would be less money there to buy from our export companies, and then Person D would lose a job there. In addition, we would see less growth and tax revenues generally. So for every person the free trader has to face and explain why he is losing his job, the protectionist has to look at around four people in the eye and explain why they are losing their job. Just because we do not have enough imagination to picture the damage that our actions can cause further down the line does not mean that it does not exist.

The government can't remove the pain, it can just move it on. The problem is that it shifts the burden from the least productive companies to the most productive ones – those that would have prepared the ground for more innovative and competitive jobs. We lose the jobs with tariffs too, but do so from a position of weakness where we cannot create new jobs and do not have the resources to help those affected. If it had not been a tariff that protected the job, but a tax-financed contribution, the effect would have been similar: the state can only create a job by taking resources that would otherwise have been used to create other jobs.

This is not a hypothetical example but what happens every time politicians promise to take action to protect domestic jobs. Maybe I was counting a little low in my example above. A detailed analysis of different US trade barriers showed that each saved job cost consumers on average six times more than the average wage in the manufacturing industry. So for each job saved by protectionism, we lost purchasing power that could have been used to employ six other workers.[46]

Britain is right now experiencing the detrimental consequences of a retreat from open trade. The pursuit of the
hardest possible Brexit has left the country not just outside
the EU but also outside the European single market that
Margaret Thatcher once worked so hard to launch. At
first, many overlooked the dramatic consequences of this
because free trade only ended in January 2021. Since then,
businesses that were used to freely exporting to any EU
country, have found themselves surrounded by new trade
barriers – what Thatcher once called 'the insidious ones
of differing national standards, various restrictions on
the provision of services, exclusion of foreign firms from
public contracts.'[47] As many small businesses give up in
the face of all this red tape, the number of buyer–seller
relationships with Europe has fallen by almost a third. So
far, it seems like Brexit mostly means that bureaucrats take
back control from entrepreneurs and consumers. 'To deny
the downsides of Brexit on trade with the EU is to deny
reality,' writes Iain Martin, the pro-Brexit columnist, for
The Times.[48]

The economy as a whole suffers from this. The pound
has fallen steeply, contributing to costlier imports and
higher prices. Even though a lower exchange rate also
makes exports cheaper, exports have not recovered after
the pandemic in the way they have for other big European
countries. Business investment also lags behind, despite
very generous tax breaks to drive it up. This will combine
to reduce productivity and hold back wages.

Some hoped that Brexit would create a 'Global Britain',
an open, deregulated economy trading freely with the

whole world. But instead, the appetite for globalization has declined and the new free trade deals have mostly just replaced deals Britain already had through the EU. And while a trade deal with Australia is welcome, it can't compensate for being part of a single market of almost half a billion people across the Channel, accounting for more than half Britain's trade.

The official forecaster, the Office for Budget Responsibility, estimates that Brexit will make Britain's trade intensity 15 per cent smaller in the long term than it otherwise would have been, and will make the country 4 per cent poorer. This is roughly £100 billion a year in lost output, depriving the government of around £40 billion of tax revenue a year. In comparison, Liz Truss's proposed cut in the top income tax rate, which spooked markets in September 2022, would have reduced tax revenue by about £2 billion.

In most discussions about trade, we forget the most important loser of all from protectionism: the consumer. And the people it affects the most are low- and middle-income households who spend a larger share of their income on internationally traded goods, such as clothing, food and consumer electronics, while spending a smaller share on domestic services like restaurant visits, real estate and legal services.

According to research published in the *Quarterly Journal of Economics*, the richest tenth of British households would lose roughly 10 per cent of their purchasing power if we stopped all international trade. Maybe they could afford it. However, the poorest tenth would lose as much as 54 per cent of an already much smaller purchasing power.[49] Each tariff barrier is a regressive tax that takes from poor consumers and gives to rich producers. This is a wave of protectionism that wipes out our middle class and our jobs.

4

IN DEFENCE OF THE
1 PER CENT

*'I'm a multi-millionaire, I'm filthy rich. You know why I'm
a multi-millionaire? 'Cause multi-millions like what I do.'*

SOCIALIST FILMMAKER MICHAEL MOORE

One thing is certain with capitalism: that wealth is not distributed equally. In recent decades, a small group of super-rich – the 1 per cent – took the lion's share and left the rest of us behind.

Why should the capitalists get so much? They are not the ones doing the work. When IKEA founder Ingvar Kamprad died in 2018, the chairman of the youth movement of the Swedish Left Party, Henrik Malmrot, who worked at an IKEA warehouse one summer, was quick to point out: 'We are 150,000 workers who should share the inheritance.' IKEA's value is not created by Kamprad but by the workers, he argued, and now it is time for them to 'take back what he stole from them'.[1]

It is a fairly extreme notion that you deserve wealth just because you happened to be in the warehouse at IKEA instead of at a somewhat less successful furniture company, but the basic attitude is widespread: only manual work is real, and nothing is created by the person who invents the business idea, risks money, organizes the work and finds new markets. That is why socialists are always so amazed when their favourite countries run out of goods and experience hunger when the government takes over companies. How come? The country has just as many muscles and brains as before, it is only the exploiters that have disappeared. And that is the answer: Venezuela has no Kamprads. That's why there is nothing to share there. As the Marxist economist Michał Kalecki concluded in 1962 after seeing the desperate poverty in then-socialist countries such as India, the problem is that there are 'too many exploited and too few exploiters'.[2]

One of Sweden's greatest authors, August Strindberg, once shared the ideas of the young socialists, but he also lived in the heyday of industrialism and could see with his own eyes that entrepreneurs were of crucial importance to prosperity. In *The Son of a Servant*, Strindberg tells the story of the worker who comes to a poor village and who has an idea.[3] He borrows money, buys raw materials and tools and asks peasant girls if they can help him weave straw and peasant boys if they can sew straw hats, and suddenly a new business is operational. He pays the workers as agreed, never misses a payment on his loans and pays for the raw materials and still manages to make a small profit. That profit incentivizes him to develop more efficient production, create better designs, find larger markets and constantly stay one step ahead of the competition. Business is getting better and better and suddenly the village is flourishing.

The workers are also better off, the hungry are fed, and the worker – who is now a capitalist – is rich. But one day a spoiled young socialist summer worker comes to the village (no, Strindberg does not write that, he calls him a 'Berliner rascal') and incites the workers: 'this capitalist has become rich off your work', he is 'a thief'. He ignores the fact that their work had always been there, and it was only this new business model that made their work so productive and valuable to consumers.

In Strindberg's story, the young socialist succeeds in convincing the workers to take the hat manufacturer's money and his machines. Now, no one is paying them unless they sell something, and no one is constantly on the lookout for the best raw materials, repairing the machines, streamlining production or looking for new markets. The villagers continue to work, but find that the profits and the salaries soon disappear. And no worker ever came up with the crazy idea of risking their savings to start a factory in the small village again – a village that soon fell back into poverty and hunger.

Strindberg's point was that the capitalist's work is highly productive, and also that he is the last in line of all those who were enriched by it. If an owner is to make money, everyone else in the supply chain must first get theirs: customers have to get a product or service that they value more than the money they give up. Employees must receive their contractual salary every month, even if it takes several years before the company succeeds in selling its product, even if it never succeeds in making a profit. One reason why most people want to work for an employer instead of on their own is that few are willing to wait to get paid or to completely forgo wages if the products do not sell.

In addition, all subcontractors of materials and machinery must be paid for their deliveries to the company, and the bank has to get their interest payments regularly. If anything remains of the revenue when employees, suppliers and lenders have been paid for their efforts, it is called 'profit' and we are very angry when it's a large sum. In fact, we should be happier the bigger it is, because it shows that everyone else in the chain has been paid first and that the company has still succeeded in its ambition to transform time and resources into something we value. That's why it's so frustrating every time someone says that successful entrepreneurs have to 'give something back to society' in order to compensate for their profits. The fact that they have made profits is a sign that they *have* given something to society.

In a free market, you make a profit if you have given others something they want, whatever it may be. Sure, I am a millionaire, the slightly embarrassed left-wing Democrat Bernie Sanders told *The New York Times*: 'I wrote a best-selling book. If you write a best-selling book, you can be a millionaire, too.'[4] Profits are not something you take from others, but a small share you get to keep of the value you create for others. How small a share? Nobel laureate and economist William Nordhaus has studied the profits that innovators and entrepreneurs make in addition to the normal return on investment when they introduce new goods, technologies and methods into the economy.

Nordhaus's conclusion from fifty years of US statistics is that these greedy capitalists seize about 2.2 per cent of the social value of their innovations, despite patent protection and the benefits of being first to market.[5]

Just 2.2 per cent! Why so little? Think of it this way: one day someone will come up with a process that makes microprocessors for half the price. Who benefits from this? The consumers, of course, but first and foremost the innovator, because she only needs to lower the price of microprocessors so much that she is a little below her competitors and yet everyone wants to buy from her. But soon the process begins to spread, she licenses it to other producers, others imitate it and still others learn in this way that it is possible and develop their own methods (and someone soon develops an even better method). After a while, most producers use the new innovation and no one earns much more than they did before. But the invention remains and so does the saving of time and effort, and hence lower prices. It has now become the profit of the consumer and of humanity. (Despite all our sometimes justified concerns that patent protection blocks imitation, it takes less and less time for innovations to spread to other companies and to consumers.)[6]

Capitalism is an improbably good deal for non-capitalists. Entrepreneurs take on debt, risk their homes, ignore friends and family and toil day and night, and if they succeed against all the odds, they get 2.2 per cent of the profits. Meanwhile the rest of us who lie on the couch and watch films get almost 98 per cent, in lower prices for goods and services, and therefore increased purchasing power. This is a beneficial form of inequality, and the greater the profits made by entrepreneurs, the more our 98 per cent share will be worth. On the other hand, 2.2 per cent of multi-billion profits are enough to become a new Ingvar Kamprad, Bill Gates or Elon Musk, and the hope of joining them can inspire many.

Sven Norfeldt, one of Sweden's most successful entrepreneurs, once described the market to me as a minefield. Over there, on the other side, there is new knowledge, capacities, products and services that could enrich the whole of society. But our path there is blocked by a minefield of uncertainty, technological dead-ends, unpredictable consumers, shifting business cycles, interest rate changes, capricious policies and plain bad luck. We have no idea where the mines are located. The only way to find a way to the other side is to get as many people as possible to venture out. This increases the chance that someone will find a safe path that we can all follow.

Nothing can inspire people to make this risky journey of discovery like the hope of getting a substantial share of the profits if they succeed. Most will hit a mine, but a few actually get there. It is not always a fair process, and it's not always the 'right' person who reaches the other side unharmed – not always the person who worked hardest or is the most sympathetic. Maybe it's simply someone who happened to be lucky. But for the rest of us, what's important is that a path is found at all, one that we can follow to the other side and then start tackling the next minefield. This is the only way humanity can move forward.

Grandpa's grandma's grandpa's grandma's time machine

Innovations can still create massive income and wealth differences. If ordinary people's average salary increases by a couple of per cent per year while a small group gets a couple of per cent of trillions of trillions, it might soon feel like we live in completely different worlds. That small group of people make so much money per second that they would lose money by stopping to bend down and pick up a lost hundred-dollar bill.

Such differences are hard to stomach. But maybe we should make an effort. Imagine for a moment, like US economist Donald Boudreaux asks us to in one of his books, that your grandpa's grandma's grandpa's grandma was transported by a time machine from 1800 to 2023 and happened to end up in the home of one of the super-rich – let's say Bill Gates.[7] What do you think she would find most amazing and enviable in his everyday life?

Think for a moment before reading on.

What did you come up with? I personally think she would first note that he does not worry about getting food on the table for himself and his family, or that there is fresh food from around the world rather than just potatoes and porridge. And she would be amazed that he could get safe water just by turning a tap – water that he has not pumped up himself. Even hot water for showering or bathing. On top of that, he can send away the family's faeces to a very safe distance – just by pressing a flush button!

Bill Gates seems to have his teeth left even though he is sixty-seven years old, can take a pill to get rid of headaches and can even get a new hip joint or liver if he needs it. When a previously unknown coronavirus hits the world, he can get a vaccine against it within a year. All three of his children are alive, even though they were born many decades ago and seem to expect to live to be in their eighties.

Bill Gates has plenty of comfortable clothes, and after he's worn them he can make them clean again by stuffing them into a big box. He can make every room bright, even in the middle of the night, by pressing the right place on the wall. He can hold up a small box against something he finds interesting or beautiful and thus generate an almost perfect image of it. Unbelievably, he can use the same little box to look at moving images from the other side of the planet, even in real time. Even though he does not have a symphony orchestra at home, he can listen to masterpieces by Beethoven and Mozart any time he likes or even obscure artists such as VNV Nation and Clan of Xymox – over and over again. The same device seems to be able to answer any question he can come up with, from how to get the weed out of your lawn to who is the richest person in the world.[8]

When your great-great-great-grandmother hears that Bill Gates can also go wherever he wants in a metal construction that travels faster than a horse gallops and that he can fly to other continents in just a few hours with a tubular variant with wings, then she would probably be convinced that she is dreaming. It feels like Gates does not live like a king but as a magician.

This is the amazing life that the world's super-rich lead. But so do you. That's what's most remarkable about this thought experiment. The most impressive things that separate your ancestors' lives from today's super-rich are mostly things that you also have access to. Of course, there are differences. Gates has his own metal tube that he can fly in while you have to share yours with others, and his house with hot water, water closets and symphonies is much bigger than yours. But the super-rich of your ancestors' time also had huge mansions and armies of servants. The amazing new things that have emerged since then you actually share with the super-rich. I would even dare to suggest that the supply of the most important goods, services and amenities is now more evenly distributed than at any other point in the history of mankind.

Why is that the case? Because Bill Gates, Jeff Bezos, Sam Walton, Ingvar Kamprad, and many, many others have been allowed to become super-rich by developing all these goods, services and amenities and creating business models and processes that have reduced them in price so much that they became available to the general public. They have got lots of zeros after the dollar sign in their bank account, but the rest of us got a better, simpler, more comfortable life that would have made grandpa's grandma's grandpa's grandma faint from rapture.

The 1 per cent

But how many of the super-rich are like Gates and Kamprad? Aren't they more often people who sit on large inheritances and passive incomes? The French economist Thomas

Piketty has shown that income from interest and gains on capital grow faster than growth ($r > g$) and that inherited properties just grow and grow until a small elite has almost everything. In the acclaimed *Capital in the Twenty-First Century*, Piketty therefore advocates what he himself calls 'confiscatory taxes' to squeeze the rich. He has no illusion that these taxes would generate large revenues. The important thing is that they end the big incomes. In that case, one must be very sure that the generation of these incomes do not add anything important to society, such as innovation and growth. Piketty is not.

His book has been praised because he is writing more about the entrepreneurs in the novels of Austen and Balzac than about their modern equivalents, and I personally found it quite a fun read, but he understands novels better than entrepreneurship. He admits that 'I know virtually nothing' about how the richest actually became rich. He just assumes that there are no pure hero stories but that everyone is somewhere on 'a continuum' between value creation and pure theft. Piketty writes that 'the courts cannot resolve every case of ill-gotten gains or unjustified wealth', so taxes become 'a less blunt and more systematic instrument for dealing with the question'.[9]

This is completely absurd, both in his disregard of businesses' social contributions and his belief that you should demand higher taxes if you are robbed instead of calling the police. His position is almost a caricature of a French intellectual sitting comfortably in his ivory tower, taking pride in ignoring what's going on down there, in garages, shops and factories, and how that might be related to the fact he lives in history's richest civilization. Piketty happens to confirm my prejudice. Since he turned twenty-five, he writes, 'I have not left Paris, except for a few short trips.'[10]

At the same time, Piketty states an explicit reason to ignore the importance of free enterprise. He believes that even entrepreneurs who profit from their own ideas and work eventually become a 'rentier' – someone who can live on interest and returns alone, for $r > g$ – and then the family's position is reproduced through inheritance. When he looks at Forbes' list of billionaires, he seems to see that over a certain limit, inherited properties 'grow at extremely high rates', much faster than the average fortune. Therefore, they will leave the rest of us behind.[11]

That is strange because when other researchers look at Forbes' list of 400 billionaires in 1982, they find that only sixty-nine of them or their heirs remain in 2014, and their conclusion is that 'dynastic wealth accumulation is simply a myth.'[12] Another researcher looked at the individuals who remained on the Forbes list between 1987 and 2014 and the 327 who left it, and calculated that their average annual wealth increase was a paltry 2.4 per cent. That is only a third of what they would have received if they had invested the money in a passive US index fund during the same period.[13] Far from accumulating more and more, the richest are losing out in terms of overall wealth growth due to philanthropy and taxes, consumption, poor investment decisions and, for some of them, hefty fines (because a few really are crooks).

What is striking when looking at the Forbes list is the absence of names such as Rockefeller, Carnegie, Morgan,

Mellon, Hearst, Stanford and Vanderbilt – the super-rich families called 'robber barons' in the late nineteenth century. When you follow rich families, it turns out that around 70 per cent of their wealth disappears in the second generation. After the third generation, as much as 90 per cent of the wealth is gone.[14]

Piketty has made an elementary mistake: he has only focused on the most successful on the Forbes list right now – the likes of Bill Gates – and how they have fared, while forgetting those whose fortunes have diminished and completely ignoring those who have fallen off the list. It's a bit like stating that humans are immortal because you've limited your observation to those who are still out and about in the city.

Interestingly, the year 1982 – a time when the Western world was exceptionally equal – is more reminiscent of Piketty's nightmare of dynastic empires than today's capitalism. Of the hundred richest people on Forbes' list, sixty had then inherited their money. As many as ten of them were heirs to DuPont's nearly 200-year-old fortune. This is what it looks like when taxes are high, most people are employed and few start new companies: equality looks impressive and few new assets are created. In that case, old money stays strong. By 2020, the number of heirs on Forbes' list had more than halved, with only twenty-seven of the hundred richest people having primarily inherited their fortune.[15] The proportion of US billionaires' inherited assets has decreased continuously, from about 50 per cent in 1976 to 35 per cent in 2001, to just over 30 per cent in 2014.[16] The proportion of the ten richest per cent who are also in the top ten in earned income – and thus seem to accumulate their wealth at work rather than at the club – has doubled since 1980.

In fact, Piketty is also wrong in his overall thesis. The share of incomes made up of capital gains has indeed grown since the 1970s, yet this is not due to wealthy capital owners but is mainly explained by housing prices. They have increased by an absurd amount but are also more evenly distributed than other forms of capital since home ownership is more equally distributed than ownership of stocks. Excluding housing, the share of capital income has decreased somewhat since the 1950s.[17] According to calculations by the scholar Branko Milanović, who is deeply concerned about inequality and wants to tax the rich harder, the distribution of capital income has been relatively stable in the United States and United Kingdom since 1975. (Given how obsessed everyone is with Reagan and Thatcher, it may be worth pointing out that the distribution does not look so different there than in countries like Germany and Norway.)[18]

As more people make money instead of inheriting it, the fortunes of the super-rich do not grow 'at extremely high rates' but more slowly than the average, and capital income does not grow faster than growth if one excludes the housing market. We also have to remind ourselves of grandpa's grandma's grandpa's grandma's time machine. Inequality in dollars and cents is not the same as inequality in access to the good things in life. A sign of this is that the increased economic inequality in the Western world has not been followed by increased inequality in the subjective feeling of well-being. On the contrary: inequality in happiness has actually decreased significantly in fast-growing Western countries, even where income inequality has increased at the same time.[19]

Another reason why happiness inequality does not increase might simply be that we have exaggerated even inequality in dollars and cents, since most studies look at market income and exclude the taxes and most of the transfers that are partly implemented to reduce inequality. The US Census Bureau claims that the top quintile receives 16.7 times as much income as the bottom quintile. However, if you include all the taxes that mostly reduce incomes at the top and the transfers that add more at the bottom, the difference is reduced from 16.7 to just four times as much.[20]

Globally, of course, inequality is more conspicuous, but thanks to the fact that low- and middle-income countries have grown faster than rich countries during the era of trade liberalization and international supply chains, global income inequality has decreased for the first time since the Industrial Revolution. This is a monumental change, and it has been dizzyingly quick. Between 2000 and 2018 the global Gini coefficient (a measure of income inequality, rated from 1 to 100) decreased from seventy to sixty points, thus erasing a hundred-year build-up of global inequality in less than two decades.[21]

Nor have we seen a rapid increase in global inequality in assets. I'm not overly pleased with Credit Suisse's popular annual compilations of global assets. A lot of it is pure guesswork and, because they do not use adjusted figures for the purchasing power of the local currency, they underestimate the prosperity of poor countries. Dramatic annual shifts

Global inequality 1950–2018[22]

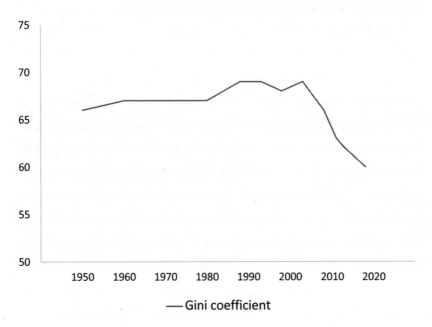

— Gini coefficient

are often simply a reflection of changes in the exchange rate. But it is interesting that these data also show that the share of the world's financial assets among the wealthiest decreased slightly between 2000 and 2020. The richest tenth decreased its share from 89 to 82 per cent and the share of the top 1 per cent decreased from 48 to 45 per cent despite the incredible increase in asset prices during this period.[23]

Nevertheless, the differences are huge. Every year, the aid organization Oxfam works hard to come up with a new calculation of how dramatically skewed global distribution is, based on Credit Suisse's reports. Recently, Oxfam announced that the world's 2,153 billionaires own more than the world's 4.6 billion poorest people combined.[24] It sounds like complete madness, and they are making it seem as if the world's problems could be solved if only the rich shared some of their wealth.

One should know that the reason why the contrast seems so sharp is that the poorest have hardly any financial net assets like stocks and bonds. There is not much left of the poorest's assets when you deduct all the debts they have from this amount. Oxfam also includes indebted Westerners who have just received their college degree in their calculation – according to their method, about a fifth of the world's poorest 10 per cent are in Europe and North America. So when Oxfam adds up the total assets of the poorest 4.6 billion, they first deduct student debt and housing loans in rich countries from the assets. I used to tell Oxfam that with their way of counting, my daughter, whose piggy bank contained a total fortune of about $20, was richer than two billion people combined.

But ignore that for a moment. Maybe the poor of the world could be helped if the rich shared their fortunes? What if we simply distributed the billionaires' assets to these 4.6 billion? If we somehow managed to avoid the problem that all the world's stock exchanges and most companies would collapse when we tried to sell these unrealized gains, it would give everyone almost $1,900. That's not peanuts. It would increase the annual income of the poorest 4.6 billion by almost 60 per cent, but unfortunately only for a year, then the money would run out – at the cost of eliminating financial incentives for entrepreneurship, investment and innovation worldwide.

Therefore, let's say that instead we give the 4.6 billion people the return on capital so that they receive an annual income boost. We expropriate all billionaires' money and invest it in an index fund, and then we assume, optimistically, an annual return with reinvested dividends that is adjusted for inflation following what we have had in the last twenty successful years in the United States. If all goes well, then each of the world's 4.6 billion poorest will receive an extra 32 cents a day (before tax). In that case, we will increase the average income level of the world's poor by roughly 4 per cent. That is not to be sniffed at, but it does not directly solve all the problems of the world.

It is also, fascinatingly, less of an increase than they receive on the market *every year* under normal circumstances. The poorest half of the world population saw their average incomes increase by roughly 6 per cent annually from 2008–18. The poorest tenth increased it by almost 8 per cent every year.[25] That is compounded growth: you increase last year's income by 8 per cent and next year you increase that new, higher sum total by 6 per cent, and so on. It is not just an extra 32 cents every year. It is through such steady growth that poverty is reduced in the long term – not by redistributing the prosperity we already have but by creating more of it, by investing in new technology and better methods. That does not tend to happen in countries that expropriate the wealth of the rich and successful, but it does in the countries where poor people can become billionaires if they have a successful idea. As Venezuela's Hugo Chávez showed, even $1,000 billion does not go very far if it is not constantly reinvested productively.

As Churchill stated in a parliamentary debate in October 1945: 'The inherent vice of capitalism is the unequal sharing of blessings. The inherent virtue of socialism is the equal sharing of miseries.'

Does inequality kill?

Take the London Underground train eastwards from Green Park on the Jubilee Line, and the average life expectancy for someone born in London drops by one year for every two stops. If you travel northbound from Hyde Park Corner to Holloway Road, a fifteen-minute ride on the Piccadilly Line, life expectancy decreases by eleven years.[26]

Books like *The Spirit Level* and *The Killing Fields of Inequality* argue that it is not just poverty that is the problem. Inequality in itself creates status stress and health issues. Therefore it is not enough to fight poverty; we must also fight great wealth.

Angus Deaton, the Nobel laureate who has done so much to focus the world on deaths of despair in the United States, is very critical of such research: '[I]t is not true that income inequality itself is a major determinant of population health… it is low incomes that are important, not inequality, and there is no evidence that making the rich richer, however undesirable that may be on other grounds, is hazardous to the health of the poor or their children, provided that their own incomes are maintained.'[27] In his book *Deaths of Despair*, written with Anne Case Deaton, he also points out that inequality is a 'false trail' in the debate: 'those in despair are in despair because of what is happening to their own lives and to the communities in which they live, not because the top 1 per cent got richer'.[28]

Almost all examples that are popular in the debate can be explained by the fact that unequal countries have on average more poverty, and it is poverty – not income difference – that undermines health. Unequal US states have, on average, a larger African-American population, which has worse health than other groups at all income levels due to a long history of racism and inferior healthcare.

Along London Underground lines, income differences are big, but even there the causality is contested. Income is often less important than the lifestyle it is associated with, as the Swedish author Fredrik Segerfeldt has noted.[29] Those who lack education smoke more, eat more unhealthily and exercise less, but not because they have less money. Cigarettes are expensive, and you can take a walk for free. A major reason for differences in life expectancy is that smoking is four times more common in the most deprived areas of England than those living in the least deprived areas. These differences are more related to the fact that it has become a status symbol in the middle and upper class to exercise, think about diet and live a healthy life. It is now embarrassing to not take care of oneself, and social stigma means such habits spread fast. It is more difficult to change the culture of others through government dictate, no matter how much social engineers would like to do so. But there is actually one thing that seems to work: in 2016, American researchers in *The Journal of the American Medical Association* discovered that low-income earners have better health if they live in cities with many high-income earners.[30]

It's a fascinating finding. Seeing people with higher incomes, better housing and a fancy lifestyle every day was assumed to make one status-stressed, humiliated and ill. But it turns out that it makes one feel better and live longer than being surrounded by people at the same income level. Why? One of the researchers behind the report speculates that it is because habits are contagious: 'So poor people living near rich people may pick up a lot of their habits. Some of these habits – say, pretentious vocabulary – aren't likely to affect one's health. Others – working out – will definitely have a positive impact. Indeed, poor people living near rich people exercise more, smoke less, and are less likely to suffer from obesity.'[31]

When does someone write the book *Inequality Saves Lives*?

Not all super-rich!

This does not mean that inequality is desirable as such. Inequality is good if it arises because a person creates something that makes her and other people's lives better. Unfortunately, not all inequality is due to such good processes – sometimes it is due to the opposite. This is often the case in authoritarian and corrupt states around the world. Russia has become one of the world's most unequal countries through the elite's institutionalized theft from the people. But the problem of ugly inequality also exists in democratic market economies.

When I fought against the anti-globalization movement

twenty years ago, black-clad left-wing activists and henna-dyed hippies had an unexpected ally among their financiers: the conservative textile magnate Roger Milliken. His generosity towards free trade opponents across the political spectrum had a simple explanation: his business model was dependent on high tariff barriers that prevented poor countries from selling clothes to the American market.

Capitalism is based on companies competing for the favour of consumers with better goods and services, but unfortunately many companies choose instead to compete for the favour of politicians to get subsidies, tariffs, regulatory benefits and bailouts so that they do not have to worry about consumers. It is not free market capitalism, it is crony capitalism – or, as it is sometimes called, socialism for the rich – and it is one of the biggest problems in our economy. Partly because it gives one group of people the legal right to put its hand in our wallets, and partly because it helps non-competitive business models to survive and drag down the entire economy.

Before the pandemic, when making a documentary for American public television, I travelled around America to study this phenomenon – from tariff protection for steel companies to restrictions on building so as not to disturb the view (or value) of the lucky ones who already live in the most attractive areas. I saw how large food companies receive huge subsidies for the cultivation of maize, wheat, soybeans, sugar and cotton – paid by consumers and by the farmers who grow fruit and vegetables that are not subsidized. I met experts who estimate that about 70 per cent of the subsidies go to the 10 per cent largest agricultural holdings. This is not just a US phenomenon, of course. OECD countries spend approximately $300 billion on farm subsidies annually – almost ten billion a day.

Among the most successful American welfare queens are the brothers Alfonso and José Fanjul in Florida, who receive around $65 million in subsidies for their sugar empire annually. They use part of that money to buy political support for a continued stream of subsidies in their direction. The best that can be said about them is that at least they don't contribute to political polarization. During the irreconcilable presidential election campaign in 2016, the Fanjul brothers protected themselves by holding one fundraiser for Trump and one for Clinton.

I witnessed a shameless attempt by large food companies to regulate a small family farm to death. The state of Indiana allows small-scale farmers to slaughter their chickens on the farm, provided they use a safe and proven technology, so that they don't have to rely on large, centralized slaughterhouses. But when Hawkins Family Farm began to achieve greater success and managed to sell its chicken to upscale restaurants, big agriculture persuaded many state politicians to remove the exemption and ban Hawkins chickens. It was not only the chicken industry but also the pork and steak industry that lobbied hard for the proposal, which they saw as a chance to stop smaller competitors overnight. This time the proposal was stopped by angry popular opinion but, as Zach Hawkins said, the most common result of such processes is for 'the small farmers to lose the battle'.

The more heavily businesses are regulated, the greater is the business community's legitimate interest in lobbying to protect itself against clumsy or excessive regulations. They must invest more and more in lobbying and political contacts as a form of self-defence. Silicon Valley's tech companies once took pride in not lobbying politically, but they soon found out that if you are not at the table, you are on the menu, and felt compelled to join the game. Now their lists of vacancies are full of titles such as 'public policy manager' and 'director of government affairs'. Then, of course, comes the temptation and the opportunity to lobby to tailor the regulations to one's own business and to stop competitors. Be on your guard when a business interest says there is chaos in the market and that it would probably be best for everyone with a little more order and fewer actors. 'When buying and selling are controlled by legislation, the first things to be bought and sold are legislators,' as P. J. O'Rourke has observed.[32]

Companies also turn tax rules to their advantage. As a Swede, I had the dubious pleasure of observing how the Swedish furniture giant IKEA opened a large store in Memphis, Tennessee, on condition that they received a tax deduction of over $9.5 million. Many large companies that are considering establishing themselves in a new region use this tactic against political assemblies: 'What do we get if we come?' When I met two local furniture companies who did not receive any corresponding deductions, they asked why they should be forced to pay higher taxes so that their rival could compete more fiercely.

Then of course we have the financial markets, full of banks and financial companies that count on taxpayers saving them when they fail, and traders who think that the central bank must avoid any risk of a bear market with promises of low interest rates and increased liquidity. This has perverted the stock market. It is supposed to value companies, and when, say, trade wars, pandemics and recessions hurt those companies, stocks should fall in value, yet instead they have often increased because central banks respond to every crisis by lowering interest rates and pumping more money into the economy. This creates speculative bubbles and makes it all the more painful when they finally burst. At any given stage, it is understandable why central banks act as they do. When a housing bubble is punctured or companies face a debt crisis, the consequences can be dire. The only problem is that the attempts to save people from the consequences of their folly is to fill the world with fools.

To help the economy recover from the dotcom bubble, interest rates were cut drastically in 2001. No one made money from savings any more, so they searched for exotic bonds in the only sector that rating agencies and governments thought bomb-proof: the housing market. This gave rise to the global financial crisis of 2008, which I wrote about in my book *Financial Fiasco*. To get out of that crisis, greater stimuli and even negative interest rates were introduced.[33] Indebtedness therefore increased even more, not least for house buyers and companies with low credit ratings – the only ones who paid any interest to speak of. When the pandemic struck, of course, interest rates on these risky loans rose sharply, and to prevent a wave of defaults, central banks bought even more, which is in effect a subsidy of hedge funds and others who have speculated in the loans least likely to be repaid. Now this unrestrained monetary expansion has pushed stock and housing prices to imaginary levels and the fall might be even deeper once we return to a somewhat normal situation.

Again, the behaviour is understandable. Nobody wants a crisis to be deeper than it needs to be, and once you have subsidized huge risks it becomes even more expensive when they fail. The problem is that in this way the state has annulled the market forces. If you just get rich enough and are sufficiently important for the financial markets, gravity will shift and you can only fall upwards. The financial upper class that owns assets, such as shares and condominiums in the big cities, have been enriched, while most people have to pay for this in inflation and more public debt. Unfortunately, a substantial part of the growing inequality in recent decades is not due to the kind of innovations and investments I wrote about earlier in this chapter but to the fact that governments coddle speculators.

This policy encourages irresponsible behaviour. Capitalism is a profit *and* loss system – profits when you do what's right, losses when you do what's wrong. The losses are absolutely crucial signals. Failing companies should be cleared out and capital transferred from them to more competitive business models, not given artificial respiration. If companies and speculators know they will be saved if their investments fail, their only driving force is to increase their leverage, seek increasingly exotic assets, ever higher risks and multiply their efforts, aware that they can always send losses to the government. In this way, we systematize mispricing of risk and stockpile more and more bad investments in the economy.

One consequence is that the economy is becoming increasingly zombified – full of business models that are the living dead. A study by the Bank for International Settlements (BIS) – an international financial institution owned by central banks – defines a zombie company as a company that has such meagre profits that it cannot meet interest payments and has a low valuation that suggests poor prospects. The share of listed companies that are zombies has increased rapidly in rich countries – from less than one in twenty in the late 1980s to one in six companies before the pandemic. There is reason to believe that this is an underestimate, as many problem companies are unlisted and the pandemic has also increased their number.[34]

One reason why zombie companies have become much more common, especially since the global financial crisis, is the prolonged era of extremely low interest rates. This made it less interesting for banks (which also face low borrowing costs) to force them into bankruptcy, which would also force the banks to record a loss and risk entering into a long-running dispute over assets. Zombie companies find it much easier to sell bonds in a market that the central banks has inflated. So they stumble on and tie up capital and labour that would otherwise have gone to more energetic newcomers in the industry.

The BIS review shows that an increase in the proportion of zombie companies by one percentage point reduces productivity growth in the economy by 0.1 percentage points. In that case, it would mean that the zombification since the mid-1990s has reduced productivity growth by one percentage point – a large part of the growth problem in Western economies.

Socialism for capitalists is no better than other forms of socialism, and few reforms could be more important than once again making capitalism a system of profit *and* loss. The market-liberal logic is merciless: either a business is competitive and so does not need support, or it is not competitive and so doesn't deserve support.

5

MONOPOLY
OR MINECRAFT?

'If you care about democracy, you need to break up the monopolies. If you care about the economy, same thing.'

TUCKER CARLSON

Alright, you might object, perhaps there are examples of entrepreneurs who become super-rich by working hard to give consumers the goods and services they have been longing for. But what if large companies, by virtue of their size, can stay in control of large segments of their market and pressure suppliers and employees into submission? And what about tech companies, who can use their dominance to obtain more and more information about us, and use it to control the way we spend our time and to silence voices they don't like? We don't seek them out, they are just there, everywhere, and the more we use their products the more psychologically hooked and emotionally drained we become.

When I wrote *In Defence of Global Capitalism*, I described a situation where the dominance of the big companies decreased. That was true then but it's not true any more. In the entire OECD area, market concentration has increased. Some large companies are taking over ever larger parts of the national markets, and they can set prices that are ever higher above the marginal cost – the cost to produce one additional unit of a product or a service. In a high-profile report, Barack Obama's Council of Economic Advisers showed that between 1997 and 2012 revenues had been concentrated in fewer and fewer large companies in ten of thirteen US sectors.[1] It conjures up the image of powerful monopolies that are devouring more local markets. Many have linked this development to disappointing productivity gains in Western economies – the problem of getting more output from the input, such as labour or capital.

Before we examine whether it is time to worry about the dominance of big companies, let's start with the question of why we should worry about monopolies. The traditional fear is that companies that dominate a market can limit product development and supply, raise prices and lower wages, because consumers and employees have nowhere else to go. If we were to see such results, all our alarm bells should ring.

As I showed in the previous chapter, there are such examples. There are plenty of companies that make sure politicians keep their competitors at a safe distance so they can continue to destroy capital and productivity. But that is not the dominant trend. On the contrary, it is large companies that invest the most in new business methods, research, development and innovations.[2] In addition, they reduce prices more often than they raise them. Companies such as IKEA and Walmart do not primarily base their strong positions on tax deductions but on efficient production and logistics systems that allow them to sell their products cheaper than anyone else. Many in the tech industry even give them away for free. And far from using their position to pay lower wages, on average, companies pay more the bigger they are. US companies with more than 1,000 employees pay about twice as much as companies with fewer than a hundred employees.[3]

This means there must be something wrong with the new monopoly narrative. What that is becomes evident when you look at the extent to which the market share is concentrated in a small number of firms at different geographical levels. Then you see that market concentration increases nationally but actually *decreases* locally and regionally. It sounds contradictory but is two different ways of looking at the same change. If there is only one cafe in your village and suddenly a Starbucks opens, this means that the concentration decreases locally, but it increases nationally because Starbucks is already the largest cafe chain. So what looks like increased monopolism nationally may locally mean greater choice and increased competition. And that is good news because we consumers live in a local environment, not in an aggregated national table.

Economists Esteban Rossi-Hansberg and Chang-Tai Hsieh estimate that about 93 per cent of increased concentration in the United States is due to large companies having established themselves in more places. This is mainly a new set of retailers that have succeeded in the difficult task of increasing productivity in the service sector. Innovative business models and large investments in data processing have made it possible for them to quickly and smoothly adapt their methods and offerings to changing demand geographically and over time. This is a more likely explanation for the increasing concentration than the usual notion that it is due to a relaxation of US competition law. The pattern is the same in other OECD countries, including in the EU, where competition law has been tightened.[4]

This explains many of the paradoxes that have given academics so much headache. The United States' productivity growth peaked in 1996–2005, one percentage point above the historical average, and that happens to be the period when market concentration increased most rapidly.[5] The fact that productivity growth has fallen since then has to do more with the zombie companies than the super-star firms. The latter have grown so large because they are more efficient, which explains why increased dominance on paper can be combined with being more productive. Their investment in information technology is very costly but can then provide cheap unit cost, which means they can set prices that are higher above their marginal cost than other companies can, while still giving customers lower prices. Rossi-Hansberg and Hsieh refer to it as an 'industrial revolution in services'.[6]

These are not some lazy monopolists who are slowing down the economy (although there are some like that). These are creative entrepreneurs who increase the pace so much that others do not keep up. It is not 'monopoly capitalism', where one gains by simply taking up more and more limited space and taking more of people's pay cheques.[7]

It is rather Minecraft capitalism, an open environment, where other players are not primarily opponents but partners, where you extract and collect resources, acquire ever better tools and, on your own or with others, stack blocks to build increasingly ingenious constructions, and in that way make the whole game more beautiful, interesting and exciting for others.

We used to be concerned about monopolies because they would serve consumers poorly. But if companies become large because they are better, that's another matter. Of course, they are a threat to other companies, but that's the way it should be. Economic development presupposes that more productive and innovative companies beat the others. I know what you're thinking: how fun is it with Starbucks, Tescos and H&Ms everywhere? Shouldn't there be room for eccentric, local alternatives? I can understand that frustration. Few things make my blood boil as much as when my charming favourite cafe is replaced by a streamlined chain serving some vanilla-bullshit-latte-cappa thing. But if the charming places are as charming as we say they are, we will express this with our purchasing power and then they will have no problem flourishing, even next to the chains. If, on the other hand, we choose not to go there, it means that our complaint was just theoretical, and so we have no right to whine about how society changes because that change is us.

In the long run, other companies will learn from these large companies and start to compete. Before we know it, many of the big ones will be swept away. And if they ever take advantage of the dominance they have created using low prices and good service and instead raise prices and worsen the service, that will be the blood in the water that signals for the competition to attack. Today, the dominant companies may look unbeatable, but companies always do that just before they fall. Capitalism is merciless against capitalists who do not deliver. When I wrote *In Defence of Global Capitalism* twenty years ago, I rhetorically asked how many people remembered that the world's largest mobile phone manufacturer, Nokia, 'just a few years ago, was a small Finnish firm manufacturing motor tyres and boots?' Today, the question is rather how many people remember that Nokia was the world's largest mobile phone manufacturer in 2001.

Only fifty-one of the companies on the Fortune 500 list of the largest US companies in 2020 have been on the list since it was started in 1955. This means that almost 90 per cent of the largest companies have gone bankrupt, been acquired, just dropped out or closed shop.[8]

For obvious reasons, established companies always fight hard to protect and develop the business model that has made them successful. However, this makes it difficult for them to develop new innovations that would cannibalize sales of their own products. Business history abounds with examples of companies that dominated the market and actually had all the technical expertise to take the next step. IBM should have developed fast personal computers, Kodak the digital camera, Sony the digital music player, Lego Minecraft, and Blockbuster video streaming. But they were a little too fond of their old markets and therefore missed the next big thing.

The Austrian economist Ludwig von Mises said that the reason why critics of the market believe it is synonymous to corporate power is that we can all see that entrepreneurs and capitalists are at the helm and control the economic ship:

'The direction of all economic affairs is in the market society a task of the entrepreneurs. Theirs is the control of production. They are at the helm and steer the ship. A superficial observer would believe that they are supreme. But they are not. They are bound to obey unconditionally the captain's orders. The captain is the consumer. Neither the entrepreneurs nor the farmers nor the capitalists determine what has to be produced. The consumers do that. If a businessman does not strictly obey the orders of the public as they are conveyed to him by the structure of market prices, he suffers losses, he goes bankrupt, and is thus removed from his eminent position at the helm. Other men who did better in satisfying the demand of the consumers replace him.'[9]

The most important anti-trust policy is to trade freely and keep markets open so that others who could steer the ship better are able to compete.

When the Obama Council of Economic Advisers concluded that US markets saw increasing levels of concentration, it made a beginner's error by looking only at goods produced in the United States. This meant, for example, that it looked like Motorola had 100 per cent market share in mobile phones because it was the only company that manufactured them within the country's borders. They analysed a market where there were no iPhones, Samsungs or Huaweis.[10] Two central bank economists looked at market dominance in US industries in 1992–2012 but also added goods that consumers bought from abroad. Then it turned out that the entire increase in concentration disappeared. The market share of the twenty largest companies *decreased*.[11]

How much did you lie today?

Was that a bit too much? Sounds like I'm idealizing corporations? As if the big bullies are just good entrepreneurs with the public interest in mind? In that case, I have not made myself clear. I know that some will be tempted to lie and deceive, and I know perfectly well that there are thieves and bandits hiding among the companies. That is why we must have free markets. Had we always been able to rely solely on their goodwill, we could have offered them monopoly power and tariff protection. It is precisely because we *cannot* count on their goodwill that we need to control them with free competition and consumer choice, as well as an independent legal system and free media. Capitalism is our way to keep capitalists under our control.

That does not stop us from regularly discovering scandals in the business world, such as Volkswagen's manipulated emissions tests, Theranos' fraudulent blood tests or the collapse of Sam Bankman-Fried's crypto exchange FTX. At the same time, such scams are getting so much attention, and causing such a strong market reaction, because they are exceptions. There is a built-in protection against crooks in the market: businesses are voluntary collaborations based on trust; no one wants to collaborate with someone who does not inspire trust. That is not always enough, because confidence tricksters use our limited information against us. Low-cost airlines continue to sell airline tickets with attractive flight times, which they then systematically change to an unearthly hour on Monday morning (didn't you read the small print?). Unscrupulous loan sharks obscure their default interest rate and use the bailiff as if it were a branch of business. And the customer service of some companies is so chronically understaffed that you can never ask for your money back. Not every businessman is a hero.

However, economist Tyler Cowen poses an interesting question to assess the reliability of entrepreneurship. Sure, he notes, companies lie but the question is: do they lie as much as normal people do? That is not a given, because we are not always in line with the truth. On average, we lie about twice in a ten-minute conversation, usually to our loved ones. Or look at our dating profiles online: according to one survey, 53 per cent admit that they have lied in their profile (and should any hardened liar refuse to admit a lie, this is of course an underestimate). Our profile pictures are so often from a bygone era (ten years and ten pounds ago) that many platforms have begun to demand time-stamped photos. And don't even get me started on the CVs we show to potential employers. One recruiter estimates that 40 per cent contain pure lies, 76 per cent improve their history and 59 per cent omit key information.[12]

With the help of data analysis, you can also find out how much we lie to our friends and relatives. On social media, we present ourselves as a happy family on holiday, who exercise, eat exciting food and read Thomas Mann's *The Magic Mountain*. But when we search online in the comfort of anonymity, we deal with relationship problems and body discomfort and try to find short summaries of what *The Magic Mountain* is really about.

Seth Stephens-Davidowitz recently studied these discrepancies and the result was the book *Everybody Lies*. Just take the difference in how women talk about their husbands. On social media, the description of the husband is usually 'fantastic', 'cute' and 'my best friend'. In anonymous searches, where they want frank advice, the husband is instead 'an idiot', 'annoying' – or possibly 'gay'.[13] Admittedly, one should keep in mind that the anonymous search tends towards the forbidden because we are looking for things that we find difficult to talk about with others. So the truth about your husband's character may sit somewhere between Instagram and Google.

The fact is we bend the truth when we need to polish our self-image, present ourselves as a little better and more interesting than we are, or just want to avoid a quarrel and the bad mood that the unvarnished truth tends to cause. Therefore, it is not surprising that we do the same in business (or in academia, journalism, politics or in non-profit organizations). The difference is that companies work hard to develop institutions and control mechanisms to reduce this risk because they know that trust sells. There is a greater chance that you will be deceived by the door-to-door salesman than at Tesco or Starbucks.

One of my favourite surveys listed the most stolen books from American and British libraries. If there was any truth in the view that moral philosophers often depict businessmen being particularly unscrupulous, one would imagine that textbooks on economics and management literature, to be studied by future capitalists, would be at the top of the list. But the books most often stolen are the ones on moral philosophy! Obscure, modern works on ethics, which are mainly read by teachers and research students, are stolen 50 per cent more often than books that are not about ethics. (Although I am embarrassed to say that books by classical liberals like Locke and Mill seem to be particularly prone to being stolen.)[14]

Undignified consumption

Several critics of *In Defence of Global Capitalism* said I ignored the fact that one form of fraud underlines the entire modern consumer society. It concerns so-called 'planned obsolescence', companies that deliberately build in errors and shortcomings that shorten the lifespan of products and therefore force us to buy new ones. According to some critics, it is a central mechanism behind the modern growth model.[15] Isn't it strange that older iPhones suddenly started to slow down after a software update? How come your washing machine breaks down after seven years, when it can continue to wash for decades in the laundromat? And why on earth do my light bulbs go out when there's a light bulb, the Centennial Light, at a fire station in Livermore, California, that's been shining for 120 years?

The answer according to the documentary *The Light Bulb Conspiracy* is that companies all over the world formed a cartel in 1925 to shorten the lifespan and raise the price of light bulbs. Otherwise we would all have had centenary lamps today. It is true that there was such a cartel, but it was quickly put out of action, partly because the Swedish consumer cooperative Lumafabriken took up the competition with cheaper light bulbs. The cartel was forced to reduce the price to the same level as Luma the same year. Interestingly, Luma did not then try to manufacture any bulbs that lasted for an eternity – it was too expensive to do so and did not provide good enough light.

The Livermore lamp shines for the simple reason that it has a carbon wire that is much thicker than modern metal wires, but it is a terribly inefficient way to make light out of electricity. At the beginning of the nineteenth century, tungsten filaments were used instead because they can withstand a much higher temperature and thus emit a stronger light. The side effect is that the wire also wears faster, but if you want to save money and save the environment, it is actually much better to change the bulb from time to time (and, unlike the Livermore firefighters, to turn it off when you are not using it, even though that also shortens its service life). Or even better – enjoy the technological development that now gives us low-energy light bulbs that produce more light from less electricity, and have a burning time of almost 100,000 hours, compared to 1,000 hours for a traditional light bulb.

In most instances, we can get significantly better products that last longer if we are willing to pay for it, but it's all about priorities. You can buy a washing machine that is built to handle much more than the one you have. There is a large selection of durable machines for laundry use that are on sale between $5,000 and $20,000. But if you go heavily into debt just to be able to afford one, what do you do when a significantly better and more energy-efficient alternative is developed in a couple of years? Choosing something that is less durable is in fact often a reasonable balance between personal finances, convenience, time spent and expectations of future development. There is no obvious right balance, so the best thing is to have different solutions compete with each other and consumers who are free to choose, then all of us can learn from these experiments.

When it comes to cars, long life gives a higher resale value, so durability becomes a key competitive advantage. That's why a car today can achieve a mileage twice as high as it did when I was a kid. Only 7 per cent of American cars manufactured in 1960 turned fifteen years old – today, the *average* age of the American car fleet is over twelve years.[16] In other cases, the development is so fast that customers will soon want a new variant, as in the case of mobile phones. Then it becomes difficult to get a consumer to pay for an expensive model built to last a couple of decades. In other cases, we are too frugal for our own good. If we just focus on the price, we will get plain products built with basic components. The drive to keep costs down means the manufacturer will not include a compartment that allows for the replacement of batteries or other parts, for example. How much do you think they can pay for components of a coffee maker that is sold for $9.90 or a printer for $39.90?

I don't rule out that there are real examples of planned obsolescence, where the manufacturer actively reduces the longevity of a product, but it is more unusual than the debate suggests and the company that is exposed doing it will quickly be punished in the market. France has a law against planned obsolescence, and it has mostly shown how difficult it is to document a single case. Yes, it was heard all over the world that Apple was forced to pay a fine after older iPhones started working more slowly following a software update. But what few observed is that Apple was never considered guilty of planned obsolescence, only of not informing users of the change. The background was that many users' iPhones crashed after an update of the operating system at the end of 2016. The reason was that older batteries could not cope with the power of all new applications when they were not sufficiently charged. To solve that problem, Apple introduced a feature in the next update that prevented phones from crashing when exposed to high workloads, by performing certain tasks over a longer period of time when they reached a peak. This is the exact opposite of planned ageing: since most people prefer a slower mobile phone to one that crashes, it prolongs its lifetime. That is also what the French court found. Apple now informs users about this function and as a user you can turn it off if you would rather have an iPhone that crashes at regular intervals.

On the other hand, capitalists don't have to make old products break down. Instead, they can regularly come up with new products that have a slightly better function and a slightly slimmer design, so we will still be tempted to upgrade quickly. This is a staple argument of anti-commercialism: that capitalism creates new needs by playing on our acquisitiveness and status anxiety. But no matter how silly the product is, such as a hoodie sewn into a blazer, a boiler suit in denim and specially designed toilet brushes, new consumer goods rarely reflect a newly created need. Humans have always sought different opportunities to enhance their beauty, status, convenience, safety, communication, transportation and entertainment. It's just the ways to satisfy it that constantly change – from cave paintings to Instagram, from smoke signals to smartphones, from tattoos to, well, back to tattoos.

Anthropologists and archaeologists have not found a single human culture that has not in any way adorned itself. One hundred thousand years before the beauty industry told us we needed to groom and decorate ourselves, our ancestors were willing to offer everything they had and even risk their lives in battle to get coveted pigments to colour their skin. The Neanderthals had no luxury brands that manipulated them, but they still fought over the best eagle claws to make necklaces and bracelets from.

Anyone who believes that consumer culture is a result of the pressure of commercial interests has a hard time explaining why people who threw off the yoke of communism immediately coveted jeans and record players. In the Taliban's Afghanistan around the turn of the millennium, women went to underground beauty salons and painted themselves under the burqas, despite being threatened with flogging. The moment the Taliban fell in 2001, Afghans lined up to buy make-up, televisions and VCRs. Undignified, thought Western intellectuals, and 'how depressing was it to see Afghan citizens celebrating the end of tyranny by buying consumer electronics?' lamented one Western journalist.[17] But that's human nature for you, says archaeologist Brian Hayden, who has lived with indigenous peoples in the Middle East, the Far East, North America and Australia. It is not commercialism – it is us: 'I can say categorically that the people of all the cultures I have come in contact with exhibit a strong desire to have the benefits of industrial goods that are available. I am convinced that the "nonmaterialistic culture" is a myth.'[18]

In this consumption we can also discern a certain restlessness that is not due to planned obsolescence but because it is deeply human to get used to an item and then be attracted by something new. There is no big brand running expensive campaigns to make us tired of old personal names and buy a new, fresh one that they have patented. Still, there are extremely strong fashion trends in the names we give our children. Just look at what they are called in nursery today. When we are naming our kids we are looking for a unique name but not *too* unique (so we will often borrow one from our grandparents' generation, so that it's both nostalgic and innovative).

That there are trends in everything has evolutionary rather than commercial reasons. We want to feel safe but also to experience the new; we want to be exciting but not weird, to stand out but not exclude ourselves from the community. That's why we always update our hairstyles and clothes a bit but not too much. We want to be different but not *too* different. Where the balance lies changes all the time and depends on what others do. When everyone constantly micro-modifies their taste in that way, fashion arises. We are not capricious because companies make money out of it, but companies make money out of it because we are capricious.[19]

Yes, I know. It is incredibly superficial and silly. The consumption of others is often silly, right? I find it quite embarrassing when others are impressed by expensive watches and fast cars, and I have never understood why you have to renovate the kitchen so often or why you need so many cushions on the sofa. On the other hand, I have covered all my walls with books and enjoy every moment of being surrounded by world literature, and the most frequent comment from visitors is whether so many books are necessary – isn't everything online anyway?[20] I confess, it is probably not necessary to own the first editions of my favourite books. Was it even necessary for you, dear reader, to buy this book?

That's one way of looking at it. It is so easy to denigrate the behaviour and vanity of others and to think they are engaged in demeaning consumption. How lucky, then, that we get to live in a free economy where you can skip it.

What does the web do to us?

No business sector has fallen from grace faster than the tech sector. Just a few years ago tech companies were perceived as exciting and creative, but are now perceived as insidious monopolies who sell out our integrity and hypnotize us to ignore real life. These companies can take advantage of spectacular network effects. You have to be on Facebook because so many people are already there, and when you join, the platform becomes even more indispensable for others. Then Facebook gets more and more data, which means they can tailor their services and their ads to even more people. Data is the new oil, so success breeds success for social media, search engines, map services, e-commerce, payment apps, streaming, app-based taxi services and other digital services.

At the same time, the debate about social media has taken a very dark turn. What was once considered the salvation of democracy is now more often seen as its gravedigger. Half of its critics are angry that too much content is censored; the other half are complaining that too little is deleted, allowing hate and lies to spread wildly. The Left thinks these are platforms for right-wing lunatics and disinformation, the Right thinks they are politically correct leftists who invented cancel culture. Many are angry at Apple for charging too much or at Facebook and Google for not charging ('then you are the product'). At best, social media is just a stupid waste of time. At worst it is a machine that creates polarization, filter bubbles, loneliness and social pressure, and exists only to glue our eyeballs to ads.

Whatever you think about these companies, when you look at how many of us flock to their platforms and what we state that we like about them, there is no doubt that they have created enormous value. An interview-based survey showed that if some of the most common services disappeared, people would be willing to pay imaginary sums for them. They would be willing to pay an incredible average of $18,000 for search engines, $8,000 for email and $3,600 for digital maps – per year. If you included just these three services in US GDP per capita by the price people would be willing to pay, the average American would suddenly appear to be 50 per cent richer.[21] These tech giants have created products of absolutely enormous value that they give to us for almost nothing.

Yes, to repeat, 'if you do not pay for it, you are the product'. We've all heard it (and I've said it myself) again and again. But if the cost of something I would have paid tens of thousands of dollars for is only that I have to look at ads that are a little more relevant than the ones I saw before, it's a pretty good deal. Most people seem to think so – and if they don't they are free to abstain. The issue of integrity is a serious one, but the critics must learn to understand what we know as individuals: that this is about trade-offs and there are no perfect solutions. I don't want to give up too much information about myself, but on other hand I get angry the moment an online shop does not remember what I purchased the last time so that I have to look it up again. (I personally believe the way forward is for users to take control of their data and for a market to emerge for information banks that systematically control the data management of websites we visit, not clumsy rules like the EU's GDPR, which has only made us click a lot of boxes without ever reading the text as we surf the web.)

It doesn't sound like it in the arena of debate, but the hopes of a democratization of communication through the internet actually materialized. Suddenly, in fact, most people can access almost all the information in the world, and can make themselves heard and find friends, like-minded people and partners all over the world. It is nothing less than a revolution. The reason there is now such widespread disappointment is that the socially progressive internet pioneers often assumed it would mean that people like them would populate the public conversation. They did not consider that if everyone can speak freely, it also means that those who do not share their values will also make their voices heard. That includes nationalists and anti-vaxxers, and because those people were often marginalized in the media, they had the greatest reason to invest properly in the digital realm. Just compare how journalists were moved to tears when the Obama campaign won voters with social media and tailored ads in 2008, while similar methods were seen as insidious manipulation on the verge of hypnosis when used by the Trump campaign in 2016. (Which, by the way, does not sit well with the fact that Trump was most popular among older people in rural areas who used the internet the least. Among users of social media, Trump actually performed worse than the previous Republican presidential candidate, Mitt Romney.)[22]

The debate about communication technology has all too often been about whether it would turn us all into cuddly latte liberals or xenophobic reactionaries. What if it instead just shows who we were all the time, for better or worse? Of course, that does not mean that it's good. The fact that we are suddenly exposing ourselves in public, with our semi-digested assumptions and prejudices, is not necessarily a civilizational advance and one can only hope that we will soon learn the difference between kitchen tables and digital mass media. However, if you are frustrated that the internet is full of idiots, you need to remind yourself that there have always been idiots, it's just that they rarely entered your field of vision before. Also keep in mind that you might only think that way because you follow political wrestling on Twitter, for example, where different fighters have to show off for their tribes and therefore are not rewarded for nuances and complexity or even normal civilized behaviour. For the vast majority of people in the world, you're crazy to even care. Instead, they use the internet to find equals and immerse themselves in their interest in the local environment, ornithology, steampunk, football, the perfect fried rice, restored outboard motors, Leonard Cohen bootlegs, or the latest insights into Russia's invasion of Ukraine. Or to quickly learn how to make a red-wine sauce, fix a zip, read an annual report, get rid of a stain or dress up for a funeral. In addition, it has exposed us to a whole universe of ideas, cultures, research, stories and music. It might be worth some craziness.

There is a lot of talk about us getting caught up in filter bubbles online, but we are actually much more exposed to opposing views than before because those who share our interests in a certain dimension do not necessarily do so in other areas. An index of how isolated we are from opposing views shows that people who read morning newspapers are somewhat more isolated than those who read news online, while workplaces, neighbourhoods and families are even more homogenized opinion bubbles. The worst echo chamber is your kitchen table.[23]

Political polarization in America is often blamed on social media, but it took off before there was social media and is led by an older generation who devote more time to talk radio and cable TV than to Twitter and Facebook. In an analysis of nine Western countries, researchers at Stanford and Brown recently discovered that polarization actually decreased in five of them – and all were countries with greater internet use than in the United States.[24]

I know, there is a lot of rubbish online as well. The bigger something is, the more rubbish there is that fits there. I also suspect that the sudden abundance of different and conflicting stories about everything can create a dangerous backlash in a small group that begins to long for simple answers, for someone who just tells us how it is, once and for all. How many conspiracy theories and hateful messages should platforms clean up? We can all see lies and harassment remaining on platforms, while completely harmless, ironic or even urgent messages (and people) are thrown out. This indicates that the companies are incompetent or possibly evil, some say. It indicates that it is a difficult task, I think. Even when something is way outside the limits of polite and sane society, it is still an open question whether it is better if those people are pushed into an even more hateful underground online environment. These are difficult trade-offs without obvious answers, where we have to try different solutions. Nothing suggests this task would be easier if it were taken over by a government authority or by hundreds of different platforms after a break-up of the large tech platforms.

Of course, we must pay special attention to how our children are affected by the availability of everything at all times. A leaked report from Facebook revealed that a substantial minority of teenage girls – 4 per cent – believe that Instagram makes them feel worse.[25] But less noticed was that the same report showed that slightly more – 9 per cent – stated that it made them feel better. There is social pressure and bullying in social media, just as there is in school. One can recognize and combat such problems without concluding that it is bad that social media – or schools – exist. After all, 81 per cent of teenagers say that social media helps them form a stronger community with their friends, and 68 per cent say it gives them the feeling that there are people who are there for them when things are bad. Large majorities say it makes them feel included and confident rather than excluded and insecure.[26]

The whole thing is complicated and it will require a lot of learning and experimentation to use the web better and reduce its negative effects. But for me, the debate about the social net effect of the tech industry was decided when I spoke to an eighty-three-year-old disabled widow who could not care less about the theoretical debate about screen time: 'I love my computer,' she said. 'You can google anything you want to know, and I never have to be alone.'

Big bad tech

Regardless of what one thinks of the tech companies' contribution, there is the risk that they cement their leadership position, buy up small rivals and create an 'innovation shadow' where it does not pay for others to even try to compete. There may be a potential competitor who could be better, but we never give them a chance because it is too costly to learn a new service, transfer our data and get a sufficient number of users to do the same.

'Will the dominant social network of our time ever lose its monopoly?' asks the *Guardian*'s tech columnist. Hardly: 'it is well on the way to becoming what economists call a "natural monopoly". Users have invested so much social capital in putting up data about themselves it is not worth their changing sites, especially since every new user that it attracts adds to its value as a network of interacting people.'

But no matter how difficult it sounds in theory, it works in practice to break monopolies if someone else offers something better. We know this, because the text above is not about Facebook today, but was written in 2007 and was about the completely dominant network MySpace.[27]

Given how impossible it is considered for new competitors to enter the market, it is a miracle that this happens so often. Just look at how novel today's big tech companies – Google, Amazon, Facebook, Apple, Microsoft (GAFAM) – actually are. When I wrote the Swedish version of *In Defence of Global Capitalism* in 2001, Google was a three-year-old newcomer who had three years left to go to IPO and was doing battle with search engine giants such as Yahoo!, AltaVista and MSN Search. 'How Yahoo! won the search wars' was a *Fortune* magazine story in March 1998. The report stated that many people believed Yahoo! even had the potential to become the next America Online (if you remember them).[28] There is actually a similarity: both Yahoo! and AOL were later bought by the telecom company Verizon, which, after large losses, recently sold them for $5 billion.

Back then, Amazon was a loss-making new online bookstore. Just one year earlier, the venerable investment bank Lehman Brothers had warned that Amazon was incompetent, bleeding money and would probably go bankrupt within a year (eight years later, Lehman Brothers was bankrupt).

In 2001, Mark Zuckerberg had not left Harvard to start Facebook – because he had not even started at Harvard. The social networks that ruled were Sixdegrees, AIM, Friendster and most importantly MySpace, which was so hot that Google saw it as a breakthrough to get a three-year advertising agreement with the network in 2006, which was signed at a glamorous party on Pebble Beach with such guests as Bono and Tony Blair. Finally, Google got to hang out with the big boys.

Apple, on the other hand, was a veteran of the personal computer age, but after a long crisis it had become a symbol of the fact that an early dominant position does not mean much in a fast-moving market. However, Steve Jobs had recently returned to the company, and the launch of the iPod at the end of 2001 gave Apple new hope. In 2003, the company was finally able to enjoy a modest annual profit. Adjusted for inflation, that annual profit is roughly what Apple currently earns in fourteen hours. But that was only after the company revolutionized the mobile phone, which was then dominated by Nokia. 'One billion customers. Can anyone catch the cell phone king?' asked *Forbes* in October 2007. 'No mobile company will ever know more about how people use phones than Nokia', so 'Nokia has a historic opportunity to become synonymous with the Web'.[29]

Of course, Microsoft had also been around for a long time, but they faltered and missed the transition to the mobile internet, making a comeback only after almost completely changing their business model from personal computer operating systems to cloud-based services that also work on Apple and Android products.

In his book *Tech Panic*, US journalist Robby Soave writes: 'If a visitor from the future had told me in 2006 – the year I graduated from high school – that within a few years I would no longer need Myspace, AOL Instant Messenger, or an MSN Hotmail email address, I would have assumed it was because I was going to die in a freak accident.'[30]

There is no reason to believe that the new giants are safer in their position than their predecessors. As long as they launch new products and services that are better, cheaper or more interesting than the alternatives, they will continue to get users – but, unlike the users, they get nothing for free. We sometimes think of them as money-printing machines that succeed in whatever they do, but that is because we look at the top sellers they have today. Yet do you remember Amazon's Fire Phone, Google Glasses or Microsoft's Zune music player? Lots of product launches from the GAFAM companies fell flat because they offered something that was uninteresting, already existed, was too complicated, too ugly, too expensive or just cringeworthy. Microsoft never succeeded with the music service Groove Music, the speaker

Invoke, the fitness bracelet Microsoft Band or the iPad clone Surface RT. To 'bing' has still not become as popular as to 'google'. Microsoft's mobile phone Kin failed badly and was replaced by the unsuccessful Windows Phone. To get back on track, Microsoft bought Nokia's mobile division in 2013. It did not give Microsoft's mobiles new life but killed Nokia's.

Facebook would probably like to forget that in 2013 it made its own attempt in the mobile market with 'Facebook Home' on a special mobile that had to be reduced in price from $99 to 99 cents after one month. It would presumably also rather forget the search engine Graph Search, the photo-sharing app Facebook Poke or its successor Slingshot, as well as Facebook Credits, Facebook Deals and Facebook Offers, and the same goes for the Facebook currency Libra.

Amazon also has a long list of projects that had to be thrown overboard when the market disapproved, such as its own Fire Phone, the photo service Spark, the game Crucible, Amazon Wallet, subsidiaries that sold fashion and baby products, and its attempts at an auction site, food deliveries, ticket sales, travel agency and pop-up stores.

Google's ability to enter new areas does not include social networks, where it in turn created and shut down Orkut, Google Buzz and Google+. The same fate befell its Twitter imitation Jaiku, the location service Dodgeball, the encyclopaedia Knol, the game Google Lively and more recently Google Stadia, the work tool Google Wave, the media player Nexus Q and the digital discount booklet Google Offers. And the much-hyped Google Glasses are currently in the 'Where are they now?' file.

Apple was the company that almost perished before Steve Jobs made a comeback, but even under his rule the company made some blunders, for example with the social network Ping, the stereo speaker iPod Hi-Fi, the smart speaker Home Pod and the connection Firewire, which admittedly could do more than USB but cost too much. Most embarrassing was probably the launch of Apple's map app, which in its first incarnation was so buggy and incomplete that CEO Tim Cook had to apologize and recommend angry users to use its competitors' products.

There is nothing strange about these and many, many other failures from established companies. Failing is a way to start over in a smarter way, with new lessons having been learned. The most successful companies are constantly launching lots of experiments to understand what works and what doesn't. And that's the point: the large size of these companies is not what makes them succeed with new products and services – as soon as they launch something a little worse, they are universally mocked no matter how many millions they spend on marketing – on the contrary, they are big because they have managed to create so many appreciated products and services that were better than the alternatives. In comparison to MySpace, Facebook was faster, less ad-heavy and constantly adapted to what users wanted to do on the site. When Google was launched, three of the biggest search engines could not even find themselves online.

The question is how long these companies can continue to be innovative and keep up with the competition. I think they can stumble faster than most people assume, for the simple reason that I've seen AOL, Digital Equipment Corporation, AltaVista, Palm, BlackBerry, Nokia, Netscape, Yahoo!, MySpace, Compaq and Kodak all hold a leading position for a certain period but not survive the next change of the technological paradigm. Before we know it, some other big, proud names will be added to that list.

Unfortunately, there is a way we consolidate the giants' position even when their time is up, and it is paradoxically the regulations we believe are a way of controlling them. Complicated regulations create a fixed cost for established companies that they handle with divisions of specialists. But for startups with few employees and little capital, these regulations act as direct barriers to entry. Research on the US economy shows that market concentration grew the most in sectors where regulations increased the fastest.[31]

It is in this context that we should see Facebook's new-found interest in abolishing section 230 of the Federal Communications Decency Act, which means that American platforms are allowed to moderate content without making themselves open to legal action for what others publish on their site. Without this, platforms would be stopped from taking any action against even hateful speech and harassment if they didn't have the resources to engage in very strict moderation to make sure that nothing ever slips through. Mark Zuckerberg's openness to abolishing it was greeted by some as a sign that he had become enlightened and realized that Facebook needs to be monitored more closely. In fact, it's just the latest round in the old game of increasing your competitors' costs. Reading, examining and moderating everything posted by the public almost in real time would be very expensive even for those who have Facebook's entire infrastructure and 60,000 employees, but what is more important to Zuckerberg is that it would be completely impossible for smaller rivals. If MySpace had succeeded in enforcing such a regulation, they might still be dominant now, and Bono and Tony Blair would still be attending their beach parties.

If there is one thing I am afraid of, it is a development where the government and big business become too close, where the government gives companies increasingly protected positions in exchange for adapting operations and behaviour to what is appreciated by the politicians in power at that moment. Between different spheres of society, there must be a certain healthy antagonism so that they balance each other in an open, decentralized system. When big government and big business team up, the small players will lose out.

Data is the new sand

One reason why lots of people think the big platforms are unbeatable is the misconception that data itself is what is valuable. However, data is not 'the new oil' but the new sand. Sand is not very valuable in itself. But if you refine it properly (to silicon), you can create the most powerful productive power we have (the data chip). So it is with data. Since the breakthrough of the web and digitization, we have been living with a surplus of information, just about everywhere. In itself, it has as little value, but if you refine, analyse and assort it you can find new information and matches that allow you to help others to find what they are looking for in a lucrative way. And that takes tremendous effort, massive investment and constant innovation.[32]

This means that no one has an impregnable lead just because they sit on a pile of data, as Joakim Wernberg explains in a fascinating study of digital paradoxes.[33] It can even be the other way around. Of course, there are economies of scale that allow companies to create better services at a lower price if they have a large market – and in that case it is good for consumers if companies are allowed to grow to that size; that's how we reap these benefits – but there are also diseconomies of scale that set a limit to companies' expansion. Since a large part of their value is created by intellectual and individual matchmaking, a platform can become too crowded and noisy. When everyone is there, it can be harder to find the person you are looking for. You get unintended consequences such as the young not wanting to share a platform with their parents, and dating apps that become too general and insipid. Then the demand arises for something more narrow and exclusive that better expresses one's individuality or one particular slice of it, and makes it possible to find like-minded people or more particular results.

Therefore, one should not expect the competition to come from another giant that offers a similarly broad platform (it's also not obvious what users would gain from having two Facebooks) but from many smaller and more niche platforms. There is another interesting implication. The innovation shadow is real. Large companies can invest more in small, incremental improvements and they can quickly imitate smaller rivals. This means it pays less for venture capitalists and entrepreneurs to invest in areas where the elephants are already dancing. But Joakim Wernberg thinks this is counter-intuitively a good thing. It means that large resources are not wasted on things that are similar to what we already have, but are channelled into areas for radical and subversive innovation that cannot easily be incorporated into existing business models. Something that will enrich us all more than having a second Facebook or a slightly bolder set of emojis.

One way for market leaders to continue to stay on top for a while longer is to buy small, innovative companies – from YouTube and Instagram to Oculus and DeepMind. It is sometimes almost considered cheating, as if the old vampires are extending their own lives with the blood of young, vibrant startups. But this is an important division of labour. It is difficult for established companies that focus on defending old business models to be radically innovative, while new companies rarely have the knowledge of the market, the capital to invest, the ability to manage regulatory systems or the infrastructure to develop, market and sell. By joining forces – like Pfizer and BioNTech when it comes to vaccines – they can ensure that true innovation quickly turns into a functioning product. That's the important thing: not who does it or why, but that it becomes a reality and benefits consumers. The opportunity to be acquired also strengthens the drive to invent, develop and start companies. Then you do not have to navigate the entire minefield yourself. It is enough to have a potentially promising idea that is appreciated by someone on the other side of the minefield.

There is more lag in this debate than in my teenagers' network connection when we're on vacation, and it freezes more often. Just as many people began to see big platforms as impregnable monopolies, they were exposed to substantial competition for the first time. In the last five years, the leading company's market share has actually decreased in online ads, cloud services, app stores, business software and ride hailing. In terms of video streaming and food delivery, the leading company has lost more than a quarter of the market.[34]

This is partly because of relative newcomers. During the pandemic, we were all on Zoom rather than established companies' video services. Snapchat and TikTok suddenly made the old social media look rheumatic. Despite it being said that no new arrivals can upset reinforced incumbents, TikTok reached one billion users in just four years – half the time it took Facebook to do the same. Salesforce is becoming increasingly aggressive in cloud services, and in five years Canada's Shopify has gone from one-seventieth of US e-commerce to one-tenth. PayPal is becoming increasingly important in online payments. In addition, long-established companies are finally getting online. Disney has entered the streaming market and Walmart and Target and all their local counterparts have invested heavily in online shopping. Amazon is constantly competing against eBay and local competitors.

Anyone who thinks the GAFAM companies lean back and count money has misunderstood the fiercely competitive pressure they are exposed to. In addition, the big firms must constantly spy on each other. Microsoft and Alphabet have started competing with Amazon for cloud services, which puts pressure on prices. Amazon, Apple and Microsoft have taken up the fight with Google and Facebook over online advertising. Facebook has started Facebook Shops to strike back at Amazon. Apple TV and Amazon Prime are simultaneously chasing Netflix. According to *The Economist*'s calculations, the share of GAFAM's revenues that overlap with their competitors has increased from 22 to 38 per cent since 2015.[35] In a more existential way, Apple has started to make life miserable for its ad-dependent competitors by offering iPhone users the opportunity to avoid being tracked online by a particular company.

Furthermore, Big Tech's impressive growth took place during a period of low interest rates and booming markets. These companies will face more difficult times ahead. Just as I wrapped this chapter up, I received the latest results from these supposedly invincible companies: in November 2022, amid slowing sales and collapsing share prices, Amazon announced that it would have to let around 10,000 workers go and there were reports that Google was preparing to do the same. Microsoft was already in its third wave of layoffs since the summer of that year and Apple announced a hiring freeze. Meta, Facebook's parent company, slashed a tenth of its workforce.

If you're afraid that a company's control over search services will give them control of what you see, think and buy, it's worth recalling that they have another eight billion competitors. The most common way to find out something, get a second opinion or recommendation on what to think, do or buy is actually not to ask Google or Facebook but to send a message to a friend or contact and ask. Big Tech's greatest achievement is to have made that form of advice easier than ever before.

6

PICKING LOSERS

'The market will always reach the most efficient economic outcome, but sometimes the most efficient outcome is at odds with the common good and the national interest.'

REPUBLICAN SENATOR MARCO RUBIO[1]

I f it's so crucial to have successful companies, innovation and growth, are they not a little too important to leave to the market? Shouldn't we help them along a bit?

When an interviewer introduces the Italian-American star economist Mariana Mazzucato by mentioning many of her assignments in advisory bodies to politicians and authorities, she replies: 'There's actually even like thirty more.' No wonder she's sought after: the thesis she pursues is that her clients are the heroes of development. In my worldview, businesses create the innovations and the growth that funds the public sector, but Mazzucato says it is the other way around – that the state funds and develops research and innovations, which private companies use to create profitable products. Mazzucato's diagram that shows how governments gave us almost everything important that makes up an iPhone has become famous. Her view is that if the government can send astronauts to the moon, it should be able to solve most other problems if charismatic politicians and visionary bureaucrats just point the way and fund the right technologies and solutions. Then knowledge will be commercialized and new innovations developed, she says. That is why we need 'moonshots', 'mission-oriented innovation', for all our societal challenges: 'First and foremost, a mission has to be bold and inspirational while having wide societal relevance. It must be clear in its intention to develop ambitious solutions that will directly improve people's lives and it should appeal to the imagination.'[2]

Active industrial policy has grown in popularity during the great financial crisis. Once again, governments are supposed to pick winners and fund particular businesses and projects to get ahead. As nations started to worry about their supply chains during the pandemic and the invasion of Ukraine, this perspective won even more adherents. Technocratic politicians who believe they can commandeer resources for the common good have been joined by national conservatives who believe that an ambitious industrial policy is a condition for survival, not just to create good manufacturing jobs but also to help the West dominate tomorrow's business sectors and to give their technological systems a chance in the geopolitical rivalry with China. In the Communist Party, we are said to have a rival who thinks strategically and plans for how the technologies of the future can be exclusively 'Made in China'.

Mazzucato has been criticized by other scholars because in this area she does not lean towards systematic research but instead tells various stories to show the government's involvement and success, and such anecdotes say nothing about overall effects. In addition, she fiddles with many of those stories. In an academic review, Christian Sandström objects that it is misleading to talk about everything important in a smartphone without mentioning the transistor, the integrated circuit, the digital image sensor and many other things developed by commercial interests. In addition, he points out that the microprocessor, LCD screen and cellular technology were developed by private companies and not by the government, as Mazzucato claims.[3] Her evidence is anecdotal and the anecdotes are sometimes fabricated.

But there is a more fundamental problem with Mazzucato's ideas – a naive view of innovation. It is not strange that she is so happy to return to the moon landing. This is one achievement that really follows her preferred mission-oriented template: the president sets a goal, NASA plans, procures and implements, and along the way technological development is stimulated. It was an extremely clear goal limited to achieving a certain capability, where the political will was so great that one could ignore the fact that the budget was constantly exceeded. But innovation rarely happens like that.

Internet, porn and politics

Another of Mazzucato's favourite examples is, of course, the internet, a powerful example of a hierarchical, foresighted authority being able to point out future solutions and get it done. It was developed by the military research authority DARPA (formerly known as ARPA), which Mazzucato is particularly fond of as it 'has always been aggressively mission oriented'. This was necessary to develop the internet, says Mazzucato. Only 'the State dared to think – against all odds – about the "impossible"': to create a communication system that would survive a nuclear war. The government was not only 'dreaming up the possibility of the internet', but only it had 'the vision, the resources and the patience to see it through' – ARPANET, which later became the internet, required 'a massive push by the state'.[4]

It's a great story, but it is not what happened. Ideas for networks between computers began to be conjured up in many places in the 1960s because universities and private companies had started developing various forms of information technology. In 1963, J.C.R. Licklider at the company Bolt, Beranek and Newman was able to propose an 'intergalactic computer network' that described many of the solutions that would become the internet's infrastructure. At the same time, Paul Baran at the private think-tank RAND Corporation came up with a proposal for a distributed communication network.

When Licklider started working at ARPA, he was involved in creating a network between its mainframe computers – the project that in 1969 would become ARPANET, the forerunner of the internet. But that project had nothing to do with the military's needs. The motivation was that his boss Robert Taylor was annoyed at having to walk between different terminals and use different log-in procedures to use several computers at the same time. It was time-consuming and made collaboration with other researchers difficult. The process of getting started had no resemblance whatsoever to any visionary five-year plan or strategic NASA committee. Taylor simply went to ARPA's manager and asked if it was OK to start work on linking their computers. Far from drawing up a plan for a massive, state push to do 'the impossible' against all odds, Taylor said (not entirely truthfully) 'we already know how to do it.' His boss replied, 'Great idea, get it going,' and gave him a bag of money. The meeting was over in twenty minutes.[5]

As Taylor himself has stated: 'The ARPAnet was not created with war in mind [and] ARPAnet was not an internet'.[6] Although it is disputed (as so much else in this creation story because so many people played an active role in different and overlapping ways at different stages), Taylor believes that a real internet – a network of networks – was created on Xerox only in 1975, where their ethernet was connected to the ARPANET.

The government was involved in many ways, through ARPA, with procurement and research money, but the result was a happy, unintended side effect of public funding and something completely different from the notion of mission-oriented innovation where charismatic leaders get people involved in large-scale projects. It was not the case that the government 'dared to think the impossible'. No president has ever given a speech saying 'we have decided to communicate in a digital global network', and no Ministry of Defence published a visionary memorandum on how to create a worldwide computer network with a massive government push. And no one, not even Taylor, had any idea how the world would change because he didn't want to walk between different terminals.

Recently, Mazzucato adjusted her story about why the internet was invented. Her latest book no longer states that the network was created to survive a nuclear war, but so that 'satellites could communicate'.[7] The interesting thing is not that she is wrong again but that she is always wrong in the same way – she always believes it must involve a big, important plan and a massive government push.

In an interview in 1989, the internet pioneer Robert Taylor took direct aim at such ideas long before Mazzucato formulated them herself. While Mazzucato claimed that ARPA was always 'aggressively mission oriented', Taylor instead complains that American politicians began to focus more and more on 'mission-directed funding' after he left and that it had 'enormously weakened the quality of the work'. Taylor believed that innovation is mainly created when you solve practical problems step by step and in this way constantly expand your knowledge and find new opportunities and suddenly happen to create a completely new world. If you follow a more mission-oriented policy, in which politicians demand a certain result in a certain way, 'then you're going to miss opportunity after opportunity to make a real advance, because a large part of what we've done over the years is stumble on things. We didn't do it by planning.'[8]

It was not that the military or politicians picked a winner, as Mazzucato claims; they did not have the faintest idea what Licklider, Taylor and the others were doing. In fact, the US Department of Defense had had a similar idea served to them on a silver platter a few years earlier. Paul Baran of RAND Corporation tried to sell his idea to the

US Air Force in 1965, arguing that such a network could withstand a military attack. So it was not the government that dreamed up the idea – it was the state that neglected it. Baran's contacts appreciated the concept, but as a result of a power struggle with the Ministry of Defense, the project went to the Defense Communication Agency, which had no technical expertise in the field and left it at that. 'I felt that they could be almost guaranteed to botch the job since they had no understanding for digital technology, nor for leading-edge high-technology development. Further, they lacked enthusiasm,' Baran said.[9] He withdrew his application and instead spent the next few years spreading the idea publicly and becoming an important source of inspiration.

When, despite all of this, Mazzucato wants to give a visionary government credit for the internet, she reduces her thesis to the fact that the government was responsible for anything that it somehow happened to touch in some part of the process, even if it didn't understand what was going on or hadn't sought this result. That is completely different to the moon landing's mission-oriented innovation. Apart from a series of erroneous and contradictory claims about the birth of the internet, she shows no causal connection but engages in praise by association. In fact, it seems enough that someone who starts an innovative tech company has received a public university education for her to say that the government is the instigator and the private sector is just parasitic.

But innovation does not happen by someone getting an idea and pressing a button on a machine, like in a children's TV series, so that an invention emerges on the other side.

Matt Ridley's ambitious contribution to the history of technology, *How Innovation Works*, shows convincingly that the great breakthroughs never come from government plans or solitary geniuses but from bustling intellectual ecosystems with constant cross-fertilization between different disciplines and activities. They rely on a complex web of collaborations, surprises, inspiration and improvisation. Big leaps can come from unexpected combinations and coincidences. This means that large numbers of people and institutions have touched every single innovation.[10]

If we are to engage in Mazzucatian praise by association, there will be a lot of praise to go around (many individuals, not just Licklider and Baran had hopeful visions about some kind of global digital network). And given that governments in the Western world account for almost half of their country's GDP, it would be very strange if those governments did not touch most things at some stage, especially in their role as a procurer and as financier of education. It's not the same as getting an idea and pressing a button, or that it would just be a process of pressing the button a little more often to get further innovations on the other side.

You could actually write a Mazzucato book like that about active industrial policy, but replace the government with the porn industry. Think about it: it is well established that pornography has played a crucial role in several technological developments. The printing press, photo, film, video streaming, online payment system, chat features, peer-to-peer sharing and virtual reality have in many cases been developed and disseminated to satisfy carnal desires. Historian Jonathan Coopersmith states: 'If it were not for the subject matter, pornography would be publicly praised as an industry that has successfully and quickly developed, adopted, and diffused new technologies.'[11]

Is there anything the government can do that the porn industry could not do? And, although the porn industry does not have half the nation's GDP at its disposal but at most a few tenths of a per cent of it, it has repeatedly touched almost all the innovations of information technology. If I were one of the new cheerleaders for active industrial policy, I would conclude from this that we should pour tax money over the porn industry to stimulate technological innovation. Yet this would be mistaken in the same way Mazzucato's whole perspective is mistaken: these innovations did not come from the porn industry's annual committee meetings, but from chaotic and ever-changing interactions and competition with other innovators and industries and the changing demand of customers.

Boulevard of broken dreams

The reason economists came to view industrial policy with such scepticism from the 1980s onwards was not that they were neoliberal but that they were disappointed. The policy had been tested on a large scale and the result turned out to have no similarities with their hopes.

The US federal programme for innovation in the 1960s and 70s 'is hardly a success story', stated economics professors Linda Cohen and Roger Noll and three other economists who initially had a positive attitude towards industrial policy. Their cost-benefit analysis of six ambitious federal projects revealed that only one of the projects was even 'worth the effort' (NASA's communications satellites). Four of them were 'almost unqualified failures'.[12] Their book was titled *The Technology Pork Barrel* as the projects often kept going because they gave politicians something to show in their home districts, not because they were successful.

In an evaluation of support for Swedish businesses, researchers found no statistically significant effects on the recipient companies' productivity, turnover, number of employees or the proportion of employees who were highly educated or were researchers. They found a single positive effect: the small companies that had received grants had higher sales than others – but only during the first year. Industrial policy is less moonshot than sugar rush. The researchers conclude: 'The lack of positive effects is worrying in view of the costs associated with selective business support, such as the direct administrative costs, the emergence of interest-seeking behaviour in companies and the distortion of competition.'[13]

When economist Josh Lerner sat down to write a book on what the government can do to actively stimulate entrepreneurship and innovation, the experience was so depressing that he gave it the title *Boulevard of Broken Dreams*. He noted, like Mazzucato, that there are successful examples of active industrial policy, especially in poor countries that use it to catch up with an already known and proven technology. But Lerner also took the trouble to look at the other side: 'but for each effective government intervention, there have been dozens, even hundreds, of failures, where substantial public expenditures bore no fruit.'[14]

An obvious reason why the moon landing has been given such a place of honour in the debate is that it worked – unlike so many other attempts at public innovation since the 1960s, such as Nixon's war on cancer, breed reactors, production of synthetic fuel from coal, French–British Concorde, Minitel, a large number of shipyards and steel plants, and now Germany's Energiewende, corn-based ethanol, municipal hydrogen strategies and attempts to make fuel from cellulose.

Perhaps you remember Quaero, the European search engine that would end Google's domination. 'We must take the offensive and muster a massive effort', otherwise we will lose 'the power of tomorrow', announced French President Jacques Chirac when he launched the project together with German Chancellor Gerhard Schröder in April 2005.[15] A massive effort from the taxpayers, however, could not help that all the politicians, companies and research institutes in the vast Quaero consortium could not even agree on what it was that the search engine was supposed to search for. The following year, the project collapsed.

Because political projects are better at selling themselves than they are at selling goods and services, the outside world often initially reacts with anxious reverence, believing they must respond with the same industrial policy in order not to lose out. Nixon wanted the United States to have a supersonic passenger aircraft just because Europeans developed Concorde. Republican politician Newt Gingrich believed the Minitel interactive computer terminals could make France 'the leading information-processing society in the world by the end of the century' and wanted the US government to do something similar. Search engine consultant Brad Fallon told *The Economist* in March 2006 that 'Quaero appears to have the edge' ahead of Google – before Quaero even came close to knowing which product to develop.[16] And today Western politicians think they have to pick winners to keep up with China's centralized innovation strategy.

The new industrial policy is often formulated in contrast to the old one. Now the idea is no longer to keep old, outdated industrial structures alive, but to encourage the new, innovative companies. But that's the way the idea was sold back then as well. It is only in retrospect that the failed projects appear to support already doomed industries. At first most of them were moonshots that used the latest technology to do what they thought would become commercially viable.

Now that we know how these projects failed, you can't expect to read about them in new books on active industrial policy, since the authors try to give the impression that this time it's different, this time it will work. With one exception: Mariana Mazzucato actually mentions Energiewende, Germany's decommissioning of nuclear power and investment in renewable energy that began in 2010. In the beginning, Mazzucato even mentioned it as 'a model of how to implement an integrated strategy', a modern equivalent to the moon landing. But nowadays she admits it has big problems and mainly praises the good intentions of the project (she would know, as she was one of the project's advisors).[17] And that's true of course: if the success of new industrial policies is to be measured in intentions, I can already predict that they will be resounding successes. For those who care more about results, the new policy is rather a magnificent failure. In 2019, Germany's Auditors General stated that the change had cost €160 billion in the last five years alone and that the expenditure is 'in extreme disproportion to the results'.[18] Attempts to transform everything from the top created instability and uncertainty in the entire electricity system, and the decommissioning of nuclear power meant that perversely Germany had to use more coal power. The result of the massive government push was that Germany reduced CO_2 emissions less than other European countries and it cost them more – in taxes and in the highest electricity prices in the EU.

When I asked the energy expert Dieter Helm about the German energy transition's three goals of reducing emissions, and increasing competitiveness and safety, he replied briefly: 'to fail on one is something the politicians should answer for. But to fail on all three, that's a pretty big achievement.'[19]

More *Vasa* than NASA

Failures are admittedly part of all innovation processes, including private ones. If you do not fail regularly, you do not take enough risks. The difference is that public support removes many of the essential mechanisms that steer resources from failures to successes. Private projects depend on ruthlessly sincere feedback from owners, financiers and customers who do not want to be a part of something they lose from. A constant stream of figures on costs, sales, profit and valuation relentlessly shows what works and what doesn't.

Public projects also receive feedback, but not from financiers who risk their own money or customers who choose. Politicians and authorities do not act in markets, which would have created a habit of dealing with opportunities and risks, and they do not invest their own resources, which means they are not compelled to find what can create greater value in the long run. Politicians have an ideological interest in certain projects. They also want to get on well with important constituencies and donors, prove that they are doing something and create many photo and job opportunities during their term in office. They want to end up in the history books as contributors to important changes and – against all economic and technical logic – by putting as much of the production as possible in their home constituency.

Authorities are often given the role of ticking boxes so that they find recipients of funding who meet a combination of what is currently politically in demand. And just like in every situation where you do not control output, you begin to emphasize your financial input as a measure of success. 'We celebrated with cake every time we managed to get money out of the door,' as a former official at the Swedish Energy Agency described their way of picking winners. Not getting rid of the annual budget can mean smaller appropriations next year and thus reduced opportunities to grow and employ. Therefore, according to the same person, the logic was: 'if you receive a credible application, you accept it. If there isn't one, you take the most credible one available.'[20] This makes evaluating the projects a bit more fuzzy, with yes-men being rewarded, problems often swept under the rug and critics marginalized. That is why the story of the government's attempt to control development more often ends up like the Swedish royal ship *Vasa* – which was built according to the king's rushed timetable and specifications, and sank on its maiden voyage in 1628 after having sailed roughly one kilometre – than the space agency NASA.

All in all, governments rarely find those amazing opportunities that everyone else has neglected, but instead follow the latest trends, where the presentations contain all the buzzwords, the food is the best and you get to hang out with the cool entrepreneurs rather than the introverted engineers. Like the glossy business magazines, governments jump from the IT industry to biotechnology to gaming to green technology and now 'real manufacturing jobs for real men'. When Lerner wrote his book in 2009, forty-nine US states had programmes to create clusters that attracted biotechnology companies from other states and I would not be surprised if the fiftieth state has acquired one since then. (If one of them succeeds, they will no doubt be included in Mazzucato's next book as an example of amazing, impossible projects that would not have happened if politicians had not dreamed about it.)

In cases where politicians discover a real shortcoming in production that they want to remedy, such as on semiconductors (which is not because of a supply chain breakdown but due to increased demand for semiconductors; production and export is at an all-time high), it is a shortcoming that everyone else has already noticed and is working as fast as possible to solve for purely commercial reasons. When the EU and the White House propose billions of dollars to subsidize the production of semiconductors, it is corporate welfare that will only generate an even larger oversupply once all the expansion plans have become reality. The German semiconductor manufacturer Infineon unintentionally displayed the absurdity of handing the taxpayers' money to large, profitable businesses in a November 2022 tweet about having 'record results in revenue', and also planning to build a new factory in Dresden, with the vaguely threatening caveat: 'subject to adequate public funding'.[21]

Every industrial policy subsidy is paid by taxpayers, who thereby lose purchasing power that could have benefited other companies. It also attracts labour to politically favoured projects, rather than to those that might have given the best returns. In addition, subsidies change companies' behaviour. In a free market, companies receive a powerful signal when it is time to stop expanding. If their last unit costs more to produce than they can sell it for, they engage in pure capital destruction. Then it's time to change business, scale back or close down. But with an active industrial policy, suddenly grants and co-financing come into play, which means that you get more money if you continue to expand. This makes it rational to destroy capital.

Governments are bad at picking winners, but losers are good at picking governments. Several researchers have identified the species 'welfare entrepreneurs', who systematically turn to various authorities to keep their business afloat for a while longer.[22] Instead of developing the best products to attract consumers, they develop the best presentations to attract politicians and officials. Instead of filling order books, they learn to fill in forms with the buzzwords that will trigger the officials' Pavlovian reflexes. In this way, they can pay qualified staff well, but with low productivity and lack of innovation they tie up resources that are in demand elsewhere in the economy.

Welfare entrepreneurship is an impressive example of how enterprising people can be in order to make money – something that is facilitated by the fact that there are many bodies at municipal, regional, national and EU level that distribute grants, often completely uncoordinated from each other. Most ingenious was the Swedish entrepreneur who managed to collect as many as thirty-eight different grants between 1997 and 2013.[23] Imagine how much such inventive people could have contributed to the national economy if they had had incentives to seek markets instead of grants and were paid for innovations instead of capital destruction.

All this turns industrial policy into a boulevard of broken dreams. What is so sad is that there are a number of initiatives that could create a much better business climate: legal security, efficient bureaucracies, good infrastructure, the freedom to build, good education systems and liberal labour immigration. Instead of investing energy and political capital in creating these conditions, politicians run off to pick specific business models to support. As Josh Lerner points out, it's kind of like serving the main course without first setting the table – it allows you to focus on the most fun activity, but you ruin the whole dinner.

The final frontier

In the recent volume *Questioning the Entrepreneurial State*, thirty scholars of innovation show that the history of top-down approaches to industrial policy has a dismal record: 'Innovation policy should be a matter of removing barriers to growth and renewal instead of handing out targeted support that tends to end up reinforcing vested interests.'[24]

Governments can contribute to innovation indirectly by financing the development and dissemination of knowledge, for example through universities. As long as it does not try to guide the activities too much, this does not presuppose any centralized knowledge or ability to predict the future. It is simply based on giving smart people money and asking them to go and be smart in some eccentric, unpredictable way and then giving the market's decentralized ecosystems the opportunity to use these insights to develop innovations that create value for society.

But theoretical knowledge is not the same as application, and invention is not the same as innovation. In order for knowledge to be transformed into processes and products that enrich society, something else is needed, and it is when governments want to stimulate a certain technology or business model that the problems arise. In this phase we instead need decentralized experiments in an ever-changing ecosystem of investors, innovators and industrialists, as well as consumers. Governments don't expand the amount of knowledge if they interfere at this stage. On the contrary, by pointing out one path and pulling capital and labour in that direction – rather than accepting a multitude of paths to find the way over the minefield – they reduce it.[25]

Another form of innovation policy that is not directly targeted by my criticism here is prizes: if you like it, put an incentive on it. If someone develops a new, important vaccine or wireless transmission of electric power over long distances, they get a bundle of millions. The prize does not have a say in who should do it or how, but gives a general incentive to everyone who thinks they have a chance to use their knowledge and to try to do it their way. It's just a matter of setting the right goals, which is not as simple as it sounds (and if it is, it is probably incredibly profitable to develop the innovation anyway).[26]

What I've written here is the reason why the nationalist attitude to research is a folly. It is based on the idea that we as a country (or at least countries that are like us) must 'own' certain knowledge complexes and technologies. But the reason we so often let the government subsidize basic research and basic knowledge is that it is less interesting for commercial forces to do so, as it is difficult to exclude a competitor from using any breakthroughs. Once someone has figured out how to fix nitrogen, conduct light through optical fibres or cut and paste DNA, it is difficult to prevent others from using the same knowledge. And that is true even if it was Xi Jinping's chosen ones who made these discoveries. The insight would soon be spread all over the world. What's more important for a country is how it decides to exploit this insight.

For a long time, it was only in the Western world that we financed this type of research on a large scale, which everyone could then use without having been involved or paying for it. There are problems related to the rise of some other countries now, such as when the research is used by authoritarian states to create military capacity or to oppress their citizens, and in that case we should do what we can to limit their access. But to the extent that other countries also start to engage in basic research, we should be happy that they help us fill the global knowledge reservoir. The key is that we have plenty of venture capital, energetic entrepreneurs and curious consumers who are constantly testing new methods to use that knowledge to develop new technologies and products that improve our lives, economies and capabilities.

This is best done in decentralized systems because technology and business development are risky, unpredictable processes where it is the sum of all experiments that creates results, not a single moonshot. If we suspect that an initially very costly technology or business idea would be a success that pays off many times over in the future, we have access to a time machine that allows us to use that future revenue instantly. It is called financial markets. Bank savers, equity investors and venture capitalists will refrain from consumption today in exchange for a substantial part of the income tomorrow.

Politicians who fund a certain technology steer resources away from the innovation and industry that would otherwise have happened. And why would they know better than millions of financiers, companies, researchers and consumers what will work? Not even the people who operate daily on the market and have hangars of data know what will succeed next time (recall the list of mistakes made by Facebook, Amazon, Apple, Google and Microsoft), so what is the chance that someone who stands outside the market looking in should be able to do it?

Perhaps I'm wrong. Politicians and bureaucrats may in fact occasionally know better than we mere mortals, but in that case we should ask them to put their own money where their tax money is. If they are so convinced that a European search engine or ethanol from cellulose is the future, we should at least request that they put their own savings in the project before they force us to chip in.

The world is big, with many different interests and many laudable ideas searching for funding. The most important reason why the moon landing should not be a model for development is that the whole of society shouldn't be subjected to a single goal from the top down. No political vision should be allowed to cost whatever it takes, because that removes resources from other people, who have their own dreams for the future, and from their attempts to solve the problems that are most urgent to them.

The fact remains that the moon landing would not have taken place in 1969 if it had not been for the US government project. As a space enthusiast, I would regret that. But what was it all about, really? We did not get any moon bases and no asteroid mining, no solar power in space, no space tourism and no journey towards Mars and into outer space. Precisely because it was all about political symbolism, the moon landing was little more than a glorified photo opportunity, and there was a complete lack of interest in building a sustainable infrastructure for space travel. And because the political interest in it was so overwhelming, the costs for the Apollo programme were allowed to soar, which made the project possible then but also completely unsustainable in the slightly longer run. The moon landing is a bizarre symbol of the new hope for industrial policy because we never got any industry. We placed a flag on the moon and then travelled back. We boldly went back home like no one has done before.

Ironically, space is only beginning to be conquered now that it is being privatized, with companies such as SpaceX, Blue Origin and Virgin Galactic. They are not going for moonshots but for experimenting, improvising, adjusting and, through incremental improvements, constantly finding new methods and sources of revenue; step by step they are reducing the cost of turning humanity into a multiplanetary species. Each launch of NASA's Space Launch System, SLS, designed to take us back to the moon, is projected to cost $2 billion. When NASA's boss suggested in 2019 that it would be quicker and cheaper using SpaceX's technology instead (projected at $10 million per launch), he got a good lashing by US politicians and had to back down. The fiercest critic was Richard Shelby, chairman of the Senate Appropriations Committee. He is from Alabama, which just happens to be home to the Marshall Space Flight Center, the lead centre for SLS development. 'I have more than a passing interest in what NASA does. And I have a little parochial interest, too,' Shelby has told NASA. 'You keep doing what you're doing. We'll keep funding you.'[27]

So industrial policy does not work in space either. Does it even work in China?

7

CHINA, PAPER TIGER

'I have fantasized, what if we could just be China for a day? Where we could actually authorize the right solutions on everything from the economy to environment.'

THOMAS FRIEDMAN ON MEET THE PRESS, 23 MAY 2010

My *In Defence of Global Capitalism* was published in Chinese translation. I saw this as a modest personal indication that the country was gradually opening up. But I knew there were boundaries: wherever I went on my Chinese book tour, I was followed by plainclothes policemen who tracked my every step and recorded who I met. Nothing has disappointed me more since I wrote that book than China. The tension was always there, but I hoped that the epoch-making economic progress the country had made over three decades would be followed by a political opening. It would be increasingly difficult for the regime to combine a richer and more educated population with an authoritarian state. In the book, I mentioned the Communist Party's labour camps, political prisoners and the oppression of the Uighur population in Xinjiang, but I saw these as a remnant of an earlier Maoist system, believing that they would gradually ease under the pressure of an emerging middle class and international opinion. I was completely wrong. Over the past decade, China has experienced an authoritarian U-turn, politically and economically. Since becoming General Secretary in 2012, Xi Jinping has concentrated power on himself and recreated an almost Maoist political model. Hong Kong's freedoms have been shattered and colossal camps in Xinjiang for forced labour and brainwashing have been erected. China is testing its neighbours' borders in the South China Sea daily and is constantly threatening Taiwan with a military invasion.

Where previously there was room for differing views as long as the party's right to govern was not questioned, censorship has now become more aggressive and all-encompassing. Dissidents are even kidnapped on foreign soil. The Chinese will no longer 'seek truth from facts', as Deng Xiaoping urged them to. Now it is written in the constitution that they should study 'Xi Jinping Thought on Socialism with Chinese Characteristics for a New Era'.

Concerns about what this new Chinese model will mean for the world and the possibility of peaceful coexistence have created a new dark narrative about China, especially in America where opposition to China is often said to be the last bipartisan issue. The narrative goes something like this: China's economic miracle was made possible by the Communist Party's strategic industrial policy and the naivety of the West. Step by step, China guided its companies until they could dominate world markets. By letting China into the WTO in 2001, we in the Western world were defenceless when they stole our technology and dumped subsidized goods here. Our industries were shattered and the Chinese could use the revenues to build the industries of the future along with its military. It was naive to believe there were ever conditions for real liberalization or democratization. We can only minimize our losses by trying to block its exports and imitating its industrial policies to win the tug-of-war over the technology and business models of the future. In short: in order to defeat China, we have to become China.

I share the disappointment implicit in this line of reasoning. I am deeply concerned about the future of China and the effect its authoritarian model has on the outside world. But the general disappointment has led to a narrative that is inaccurate on almost every point and, if we embrace it, it could lead to major mistakes both in China and in the West.

When China became capitalist

To start from the beginning, it is a Communist Party myth that its strategic planning made China rich. On the contrary, as Ning Wang and Nobel laureate Ronald Coase showed in their book *How China Became Capitalist*, it was a series of popular revolts that created grassroots capitalism and set the entire reform process in motion.[1] Hungry farmers began to dismantle collective farming and privatize land in the late 1970s. They wrote secret documents that stated the land would be divided between families, and they promised to raise the children of the villagers who were sent to labour camps if the party ever found out about their conspiracy. But it was difficult to keep it a secret when their production increased so rapidly. Private farming spread 'like a chicken pest', as one farmer put it. 'When one village has it, the whole country will be infected.'[2]

The rapidly increasing agricultural productivity enabled the rural population to use part of their time for non-agricultural purposes. They created small companies that operated outside the planned economy and therefore sent their own buyers to obtain material and their own sellers to seek consumers. As a result, they outmanoeuvred the old rigid state-owned companies and made consumers accustomed to simple but more varied products at market prices. This success meant unemployed young people in the cities started demanding the right to start similar companies in the early 1980s. Around 20 million young people had been sent to the countryside under Mao's rule because there were no jobs for them in the state-owned companies. After his death, they returned to the cities and demanded employment. They began to protest, sometimes in a subversive manner. In several cities, they blocked railways. It forced the government to allow small-scale businesses in cities from 1983, which revolutionized the restaurant industry, retail and soon even manufacturing.

The party learned some tricks and began to allow special free trade zones where companies were freed from the plan and allowed to experiment with technology and investment from abroad, even from Hong Kong and Taiwan. It was intended as a limited experiment at a reasonable distance from the big cities so that the planned economy would not be affected too much by a failure – or a success. 'We [had] to put up a fence around the provincial border of Guangdong,' a deputy prime minister said, 'so that other provinces would be sheltered from the bad influence of capitalism.'[3] But like with chickenpox and private farming, it was difficult to isolate any part of the country from the remarkable innovation and productivity these zones made possible. The Guangdong backwaters soon became the country's largest economy. The old fishing village of Shenzhen with a population of 30,000 grew to become a global economic centre with more than ten million inhabitants.

This entrepreneurial explosion in villages, cities and special zones began to put pressure on state-owned companies, which lost consumer markets and bled money. Therefore, after much hesitation, the party initiated a harsh restructuring that meant state-owned companies were disciplined, privatized or closed down. Between 1996 and 2002, the workforce in state-owned companies decreased by more than 40 per cent.[4] In combination with the abolition of price controls and a major tax reform, this created an integrated national market, where market forces that had previously been allowed to exist only on the margins in effect replaced the planned economy. The periphery took over the centre.

However, the decline of state-owned companies created a new problem in that workers' housing was owned by the work units of these companies. How would they ensure people were not left homeless because their employers went bankrupt? The answer was to privatize housing. From 1998 onwards, the cities' properties became the property of the workers. They saw in turn that they now owned an asset they could invest in, mortgage, sell or exchange, so the result was a housing market, a real-estate boom and a construction sector in full swing.

The reform process created a new imbalance. Rural workers lost their jobs when agricultural productivity increased, while dynamic markets in the cities needed labour. Migrants wanted to migrate to cities, where the factory jobs were dirty and dangerous but also offered an income five times higher than the one they had left. It prompted the Communist Party to embark on the greatest reform of all – to dismantle the internal borders. During Mao's time, no one was allowed to leave their home village, and anyone who somehow managed to get to a city was not even allowed to buy food. Now the system began to erode. In 2003, a law was revoked that had allowed the police to forcibly relocate people back to their home village, leading to the biggest wave of migration in history, and this gave further impetus to entrepreneurship and the real-estate market that had previously opened. Within a few years, a quarter of a billion people had sought refuge in the cities and become the economic engine of the twentieth century in their roles of workers, consumers and new entrepreneurs. Between 1980 and 2010, Beijing grew from 9 to 21 million inhabitants and Shanghai from 11 to 20 million.[5]

The last major reform was China's accession to the WTO, which was finally approved in 2001. The notable consequence was a rapid increase in Chinese exports, but the main intention of Chinese reformers was to make their own companies stronger by exposing them to competition, both internationally and at home. The most important outcome was a continued opening of the Chinese economy.

Average Chinese tariffs fell from 40 per cent in 1992 to less than 10 per cent in 2004.[6]

As I described in chapter 3, the notion that China devastated Western industrial landscapes is all wrong. This trade enriched both us and the Chinese. Many Chinese exports are in fact exports of products Western companies have had made in China. Unfortunately, many such collaborations have been allowed only on condition that technology and intellectual property are transferred to Chinese partners. Even if that condition has not been stated in the agreements, it does not matter much. Often, soon after a Swedish or British company has opened a factory in China, a Chinese factory pops up nearby that produces a slightly cheaper variant of the same product.

The theft of knowledge and technology has been massive and shameless, but it is by no means unique. Swedish and British companies did the same thing at a corresponding level of economic development. The United States even had an official policy of smuggling inventions and bribing European artisans to reveal their secrets.[7] What changed was not that Americans were forced to change policies by outsiders, but that they became more inventive themselves and therefore began to realize the value of protecting patents and copyrights. The same thing is happening right now in China. For ten years, the US–China Business Council has asked US companies how China's intellectual property protection has changed over the past year. The proportion who experience an improvement since the previous year is on average 47 per cent during these ten years. The proportion who experience a deterioration is just 3 per cent.

Forced technology transfers is a major concern but only ends up in twenty-fourth place among the twenty-seven biggest concerns that US companies experience in China.[8]

One of the best ways to deal with such abuses is to use World Trade Organization rules, because several issues about intellectual property and government subsidies are covered by WTO agreements. Critics of the WTO claim that the organization is toothless, that the dispute resolution mechanism has been unfair to the United States ('you lose almost all of the lawsuits in the WTO,' Trump complained) and that China still does not follow rulings when they lose. However, of the complaints dealt with by the United States against China, the US has won twenty out of twenty possible, while China has won only about a third of the complaints it has brought against the United States. In addition, in all but one case (which the US chose to abandon), China has taken action as a result of the ruling, meaning that – despite all the flaws and shortcomings in the process – it follows the process better than the United States, which has sometimes completely disregarded WTO rulings.[9] The way to get China to engage in fair play is not to withdraw from multilateral trade cooperation but to expand and deepen it – and perhaps even to follow the rules ourselves.

Why am I taking up your time with this review of the waves of reform in China? Because how China's economic success is interpreted is crucial to which model the country chooses and how the West should perceive it. The Chinese Communist Party gives itself the credit for the economic development since the late 1970s, which is a view shared by China's angrier critics in the West. This creates a false image of how strategic and wise the party is and what can be achieved with centralization and industrial policy. So the party wants more of it, while the critics in the West believe they must borrow China's instruction book if the West is to make its own economies strong. This is based on a fundamental misreading of China's modern history. The waves of liberalization were not initiated by the Communist Party and were not even foreseen by it. Observers often date the start of the reform process to the Eleventh Central Committee's third plenary session in December 1978, in which Deng Xiaoping took power. But as one of Deng's closest advisors, Bao Tong, later acknowledged: 'In fact, reform wasn't discussed. Reform wasn't listed on the agenda, nor was it mentioned in the work reports.'[10]

As we have seen, many reforms were initiated informally, by brave villagers, such as land privatization and the opening of small businesses. Deng Xiaoping's greatest achievement with his Reform and Opening Up programme was to acknowledge the development and not to punish the pioneers, since it turned out that they produced results superior to the planned economy. Other reforms were reluctantly implemented because the popular demand was too great, such as free enterprise in the cities. Still others came about because previous changes had created unintended consequences and pressured the party to solve urgent problems, such as the reforms of state-owned companies or the opening-up of internal migration. This was 'crossing the river by touching the stones' as Deng put it, and it was the Chinese people who had put the stones in the right place. The economist Weiying Zhang says the reform process was about 'becoming good at using spontaneous forces and turning spontaneous forces into conscious policy.' The process was not planned, controlled or even foreseen. It was, Weiying writes in an explicit reference to Adam Smith, as if it was controlled by an 'invisible hand'.[11]

Everything that took China out of poverty happened outside the five-year plans. By the mid-1990s, the last four five-year plans had been abandoned before they reached halfway, and the plans thereafter were more about vague objectives than governance and commands. 'How much of that success can be attributed to industrial policy and planning?' asks Barry Naughton, an expert on China's modern economic policy, in a recent book. 'The answer is simple: none.'[12] The reason he can speak so categorically is that, by the middle of the twentieth century, the planned economy had collapsed and China still had no industrial policy.

In 1978, more than 99 per cent of China's urban population worked for the state. In 2011, only 18 per cent did so. Almost all of the 250 million urban jobs created since 1978 were private. The private share of the export sector increased from a third in 1995 to almost 90 per cent in 2012.[13] Poverty plummeted on a larger scale than anywhere else at any time before. Between 1981 and 2015, extreme poverty in China fell from 88 per cent to around 1 per cent according to the World Bank. Masses and markets had defeated Maoism.

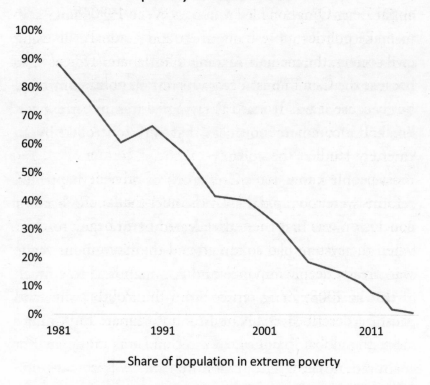

Extreme poverty in China 1981–2015[14]

— Share of population in extreme poverty

Mao strikes back

But then, towards the end of the first decade of the new millennium, everything started to go wrong and Maoism started to make a comeback. Although there was always such a risk, it was by no means decided by fate. In fact, for a while longer, most party documents talked about continued reforms, both economically and politically.

During the period 1995–2008, it was even possible to believe that China was on the verge of democratization. When I wrote *In Defence of Global Capitalism*, experiments with elections at village level were going on, and the influential Zeng Qinghong led attempts in the 1990s and 2000s to make politics more transparent and gradually liberalize civil society, the media and the public debate. This was not because the Communist Party appreciated political freedom but because it was worried that what does not bend might break. It is common knowledge that the Chinese authorities carefully studied the collapse of Soviet communism, and most people know that they thought Gorbachev's political reforms were too rapid. Few remember that another central conclusion was that the Soviet reforms had begun too late, when the system had solidified and the Communist Party was already deeply unpopular.[15]

But in 2008, Zeng retired from the Politburo in what must be described as historically unfortunate timing. Just then, the global financial crisis hit and was interpreted by many around the world as the end of the 'neoliberal' era. The United States was stuck in Iraq and Afghanistan after military invasions. Conservative groups in China's Communist Part saw it as a sign of the decadence of the West, while at the same time their fear of political change escalated when revolutions took place in former Soviet republics such as Georgia (2003), Ukraine (2005), Kyrgyzstan (2005) and Moldova (2009). The Arab Spring would soon make it seem even more worrying. In *China's Leaders*, China scholar David Shambaugh describes how four groups who felt threatened by the reform effort – the party's propaganda apparatus, state-owned companies, the security forces and the military – used this opportunity to convince the weak General Secretary Hu Jintao that continued liberalization risked undermining the party's position. Without Zeng at the top, there was no one to oppose them, and the initiative passed to the conservative faction, which would later consolidate its power under Hu's successor Xi Jinping.[16]

Not only did this new centre of power reverse the incipient political openness but they also began to dismantle the liberal economic model. They had never had any preference for spontaneous order and grassroots capitalism but instinctively believed in command and control. These were the groups that got high on their own propaganda, which stated it was the party that in its infinite wisdom had led people to prosperity. Now they tried to get reality to imitate fiction. Instead of clearing up large-scale malinvestment after the financial crisis, they created a massive stimulus package where indebtedness and government spending would lead the way instead of productivity and innovation.

Even this faction believed China's economy needed to be modernized but, where previous generations of leaders were willing to accept that liberalization had snowball effects, this group has repeatedly rolled back reforms when they've faced the consequences.[17] Attempts to discipline banks that speculated with easy money from the central bank in 2013 were abandoned when it caused short-term interest rates to soar. In 2014, Chinese companies were allowed to start investing abroad but were stopped when it led to a massive outflow of capital. In 2015, the bank interest rate was liberalized, but concerns that small banks that offered higher interest rates would attract money away from the state-owned companies meant an informal rule was created that no one could be too far from the interest rate benchmark.

In 2016, an aggressive tightening of speculative loans began but, when new construction and infrastructure decreased, it was also abandoned, and this has turned into a painful stop-and-start process. Tech companies were given freedom from regulations and protection from foreign competition, but when they became too big, policy turned around and the state started chasing them to the brink of ruin.

This pattern has been repeated time and time again during Xi Jinping's time. This confusing dance back and forth is not about any elegant fine-tuning of the economy, as some foreigners believe. Nor is it about any conviction that the economy does not need more liberalizations. The party has cautiously initiated reforms that it has seen as necessary but, as soon as it has created unforeseen consequences, the leadership has panicked and turned 180 degrees back to the secure, low-productivity command structure it is used to.

When one does not dare to liberate market forces, state-commanded innovation emerges as the only remaining source of growth. The active industrial policy that now suddenly dominates China's economy – where the government makes plans that define crucial technical and economic areas and steers companies towards them – began to appear in documents in the middle of the 2000s and was realized on a large scale only around 2010. State-owned companies have once again been given a prominent role. Instead of doubling down on international trade, the government has begun to strive for self-reliance in many industries, partly as a reaction to Trump's trade war, which Biden has essentially continued. The aim of reducing economic connections with the West reinforces the party's sense that they can now safely ignore what the rest of the world thinks of their human rights violations and aggressive foreign policy.

Both the party and its critics now see today's command policy as defining China's economy, and believe that it explains their success. That is reading history backwards, as Barry Naughton explains:

'China's emergence as an economic and technological super-power is due primarily to the policy package that it followed from 1978 through the first decade of the 21st century, that is, until about 2006–7. China's policy package today – that is, the policies that started tentatively after 2005 but were fully in place by 2008–2010 – are radically different. Because of this, it is a mistake to attribute China's success to the policies China is currently following. These policies are simply too recent to have had a determinative impact on today's outcomes.'[18]

Would a poorer China have been less destructive?

I am the first to say that China has gone completely in the wrong direction in the last decade. I also think the free world has been very bad at sticking together against China's new aggressive foreign policy and its economic punishment of countries that criticize its human rights abuses. Democracies in the Pacific region must deepen their security cooperation to prevent China from subjecting one country after another through economic warfare or threatening military might. I am also convinced we have been naive in our view of Chinese investment abroad. It is not a problem when it comes to chairs or sunglasses, but investments in important digital or physical infrastructure can make us vulnerable. We must be aware that after 2010, no Chinese companies are completely private. They are all expected to submit to the party's plans.

But the popular notion that it was wrong to support China in opening up to the outside world because it enriched an enemy is something completely different. Well, if the expectation was that trade would make China a free, democratic country, it has clearly failed. But the goal of the Western world was not to try to reach heaven but to avoid hell. Nixon did not go to China in 1972 to turn them into cuddly liberals but to split a communist bloc with which the West was in existential conflict, and to shake up the Soviet Union until it was willing to come to the negotiating table.

There was also a worried realization that a poor but technologically sophisticated China would find other ways to raise money if it were not allowed to sell clothes and toys. In the 1980s, China not only provided the instruction manual for an atomic bomb to Pakistan but sold the entire kit, including uranium and ballistic missiles. There were great fears that China would become a large-scale exporter of weapons of mass destruction to every villainous regime around the world. After decades of negotiations and relationship-building, China is now an active opponent of nuclear proliferation. The diplomats of the 1980s would have seen it as a great success that has made the world much safer.[19]

The idea that it was always naive to expect China to continue towards openness is based on the notion of a monolithic China that has acted according to a unified long-term plan, whereas there has always been a struggle within China over both means and goals, between reformists and market liberals on the one hand and conservatives and neo-Maoists on the other. Interestingly, it was the former who supported economic modernization, while the latter group opposed it. Could both groups really be so wrong?

For the Western world, the question boils down to whether China today would have been less authoritarian and destructive if it had been poorer and more isolated internationally. Of course, that is not impossible but I have still not heard any convincing arguments for it. Just look at other dictatorships like Iran and North Korea, which were isolated and kept in poverty by despots and sanctions. None of them are WTO members. As is well known, none of them mitigated their foreign policy aggression or implemented democratic reforms. Instead, both countries have moved in an increasingly despotic and threatening direction and continue to develop their nuclear weapons programmes despite sanctions from a far more united world than we could ever have mustered against China. And Iran and North Korea have not even had nuclear technology since the 1960s, as China has. Nor do they have a fifth of the world's population and a self-image of being a historically dominant power only temporarily humiliated and held down by the Western world.

Counterfactual history is always difficult, but my guess is that if we had closed our markets for Chinese goods and our universities to their students in the 1990s, not only would many more Chinese still be living in deep poverty but the Chinese people would also have been much more likely to have generally perceived Westerners as irreconcilable opponents, instead of the present situation where many consider an open, peaceful world as the goal and Western democracies as models – something that might be pivotal for the country's future. The risk is that in the alternative timeline, where we continued to shut China out, we would not only have talked about a possible future war between China and the United States but perhaps already have been in one.

Even though, as I said, I share the view that we need to look at Chinese investment abroad in a whole new way, I am afraid that a policy of trade barriers and isolation for fear of an aggressive China could become a self-fulfilling prophecy that strengthens the most reactionary and nationalist forces in China. The reason the Communist Party has not gone all in with supporting Russia's invasion of Ukraine is not that it treasures peace and human rights but that it fears secondary economic sanctions from the West. If our economies were to decouple completely from China, that limitation would disappear and the dictatorship would be free to act according to its character. That would be a more dangerous world.

Going backwards

One reason the Chinese Communist Party performed unexpectedly well for such a long time was that it learned a crucial lesson from Mao's autocracy, which resulted in the greatest famine in history and the horrifying cultural revolution. One-man rule limits the amount of knowledge that reaches the top, and leads to yes-men, paranoia and purges. Major mistakes can be made when witless loyalty is rewarded. Therefore, a more collective leadership with ideological flexibility was developed within the top echelons of the party. Internal debate meant that different factions could make their views and objections heard, and consensual decisions meant that no individual lost face when they needed to change their mind and set a new direction.

Xi Jinping has overthrown this order. Xi and the other conservatives were worried that dissatisfaction with the party was growing. The party cells in business, state-owned companies and organizations had fallen into disrepair and, even though the party membership grew, it no longer meant anything – you could have any opinion on various issues or none. Since the leaders rejected the idea of creating loyalty through democratic experiments, their only solution was to return to a more Maoist control, with centralized power and a personality cult. Like Mao, Xi rules through purges, in the form of perpetual anti-corruption campaigns, creating fear and submissiveness. Officials and students practise Xi Jinping's thinking via apps on mobile phones, and eighteen research institutes have been set up to study his speeches and texts.

Yet this is precisely what makes the new system extremely vulnerable. When decisions are presented as the will of an infallible leader, it is no longer possible to pragmatically cross the river by touching the stones and adjust direction when you've gone wrong. It builds tensions within the party and makes it more difficult to respond incrementally to problems and dissatisfaction. It increases the risk of catastrophic decisions – like the brutal zero-Covid policy that hurt people and the economy, and then at the end of 2022 the rushed, almost panicked abandonment of it without preparing for it, by importing foreign, efficient vaccines for example. Centralised authority also makes it more difficult to admit a mistake since it's more difficult to escape individual responsibility for it.[20]

It is often said that China shows political stability, but it's too early to tell since this is a system that has yet to be tested by an economic depression or a military defeat. In its current form, the model is not much more than a decade old. The party, of course, presents itself as popular, but its need to constantly sharpen censorship and persecute every dissenting thought suggests a lack of self-confidence and a fear of brewing discontent in the population. Political models that give people the right to choose and build their own lives will always have an attraction to people. But a technocratic dictatorship like China has to prove its worth by delivering growth and higher wages. That means it can never feel safe and it must constantly prove itself, which will not be easy with the new economic policy.

The more economic power the Communist Party takes, the more knowledge and outside initiative is lost. The difference between the popular image of China and what research actually shows about it could hardly be greater. Our politicians and media paint horrifying images of China's brilliant strategic planning, but in the vast literature on China's economy there is hardly a single study that even attempts to argue that a specific industrial policy has created real commercial success.

The Westerners who now assume we need an active industrial policy in order to compete with China thus choose not to imitate the Chinese policy that created the country's successes but the post-2010 policy that involves enormous risk-taking. To the extent that the new policy has achieved any results, they are negative. Capital has been transferred to less productive state-owned companies. Despite the fact that they only account for around a quarter of the country's GDP, they get about 80 per cent of the banks' lending. Growth per capita, which in the 1990s and 2000s was around an incredible 10 per cent annually, declined to 5 per cent before the pandemic (and some observers believe this was an exaggeration). Under the current economic model, China finds it hard to squeeze any growth out of the economy. You can afford to make many big mistakes if you have double-digit growth. A slower economy cannot buy itself out of structural problems in the same way.

The problem is that China's impressive growth was based on reforms that were made far back in time. One after another, changes were undertaken that gave a new boost to the economy. But since the liberalization of migration and the WTO membership, no major new reforms have been implemented. After the financial crisis, the economy was sustained through massive government investment, but since it was not supplemented by increased productivity and innovation, ever more money is needed to get any growth out of it. After rising 1.1 per cent annually from 1982 to 2010, growth in total factor productivity (what you can squeeze out of the resources you use) declined by 0.6 per cent during the period 2011–2019.[21]

In addition, the working-age population is declining and any time now the population as a whole will start declining as well. China can no longer build its economy on rural farmers moving into factories, or its housing boom on more of the population moving into brand-new apartments in cities. Real estate is no longer the engine of the economy but a drain on it. At the time of writing, the real-estate market seems to be in free fall. By 2033, almost a third of the population will be over sixty years old. As the Chinese get older, they will also need the savings that the government has previously used to keep state-owned companies under arms.

All this would have been easier to deal with if China had been a rich country. But that it is the world's second-largest economy is because the population is large not because it is rich. Measured in GDP per capita, China is about as poor as Turkmenistan and the Dominican Republic, at about a quarter of Britain's prosperity level. Other fast-growing Asian economies began to grow more slowly only when they were already relatively rich: Japan in the 1970s, and South Korea and Taiwan in the 1990s. When they reached China's current level, Taiwan grew by 7.5 per cent annually for another decade and South Korea by 6.3 per cent.[22] The only way for the current Chinese model to reach such levels is to falsify numbers.

One should not underestimate what was required for China to grow so fast in recent decades, but the first step in the growth saga – to catch up – is, after all, the easiest. It is about getting low-productivity farmers to move to modern factories and about making these factories more productive by utilizing technologies and processes that have already been tried and tested in richer countries. The next stage is much more difficult. When there are not many farmers left who want to move to the city and the old technology is already imitated, you have to come up with your own innovations, new methods, products and business models to create growth on your own merits. The problem for the Communist Party is that these innovations can only come from the unexpected, from creative and seemingly chaotic processes, and if there is something authoritarian rulers do not like, it is surprises. As long as the Chinese state only has a market for goods but not for ideas, it will always be handicapped.

In several areas, however, China has been surprisingly good at innovation. One reason is that the dictatorship has paradoxically given companies great freedom if they are focused on an area that is perceived as politically prioritized. It is not uncommon to hear Western entrepreneurs at the frontiers of technology say they have significantly greater freedom from regulation in China than in the West (which should give us pause for thought). But on the other hand, Chinese companies have significantly less freedom as soon as something does not fit into the plan, and as China moves in an authoritarian direction, the plans become increasingly comprehensive and more arbitrary. In addition, successful private entrepreneurs are always a threat to groups who want total control and cannot accept a variety of power sources.

The ongoing attack on China's tech sector is an example. Unlike the tightly controlled financial and energy sectors, tech companies were unregulated for a long time. They are not just imitators but often genuinely innovative companies that have surpassed their Western models in e-commerce and digital payments. But they became a little too successful and a bit too bold in public, and the Communist Party has responded by attacking the entire sector. The most dramatic example is the payment giant Ant Group, which was on its way to the largest IPO in history in the autumn of 2020. After its popular founder, Jack Ma, gave a speech criticizing the country's banks, the launch was blocked, the company castrated and China's highest-profile business leaders were forced out of the public life.

In part, this might have been about the regulatory system trying to catch up with the new superstars, but the drastic change in attitude and arbitrariness of the decisions reveal the weakness of the authoritarian model. By striking so fiercely, the Communist Party has deterred other entrepreneurs and chased capital away. What could have been China's next big success story, with the potential to conquer world markets, now looks more like a crisis industry. Since then, the attacks have been extended to the gaming industry and education companies. No one knows where such persecution ends once it has begun. In an article that was quickly scrubbed off the net, economist Weiying Zhang warned that Xi Jinping's policy of 'common prosperity' risks leading to 'common poverty'.

Experiments and innovation always look messy and you never know what you will get, and this will never be welcomed by rulers with an excessive sense of order. Many despots have succeeded in creating rapid growth by moving farmers to factories, but so far no one has managed to take the next step and become a complex, innovation-driven growth economy. Most foreign observers still hope the Communist Party will learn from its mistakes and once again reverse course, but that is exactly what is so difficult with the new personality cult. It would probably presuppose a coup against Xi.

I know I'm sticking my neck out when I predict that China's authoritarian model will not survive. I got it wrong last time. But I think the reason I got it wrong was that the Communist Party identified exactly the dilemma I pointed to: continued economic liberalization will lead to openness and diversity that will eventually undermine the dictatorship. Precisely for that reason, the party chose to step on the brakes and start rolling back the liberalization. They don't do it out of self-confidence, but because they fear they are losing their grip.

That is not to say that I believe that China will necessarily become a liberal democracy. It could also crumble in factional struggles and separatism, it could become a failed state, and the Communist Party might also decide to be content to become the kind of semi-rich regional middling power that an authoritarian system can bear. What I don't believe is possible is that a totalitarian superpower will be able to replace the leading role of the United States and Europe.

To sum up: many in the West believe China is winning and that the West's only chance to cope with this economic and technological rivalry is to become more like China. But they confuse China's unparalleled successes during the opening years 1978–2010 with the centralist policies after 2010, which in fact hold the country back and put its future in peril. As long as China does not allow capital to flow to the most promising ideas, refuses to let entrepreneurs pursue innovations and surprises, and only allows markets in goods and not in ideas, China will never be an innovative, rich economy. And the more Xi Jinping concentrates power on himself and his clique, the more vulnerable he makes the country when it encounters unpredictable but inevitable problems and manifestations.

The despotism that makes the country dangerous is also what sets a limit to how powerful it can become. It is not the free world that has to become like China to beat China. It is the other way around. If China wants to 'beat' the free world, then China has to become free.

8

BUT WHAT ABOUT
THE PLANET?

*'We are in the beginning of a mass extinction, and all you
can talk about is money and fairy tales of eternal economic
growth. How dare you!'*

GRETA THUNBERG, AT THE UN'S CLIMATE

ACTION SUMMIT 2019

When I read *In Defence of Global Capitalism* again,
I am struck by a startling oversight. I flip back
and forth but find it nowhere. Where is climate
change? I write about the environment, resources and emissions, but I do not address with one word what almost
everyone today considers to be the most serious threat to
our planet. It feels like an oversight that will be difficult to
explain to my children.

I underestimated the risks of greenhouse gases, in part
because so many of the environmental movement's warnings had previously turned out to be exaggerated or outright
false. According to the environmentalists, we would suffer
from overpopulation, food would run out, water would run
out, oil would run out, we would have silent springs without
birdsong, forests would be replaced by a 'chemical desert'

and genetically modified crops were 'Frankenfoods'. The first environmental issue that concerned me as a child was the belief that we would all soon die due to nuclear power. The environmental movement had cried wolf so many times that I did not see when a real wolf actually snuck up on us. It says something about how one can deceive oneself with simplified historical analogies.

But it also says something about how the climate threat has worsened and our knowledge of it has improved. When I wrote *In Defence of Global Capitalism*, the latest available report at the time from the UN's climate panel IPCC spoke of a warming of between 0.3 and 0.6 degrees over the last hundred years, 'a change that is *unlikely* to be *entirely* natural in origin' (my emphasis). The IPCC wrote that there was not enough knowledge to say whether warming led to more extreme weather such as storms and cyclones.[1]

Everything has certainly not improved in the last two decades. Our greenhouse gas emissions have increased rapidly and now there is no doubt that they have made a strong contribution to global warming. According to the IPCC's latest assessment, humans have increased the global temperature by around 1 degree and are increasing it by a further 0.2 degrees every decade. We have also begun to see the consequences of this warming in the form of new temperature records, extreme weather events, more droughts, more floods. The climate is extremely complex, each effect has a variety of causes and it is almost impossible to isolate how much humans have contributed to a particular weather outcome. Climate change strikes locally and randomly, sometimes in a favourable way. But what we do know is that a large amount of change is now occurring around the world at a rate that exceeds previous forecasts. In addition, there is the risk of tipping points: rapid, irreversible changes that risk completely changing conditions for life on Earth. Although the risks of their occurrence may be small, the consequences would be so enormous that it is worth investing quite a bit to insure ourselves against such an outcome.

Reducing global warming and its consequences will require major changes. But which ones? A common line of argument is that the problem is the whole idea of an ever-growing economy with ever more planes and trucks ferrying people and goods across the continents around the clock. Leftists like Naomi Klein claim this is the inevitable result of global capitalism and ever-increasing production. But even a climate activist like Greta Thunberg complains that world leaders only talk about money and 'some technical solutions'.[2] This alludes to the widespread perception that we cannot rely on the growth and technology that have created the problems to solve them. Many greens want 'degrowth' and say we should consume less, travel less and settle for less to give the planet a chance.

It is my sincere conviction that this would be the worst thing we could do for the world – and for the climate. My exhibit A is the fact that we just tested this approach. The 2020 pandemic was an unforeseen and undesirable experiment in degrowth. Almost overnight, the machines stopped and the borders were blocked. The planes stayed on the ground, cargo ships anchored outside the ports and half the world's population was barred from leaving their homes. The result was disaster. People lost their jobs and their livelihoods. According to the World Bank, nearly 70 million people were thrown back into extreme poverty as a result of the pandemic. Hunger increased rapidly and the United Nations Food and Agriculture Organization (FAO) estimates that between five and seven million children may be hampered in their physical development due to pandemic-related malnutrition.[3]

And how much did this global lockdown reduce 2020's global carbon emissions? By about 6 per cent. It is the largest reduction ever but nowhere close to what would be needed. If we were to meet the Paris Climate Agreement by 2030 just by doing and travelling less, we would need to suffer a pandemic like this *every year* for the next decade, without allowing us to have any recovery between the pandemics. Which, of course, would lead to an unprecedented social collapse.

Even under this global state of emergency 94 per cent of CO_2 emissions remained. It shows that the solution was never to stop flying and settle for less. The large emissions are built into our societal infrastructure and our energy systems. We can get rid of them too, through a transition to non-fossil fuels and energy sources, but it will cost tens of thousands of billions of dollars. And if there is one thing people who are fighting for their jobs and for food on their tables do not appreciate, it is spending tens of thousands of billions more. This is why people always see the environment as less of a priority during recessions.

If we were to achieve carbon neutrality through negative growth, it would require us to phase out approximately 85 per cent of the global energy supply by the year 2050. It would have the potential to become the greatest catastrophe to hit humanity. About half of food production would be threatened, as it is dependent on fertilizer produced from coal and gas. We would have to give up agricultural machinery and cold storage. The result would be large-scale starvation. Even more people would die when healthcare clinics lose lighting, medical technology and the ability to cool vaccines and medicines.

A few years ago, I visited a small, poor village in the Atlas mountains in Morocco. I got to spend time with a friendly family who lived close to each other and close to nature. From the outside, it looked like a simple but good life, far from the stress and pressure of the modern world. But when I asked the father about their lives, he gave a long list of everything they were missing and desperately longed for: a water pump so the family could shower off the desert sand and water the crops, a refrigerator to store food and lighting so kids could read in the evening. He wanted to be able to charge a telephone to keep in touch with the outside world, especially his eldest son, who had moved away to university in the big city. All these needs could be summed up in a single wish: that the power lines would finally reach all the way to their little village. Worst of all, without electricity and gas, the family cooked and warmed itself in the same way as three billion other people do: by burning solid fuel indoors – a dirty everyday activity that results in respiratory diseases and lung conditions that kill around two million annually (still the world's most fatal environmental problem).

An Indian study shows that for every million children born, 8,000 die from lack of electricity. A report from

Bangladesh documents that infant mortality is more than a third higher in villages without electricity. These numbers would be much worse if the energy-poor could not use technology and goods produced in places with electricity but, in a world of energy starvation, the entire world's production, trade and transport systems would collapse.[4]

And that's not all. Paradoxically, degrowth would also make global warming even more dangerous for humans, as we need prosperity and technology to adapt to it. Rich countries have no fewer natural disasters than poor ones, but they are much better at minimizing their damage to life and health. According to the International Disaster Database, the global risk of dying in a climate-related disaster – such as droughts, floods, storms, forest fires and extreme heat – has decreased by more than 90 per cent since the 1950s.[5] That's not because the number of natural disasters has decreased, but because prosperity, technology, construction and healthcare have improved. If we had had zero growth since the 1950s, we would have had less CO_2 in the atmosphere, but almost half a million *more* people would have died from climate-related disasters every year.

Lower growth is one of the costliest ways to reduce CO_2 emissions, both in terms of money and human life. According to one estimate, each tonne of CO_2 that was reduced because of negative growth in 2020 cost approximately $1,750 (in the form of reduced GDP), which is many times more than the cost of most technologies to reduce CO_2 emissions available even today.[6] Poverty is one of the most expensive ways to save the planet, even apart from its effect on the poor themselves.

We cannot save the climate by becoming poorer, we can only do so by becoming richer, in a smarter way. And if we want to find out how it can be done, we should learn from previous environmental progress.

Environmental progress

Many environmental problems have been dealt with surprisingly well. We did not run out of natural resources. In the last hundred years, the amount of material used for a certain amount of economic growth has decreased by around two-thirds in the Western world. That did not suffice when at the same time the population grew rapidly and each country produced much more goods and services. The use of resources still increased in absolute numbers – until now. Rich countries now use less aluminium, nickel, copper, steel, stone, cement, sand, wood, paper, manure, water and fossil fuels every year. The use of sixty-six of the seventy-two resources important enough to be documented in the US Geological Survey has declined in recent decades.[7]

The problem is rather that the residual products end up in the wrong places, although we have also started to clean this up. Freons were phased out and the ozone layer began to heal. The leading pollutants have fallen dramatically in the United States and Europe. One remarkable success story is sulphur dioxide, which tormented our lungs and acidified our soil and water. Between 1990 and 2013, emissions of sulphur dioxide in the EU decreased by 92 per cent. The dreaded forest death did not occur.[8]

These improvements have also cautiously begun to spread globally, not least because cross-border trade and investment make new technologies available to more people. The World Health Organization has a measure of Disability-adjusted life years (DALY), which it uses to assess the total disease burden that something causes in a population, both in terms of premature death and disability. Globally, from 1990 to 2017, the number of DALYs lost to air pollution has decreased by 49 per cent and to water pollution by 65 per cent.[9]

Environmental damage to life and health[10]

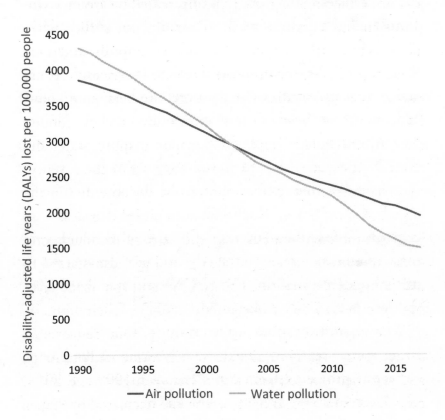

One important exception is CO_2 emissions, which have continued to increase as more parts of the world have been electrified. However, this electrification has been crucial in reducing the number of people who cook with biofuels. Between 1990 and 2019, the number of deaths from indoor air pollution decreased by more than two million. The death rate has dropped by two-thirds, one of the biggest health triumphs of recent decades.[11]

Yet biodiversity is under increasing threat as humans encroach on the wilderness, mainly to turn it into agricultural land. It is often said that we are in the midst of the sixth mass extinction, this time a man-made one. But almost all the figures we hear about how many species die (such as '150 a day') are based on 'pessimistic projections' about the relationship between space and species and have been shown to be incorrect, according to Claude Martin, former head of the World Wide Fund for Nature. The International Union for the Conservation of Nature (IUCN) has documented fewer than a thousand species that have become extinct in the last five hundred years, mostly invertebrates, which is about one-twentieth of a per cent of all described species.[12] On the other hand, even these numbers represent a tragedy, and with great certainty it is an underestimation. The IUCN estimates that 37,000 species are currently endangered.

Many countries try to deal with this problem by creating larger nature reserves. Today, 13.5 per cent of the Earth's surface is protected from exploitation, more than double the figure in 1990. Development has been even faster for coastal areas and nationally administered zones in the oceans and seas. The proportion protected today is fifteen times greater than in 1990,[13] even though that does not help much when the rest of the sea is overfished by huge, tax-subsidized trawlers.

One of the biggest threats to biodiversity is the continued loss of virgin forests. Every year, an area of forest corresponding to the size of Hungary disappears. However, the rate of deforestation has fallen by 40 per cent since the 1990s, according to the FAO. Deforestation has ceased in rich countries. In the United States and Europe forested areas are increasing. In China and India, too, forests are now growing, suggesting that rising populations and economies do not have to cause overexploitation.[14] Were it not for deforestation in seven countries – Brazil, Paraguay, Angola, Congo, Tanzania, Indonesia and Myanmar – the world's forests would have grown in the 2010s. That is not much of a comfort, given the unique natural values lost with those forests. But it shows that the notion that we are experiencing a relentless global deforestation does not hold.

If we are to save biodiversity, the human footprint on the planet must be reduced, which can only happen through urbanization and more productive agriculture. Half of the world's ice- and desert-free land is used for agriculture, so everything we can do to make the soil give higher yields is important. We have already seen tremendous progress in this regard thanks to the productivity improvements of the Green Revolution. If Indian farmers had grown wheat as they did in the early 1960s, they would have needed another 65 million hectares to achieve the 2010 harvests, and Chinese farmers would have needed 120 million more hectares just for corn. In total, higher agricultural productivity has probably saved around three billion hectares of forest and grassland since 1961. Without it, an area equivalent to the size of two South Americas would have had to be put under the plough.[15]

In recent decades this has led to 'peak farmland' and, for the first time in history, we have allowed pastures to grow again.[16] If urbanization and agricultural productivity continue to increase – with the help of genetically modified crops, for example – we have a historic chance for rewilding, where wildlife recovers lost land with flora and fauna in diverse combinations.

The economists Jonas Grafström and Christian Sandström have compiled an impressive set of statistics for Sweden showing that in almost all environmental areas there has been striking improvements since 1990. Despite the fact that the population has increased by 1.6 million and the economy has almost doubled, emissions and resource use have decreased. Sweden now uses less water and pesticides and almost half as much petrol. The amount of nitrogen and phosphorus with which the country eutrophicates its sea areas has decreased by 40 per cent. Emissions of metals such as chromium, cadmium and mercury from treatment plants have plummeted by more than 80 per cent. The amount of waste has increased by almost a quarter, but the emissions from its treatment have decreased by almost 40 per cent – CO_2 emissions from the waste by 67 per cent. Of the twenty-six harmful emissions into Swedish air, twenty-four have decreased since 1990, nineteen of them by more than half. Particulates have been halved, nitrogen oxides have decreased by 54 per cent, volatile organic compounds 63 per cent, carbon monoxide 69 per cent and lead 97 per cent.[17]

This is no longer just about a relative decoupling, where we use fewer resources per person or unit of GDP, but an absolute decoupling, where we get more from less even as the population and economy grow. As economist Paul Romer has stated, growth does not have to come from using more ingredients but from coming up with better recipes and creating many of the best ones with fewer ingredients. If growth was only created when more things were put into the pot, there would obviously be limits to growth, but only our imagination and our freedom set the limits for what recipes we can come up with.

What went right?

What happened? Wasn't capitalism supposed to destroy the planet? Leftist thinkers like Naomi Klein and Göran Greider still claim we need a planned economy to save the environment. But a look at the planned economies that actually existed in the communist states in Eastern Europe provides an insight into what works and what doesn't.

The communists tortured the environment. There were many reasons for this, but one of them relates to resource use. In the 1980s, Soviet economists calculated that their factories needed to use 50 per cent more materials and more than twice as much energy to produce the same amount of goods as American ones. The Soviets used almost twice as much steel and cement but produced only half as much with it. Their machines and tools weighed 15–25 per cent more than foreign models.[18] Of course, this was because machinery and methods were outdated, but why should they not be? If the planners thought that a certain form of production was a priority, it received the material and energy it needed. In the socialist system, the factories faced no pressure to constantly streamline production in order to cope with competition from others who were better at managing materials and energy.

It is very different in a capitalist economy with competition, profit motives and free pricing. The company that comes up with methods to reduce the thickness of a soda can by just a tenth of a millimetre can earn millions in material costs (something that has reduced its weight from 85 to 13 grams in a century). This means that production is constantly being revolutionized. The one who succeeds in developing more environmentally friendly technology can be the next green tech billionaire.

It always looks like the resources we use will soon run out if we ignore human ingenuity and assume that they will be used in the same way and in the same proportions. The nineteenth-century economist William Stanley Jevons – known for his prediction that coal would soon run out – collected tons of writing paper and wrapping paper because he believed there would soon be no trees left.[19] But as long as resources are privately owned and priced, myriad innovators and entrepreneurs will constantly come up with new ways to manage them better, find substitutes and recycle – new recipes, in other words.

None other than Karl Marx admired how effectively the capitalist economy turned waste into wealth. He noticed how the meat industry realized that leftovers could be used to make buttons, handles, glue, soap and tallow instead of throwing the leftovers away. As long as they were exposed to competition from others and there were no commons where they could freely throw their rubbish, they had to find ways to recycle their waste in a profitable way.[20] Now, however, there are plenty of commons in the form of forests, water and sewage, and the links between the person who emits and the damage it does become increasingly complex during industrialism.

But the damage was no less simply because it happened somewhere else. We built higher chimneys to send our sulphur dioxide away, but they always ended up in another lake and emptied it of life. The lead that lubricated our engines also ended up in children's nervous systems. This form of environmental degradation runs counter to the fundamental capitalist principle that everyone should bear the costs of their own behaviour. Polluters privatize profits (for example, from production or transport) but socialize costs (for example, through emissions that harm others, the waters they fish in or the climate we all depend on). If companies are free to use other people's resources or dump their waste, they will do so, but if they have to bear their own costs – either by negotiating a price with those affected or by the government putting a price on the environment – they will invest in new ways of using fewer resources, developing green technology, cleaning up or exploiting waste, just as Marx observed.

The free market solution is that no one should profit from passing costs on to others, and the only reason to accept emissions is that they are the by-product of a process that creates such great value that they can be justified even to those hurt by them. There could be – and historically sometimes have been – legal processes where polluters bear strict responsibility for the consequences of their actions, with those affected being compensated financially. But in a complex world with increasingly diffuse relations, it is not always applicable. Can a few billion people bring a class-action lawsuit against a few million CO_2 emitters? How do you compensate for an increased risk of a forest fire? How do you track specific damage to a particular car, flight or cow?

Therefore, it is an important political task to imitate what an environmental market based on property rights, liability and negotiations would have done to 'internalize the externalities' as economists say – or to put a price on the environment, in the layman's language. Some emissions are destructive and yet have alternatives so that they can be banned outright, such as freons in refrigerators or lead in petrol, while other emissions are so central to human well-being, like the greenhouse gases that our lifestyle relies on so far, that it is better to put a price on them so that there is an incentive to reduce emissions and find alternatives. This creates difficult demarcation problems to which I cannot give any precise answers, but the principle is important and, as always, it is better to be approximately right than exactly wrong.[21]

One reason for Sweden's environmental success is that they started setting prices for emissions in the early 1990s in the form of, for example, the nitrogen oxide tax and the sulphur tax. It harnessed the creativity of the market by giving all producers the incentive to look for better technology and fewer emissions. This meant progress did not depend on the assumption that politicians could predict which technology would work, but only on the assumption that innovators and entrepreneurs wanted to make money.

We could afford the west coast

Free markets make us richer and that is crucial. In a famous statement from 1972, the Prime Minister of India, Indira Gandhi, declared: 'Are not poverty and need the greatest polluters? ... How can we speak to those who live in villages and in slums about keeping the oceans, the rivers and the air clean when their own lives are contaminated at the source? The environment cannot be improved in conditions of poverty.'[22]

That is not entirely true. It is possible to improve the environment at all economic levels, even in deeply poor countries, but it is more difficult to get broad support for expensive measures before people have food on the table. We should be grateful to the green movement for our insights into the importance of environmental problems, but the fact that it emerged in the 1970s is in itself an illustration of the importance of prosperity. Before that, we in the Western world were still struggling to provide our children with a proper education and our old with care and pensions. Then we were still prepared to sacrifice nature for a few dollars more.

'If you want this town to grow, it has to stink', as one American mayor put it in the 1960s. Or as the Swedish Social Democratic State Secretary to the Minister of Finance explained in 1970 when big industry wanted to set up on the beautiful west coast: 'If we look at this from the point of view of economic efficiency and growth, it is obvious that we should sacrifice the west coast. I can't find any other solution that gives better returns... There are hundreds of miles of coasts around the Mediterranean and other seas.'[23]

The best thing about having money is that you can think of other things than money. Prosperity changes our preferences. As individuals we begin to think about how our behaviour affects the local environment, as consumers we think about how our goods are produced and as voters we elect politicians who protect the west coast instead of sacrificing it. In addition, richer economies can also devote more resources to research, development and consumption of greener technologies. It is richer countries who have developed new processes and technologies that enable us to produce and transport goods in a better way and to take care of and manage waste and dirty water. This is where we have had a rapid development of the catalytic converter, cyclonic separation, scrubbers and sorbents that purify emissions and take care of hazardous chemicals. This is where we have the resources to develop unleaded petrol, oil with less sulphur, electric cars, more fuel-efficient aircraft, domestic appliances that consume half as much energy as in the 1990s and lights that consumes a fifth. It is also these countries who are leading the development towards replacing physical products with ones and zeros. Radios, cameras, calculators, alarm clocks, telephone directories, calendars, maps and compasses now fit in a single mobile phone.

Prosperity gives us resources to take care of and treat our waste. In recent years, our plastic consumption has been much discussed and we have seen wildlife documentaries where animals get stuck in or eat our plastic waste with heartbreaking consequences. But we cannot do without plastic. Although a tonne of plastic has a slightly greater environmental impact than a tonne of replacement material, like wood or glass, the problem is that no other material is as light, strong and flexible, meaning we'd need more tonnes of the replacement, which is not necessarily better for the planet. Plastic reduces food waste by protecting food from moisture, dirt and insects, and plastic packaging allows us to pack goods so efficiently that we can manage with one truck instead of two or three.

So the more interesting question is about where the plastic goes after we have used it. In rich countries, plastic very rarely ends up in nature or in the oceans. It is collected, recycled or incinerated and becomes electricity and heat. Even if every European and American citizen ceased all use of plastic bags, straws, sterile disposable bags in healthcare, the plastic in the cars (which makes them lighter and more fuel-efficient) and *all* other plastic beyond that, it would not even reduce plastic emissions in the oceans by a single per cent.[24]

In poor countries, plastic is often thrown onto leaking landfills, and where these are close to rivers, the plastic often eventually ends up in the ocean. The Philippines alone accounts for seven times more plastic in the oceans than the whole of Europe and North America together. Although Asian and African countries use very little plastic per person, they account for almost 90 per cent of all plastic that ends up in the oceans.

All this points to a clear conclusion: to 'talk about money' is not the problem but the solution. *The Environmental Performance Index* (EPI) is an ambitious project from Yale University, in partnership with others, to regularly rank the ecological sustainability of 180 countries according to thirty-two different environmental measures, from biodiversity to climate emissions. In fact, the regions of the world line up in relation to their level of prosperity, and it looks the same within each region. Wealthy Western democracies occupy the first thirty-seven places in the list, and at the bottom you find mainly African countries and the poorest Asian countries. The EPI concludes that 'environmental performance correlates strongly with a country's wealth', although there are also countries at each level of prosperity that perform both better and worse.[25]

In the literature there is a discussion about a possible 'Kuznets curve' for the environment. Many forms of environmental degradation follow the pattern of a 'U' turned upside-down, a shape that the economist Simon Kuznets had previously used to describe the relationship between growth and inequality. As countries begin to urbanize and industrialize, the damage to nature and health increases

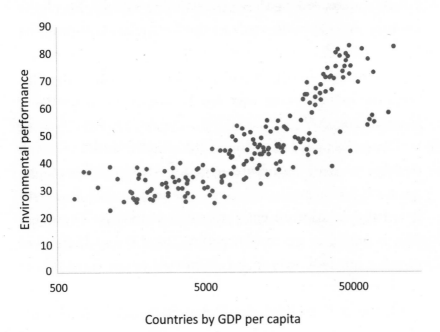

Wealth and environmental protection[26]

Countries by GDP per capita

rapidly, but after a certain point increased income is associated with environmental improvements. The hypothesis is controversial and many researchers object that there is no automatic connection and that it does not apply to all forms of environmental damage. However, a review of more than a hundred empirical studies between 1992 and 2009 shows that there is such a connection for many of our most serious environmental problems.[27]

There are even indications that this might apply to biodiversity. The Living Planet Index, which is published by the World Wide Fund for Nature, shows an improvement since 1990 in high-income countries, even though that study only covers vertebrate animals. An OECD review of biodiversity shows it is declining in most regions but has increased in Western Europe over the past half-century. An in-depth study of the Netherlands shows that biodiversity declined rapidly until 1970, but since then it has increased rapidly, 'a pattern that is broadly consistent with the notion of an inverted U-shaped environmental Kuznets curve'.[28]

The challenges facing the world are great and how much damage we will do before it gets better is still an open question. What we have learned, though, is that degrowth is not the solution to environmental problems. The question is not how we can keep the Chinese and Indians in poverty, but how we can get them over to the right side of the Kuznets curve.

One way is to keep the global economy open. Long-distance trade is often blamed for creating more emissions and we are encouraged to buy local products. After reviewing the research, Hannah Ritchie from Our World in Data writes: 'While it might make sense intuitively – after all, transport does lead to emissions – it is one of the most misguided pieces of advice.'[29] The reason it sounds intuitive is that we overestimate the environmental impact of transport compared to other factors. According to a review of the average European diet, transportation does not account for more than 6 per cent of the average grocery bag's climate impact, and much of it is the last mile – from store to home. The rest comes from land use, production and storage. Surveys of such diverse goods as shoes, beer and iPads show similar results – nine-tenths of the emissions come from other things than trade.[30]

This means that the green choice may counter-intuitively be to buy something from the other side of the globe if it can be produced in a little more environmentally friendly way than it can locally, such as onions from New Zealand or roses from Kenya instead of from the Netherlands, where the same rose gives rise to emissions more than five times larger.[31]

Instead, the great effect of trade is to stimulate technological development globally. It drives down the price of greener methods and products so local companies can use them to a greater extent. This makes it easier for poor countries, who face the greatest environmental challenges, to learn from our mistakes and from our progress. They can use technology that it took us many generations and many billions to develop. (From that perspective, tariffs on green technology are even more idiotic than tariffs in general.)

To get rid of lead in gasoline, we needed to invest in advanced refineries that made it possible to get higher octane levels even without lead additives, and research sodium additives to replace the lubricating effect of lead on the engines. It was not until 1995 that lead in petrol was banned in Sweden. China and India could do the same only five years later, when they had a per capita income at around one-tenth of the Swedish level. Since Iraq and Yemen banned lead in petrol, the UN Environment Programme states that the last country to use lead in petrol is Algeria. As I write this, however, the news comes that Algeria has also abandoned it. From having completely dominated the market when I was growing up, today there is no longer a single petrol station in the whole world that sells leaded petrol.

Such a spread of greener technology makes it possible to be cautiously hopeful about even some of the most affected countries. As China's economy has grown, it has become one of the world's largest polluters in almost every category, but the risk of a Chinese person dying from any kind of air pollution has decreased by almost two-thirds during the period 1990–2019.[32]

If you are still not convinced that we can combine free markets and a healthy planet, you might be interested in learning that in the latest edition of the *Environmental Performance Index* researchers use two different indices of economic freedom and test them against environmental indicators. The results, surprising to some, emphasize that one does not have to choose between the economy and the environment: 'we find that economic liberalism is positively associated with environmental performance. While our results do not give countries carte blanche to pursue laissez-faire economic strategies without regard for the environment, they do cast doubt on the implicit tension between economic development and environmental protection.'[33]

But, hey, wasn't this chapter supposed to be about the climate?

So what does all this mean for our ability to cope with climate change? Unfortunately, it illustrates once again why it has been so difficult to get anything done. No one owns the atmosphere, and polluters do not have to pay for imposing environmental costs on others. The effects of pollution are unpredictable and spread over time, and they are often not limited to one country with a political assembly that can set rules, so it is difficult to get an overview of causes and effects. But that does not mean that nothing has been done. In the world as a whole, the amount of energy required to produce a unit of GDP decreased by 36 per cent between 1990 and 2018. Low- and middle-income countries have made an even faster journey as they have been able to move quickly from old, dirty technology to the very latest. China's energy intensity decreased by as much as 70 per cent during this time.[34] In addition, an ever smaller part of the energy that is produced requires fossil fuels as renewable sources become more affordable. Between 2009 and 2019, for example, the price of electricity from non-subsidized solar power plants fell by an incredible 89 per cent.[35]

With a longer-term perspective, we see extraordinary gains. Britain and other countries that industrialized in the nineteenth century needed to emit around 1 kilogram of CO_2 for every dollar of GDP (in today's value) they produced at their peak. When China and other emerging economies did the same a century later, they only emitted 500 grams for every dollar at the dirtiest point. The present generation of fast-growing economies in Africa and south Asia have already peaked at 300 grams per dollar produced and are moving towards a greener energy transition.[36]

But the fact that we emit less per person and per unit of wealth produced is unfortunately not enough, for the simple reason that tomorrow there will be even more of us on this planet and we will produce more units of wealth. Energy use therefore increased by 59 per cent during the same period and CO_2 emissions by approximately 38 per cent. But it means the underlying trend is the right one and that we shouldn't back-pedal but step on the gas. Those who long for degrowth should take a look at countries that have experienced economic crises in the last decade, such as Greece and Portugal. Yes, in the short run they reduced emissions because production declined, but the long-term effect is that they put fewer resources into investments. Since 2010, unlike the planet as a whole, they have *increased* the amount of greenhouse gases they need to produce a unit of growth.[37]

In the last decade, about fifty countries have reduced their CO_2 emissions even in absolute terms, and these are mainly the richest countries, such as North America and those in Western Europe. This is not due to them having outsourced emissions to dirty factories in poor countries. The carbon emissions imported by OECD countries through trade have been reduced by more than a third since 2006.[38] It seems like there is a Kuznets curve even for CO_2 emissions, but it peaks and starts declining at a much higher level than the other emissions.

How do we get more countries onto the right side of the Kuznets curve, and accelerate the pace for the fifty countries that are already there? Well, I don't know. And you don't know either. Nor do our political representatives. Maybe electric cars or extremely fuel-efficient combustion engines, better biofuels or completely different modes of transport? Should we get energy through the sun, wind or a new generation of cheap and safe nuclear power? And if it's the sun, is it by building massive, industrial solar parks or by wrapping solar panels around everything or placing them in space where the sun always shines? Should we become vegetarians, start eating laboratory-grown meat or develop other diets and new additives so livestock do not need as much grazing land or emit as much methane? Or should we continue with certain fossil fuels and separate the CO_2 and store it, perhaps by sucking CO_2 from the atmosphere? And if we do that, should we do it by cultivating more trees, with all that means in terms of colossal monocultures and its demands of huge amounts of water, or through industrial processes that companies such as Climeworks, Carbon Engineering and Global Thermostat are experimenting with right now, where the hope is that the cost of capturing a tonne of CO_2 could be brought below a hundred dollars? (You may remember that the same process cost around $1,750 per tonne when it happened through negative growth during the pandemic.)

No one knows which technologies will work best in the end, which innovations will drive that technology down in price or which scientific breakthroughs will suddenly result in a completely unexpected solution. That is why we need to mobilize as many people as possible to perform different experiments based on their local knowledge and individual beliefs and skills. The goal is to accelerate the trend towards energy efficiency and non-fossil energy so that difficult international agreements are not required for us to use green technology and instead we do so because it is also in our economic interest. My friend Mattias Svensson surprised me with the fact that illegal poppy fields in Afghanistan are irrigated with pumps powered by solar energy. Not because the poppy farmers care so much about government orders or even the environment, but simply because it is the cheapest way to do it. When we all face the same incentive as Afghan opium producers, the problem is solved (in terms of energy consumption, at least).

The best way to encourage such development everywhere is to make people pay for the consequences of their actions. A tax on all forms of fossil fuels at the wholesale level means that the cost of them is spread to industries and consumers at the next level. It makes everyone feel their contribution to global warming, not only in their conscience but also in their wallets. It gives everyone an incentive to direct their consumption towards goods and services that create less greenhouse gases, and motivates everyone to come up with their best ideas on how to reduce CO_2 in the cheapest way possible and develop new technologies that minimize emissions.

With a carbon tax, politicians could stop trying to predict which technology will work best to reduce greenhouse gases. They could stop handing out subsidies and benefits to potentially green companies with which they have private contacts, personally believe in, like for ideological reasons, make for a good photo opportunity, create jobs in their constituency or are needed for campaign contributions. Companies would not make money in relation to how well they manage to charm decision makers but in relation to how much they reduce emissions. Then you could remove detailed regulations telling you what kind of light bulbs you should use, how large windows may be or what year we should all stop driving a petrol car.

It would avoid a sham Potemkin-like environmental policy that sets specific goals for a specific technology and subsidizes an expansion that does not always have any relation to what it delivers. A current example is China's planned economic expansion of wind power, which led to many turbines but little electricity, as quality is low and inefficiency high. Despite the fact that China has twice as much wind power as the United States on paper, they generate about the same amount of electricity. Up to 30 per cent of the capacity is not even connected to the electricity grid, but what does that matter when the goal is to fulfil the plan and impress the outside world?[39]

About forty countries and many cities, states and provinces have set some kind of price on CO_2 – usually the richest countries and, within these, the richest regions. But it still means that only around one-fifth of global emissions are priced. And here we come to the central political problem: how do you get people to agree to pay for something that was previously free, if the reward comes in the distant future and perhaps mostly in other places?

Sometimes it feels like a hopeless task and, therefore, in the EU work is underway to start punishing countries without a CO_2 price by imposing a border tariffs on their exports. Yet I fear that this is not a way to save the climate but to destroy world trade. As it is completely impossible to find out the individual emissions of all foreign exporters, they would be subject to customs duties based on the amount of greenhouse gases such exports *usually* generate. A company that has made costly investments in greener production would therefore be punished as much as those who haven't. It is difficult to imagine a worse incentive for environmental progress. And what to do with regions within a country that have introduced emission markets or taxes? Should EU customs officials start separating goods from Virginia and West Virginia? North Carolina and South Carolina?

Carbon border tariffs are a blackmail tactic for countries that do not have the right environmental policy, but they risk inviting a perpetual trade war, where other people's policies are used as an excuse to prevent their exports. Perhaps other countries should respond with tariffs on EU exports for its overfishing of the world's oceans? Personally, I would prefer us to do the exact opposite. We could entice other countries to introduce carbon pricing by saying that, if they do, they will also have free access to our markets without tariffs or quotas. The important countries we need to take climate action have exports that are still facing high tariffs in rich countries. China and India, for example, would like to see tariffs abolished on textiles, while Australia and Brazil would love free trade in food. A grand bargain could see them price emissions in exchange for us abolishing all our tariffs on such goods.[40]

We don't have to include all countries, but the more countries that are involved, the less the risk that fossil-dependent production will move elsewhere. Initially, the most important thing is to get the big emitters on board. If the EU could only agree with the five other countries that emit the most, it would cover almost 70 per cent of global CO_2 emissions. In that case, we could encourage poorer countries to join the programme on condition that they are allowed to introduce the levy gradually as their GDP per capita rises.

One way to encourage voters is to give the money back to them. A carbon tax should function as a price and an incentive, not as a source of revenue for the state. The money should therefore go back to the population in the form of a reduction in other taxes. One way to avoid threatening our own business competitiveness in a world where few countries have taxes on emissions is to use a substantial part of the revenue to reduce capital and corporate taxes. But before we get there, we can do something even easier: even if we do not demand payment for the damage, we do not need to subsidize it. The world's states spent a total of $440 billion on fossil fuel subsidies in 2021, mainly involving large developing countries such as China, India and Iran.[41] That's almost ten billion every day. If politicians are afraid of how consumers will react to higher electricity and fuel prices, they can still abolish all subsidies and instead give the $440 billion directly to consumers, so they can decide for themselves whether it is fossil fuels they want to use them for or maybe something else.

Wait, I'm not done. There is a final paradox that doesn't get enough attention: if we are *too* green in the short term, we will never be green in the long term. Climate change and electrification will require copious amounts of copper, aluminium, lithium and other metals and minerals, but we in the Western world now believe that mines and smelters are too rough and dirty. Increasingly complex permit processes make many investments impossible and delay them all. It is natural that we don't treasure such dirty extraction business any more – we have slipped far down on the other side of the environmental Kuznets curve. The only problem is that we risk becoming completely dependent on importing such materials from authoritarian states with lower environmental requirements, where the pollution and natural impact from such processes are significantly worse. In addition, it raises prices, which delays the entire transition.

This is understandable if our environmental commitment is nothing but an aesthetic attitude, but if we really believe that global warming is a crucial problem for the world, we cannot have an environmental policy that is mostly focused on delaying, limiting and shutting down. Then we cannot block every new mine, delay all permits for power lines, wind and solar power parks, ban genetically modified crops that can make agriculture greener, or phase out the nuclear power that gives us fossil-free energy. And for all intents and purposes, we must not become a NUMBY – 'not under my back yard' – and protest against any project to capture CO_2 and store it underground. If we are not willing to get our hands dirty, we will never be able to clean up all the dirt.

9

THE MEANING OF LIFE

'Forty years of neoliberal capitalism has at best marginalised values such as solidarity, community, togetherness and kindness. At worst, it has cast these values summarily aside.'

NOREENA HERTZ[1]

O K, say that the economic case for free markets is true then. Capitalism makes us freer and richer, creates better jobs and greater opportunities and helps us solve environmental problems. But does it make us happier? Is it really the purpose of life to work, perform and stress, to sharpen our elbows to beat the competition, to collect even more stuff that we do not need and cannot take with us when we die? Free markets and individualist societies make us obsessed with being independent, but this also liberates us from what makes us human – communities, relationships, fellow human beings, faith and family. Self-realization becomes nothing but a beautiful word for the emptiness of modernity, the loneliness of the mall.

This is the last line of defence against free markets, from the statist left, the national conservatives and collectivist intellectuals. Once upon a time the critics said liberal capitalism could never produce wealth, then they had to admit that it does albeit only to a small elite, then they admitted that everyone might get richer but poor countries will suffer, but eventually then they said OK, everyone might be better off, but why would that be such a good thing? Capitalism may make us materially rich but spiritually poor.

The American conservative Patrick Deneen believes that liberalism makes us 'increasingly separate, autonomous, nonrelational selves, replete with rights and defined by our liberty, but insecure, powerless, afraid, and alone'. By liberating us from 'particular places, relationships, memberships, and even identities', liberalism and markets 'render us ever more naked as individuals'.[2] Under the fantastic and exhaustive headline 'Neoliberalism – the ideology at the root of all our problems', the British leftist George Monbiot explains that these problems include (but are by no means limited to) 'epidemics of self-harm, eating disorders, depression, loneliness, performance anxiety and social phobia.'[3]

Freedom 'doesn't make us free, it makes us lonely,' adds Christian conservative Joel Halldorf. 'Increasing mental illness, isolation and populism are signs that liberalism cannot sustain itself.'[4] Society must be something greater than the sum of all individual market relations. We need something *more* to heal our spiritual emptiness.

Just look at how free markets distort our very soul. In *The Lonely Century*, the leftist economist Noreena Hertz writes that 'Neoliberalism has made us see ourselves as competitors not collaborators, consumers not citizens, hoarders not sharers, takers not givers, hustlers not helpers'.[5] Similarly, the socialist author Nina Björk claims that the urge to improve our situation invades every corner of our lives and makes us ask in every situation and in every meeting: 'What do I gain from this?' It makes us compete and fight: 'Living in competition breeds fear... We turn each other into a threat.' In the end, therefore, it leads to relationship fear: 'If we are dealing with each other primarily as competitors, maybe we do not want so much to do with each other?'[6] Since John Locke taught us the value of freedom of choice in the late seventeenth century, personal relationships have become based on 'the calculation of personal self-interest', claims Patrick Deneen: 'Liberalism encourages loose connections'.[7]

Why on earth would anyone want individual liberty and free markets if this is the result? According to these descriptions, it sounds like an infernal machine that destroys all the humanity within us. Anyone who actively advocates it must be completely mad.

If one claims that political opponents create human isolation and mental illness, one takes on a rather heavy burden of proof. Incredibly, such sweeping statements are only very rarely followed by attempts to document any causal link or even a correlation. Surprisingly often, a quick misreading of classical liberals is enough to prove the connection between liberalism and greed and loneliness. As if the resistance to forced relationships was based on a resistance to relationships.

But John Locke, the father of classical liberalism, wrote in 1689 that 'God having made man such a creature, that

... it was not good for him to be alone', and went on to explain why one cannot imagine the individual without the family and her other communities.[8] Adam Smith, the stepfather of economic liberalism, declared in 1759 that nature 'formed man for society', and set out in a sophisticated way how our behaviour and our morals emerged from our social interactions as a result of our empathy, in a period when his conservative opponents just assumed that they had been given to us by God.[9]

The point is that Patrick Deneen spouts nonsense when claiming that traditional liberals 'rejected the classical and Christian understanding of human beings as fundamentally relational creatures – "social and political animals"'.[10] Both liberals and anti-liberals saw man as a social animal. That was never the bone of contention. They both believed that the individual needed the family, culture and communities, and that we are all in fact created in such contexts. The disagreement was about something else.

Opponents of liberalism did not just see humanity's social nature as a fact but as a moral obligation. For them, it was not just descriptive but normative. So if we belonged to a particular community, family or faith, we had an obligation to stay there and submit to the literal or figurative father of the family, no matter how he behaved: support your country, right or wrong, and stick to this lord or church, even if they abuse you or your conscience. But this does not follow from man's social nature, and the historical achievement of liberalism and capitalism was that it gave people the freedom to leave exploitative collectives, demand that they be changed if they were to stay, or create entirely new ones that better suited their needs and interests – like the labour movement that leftist communitarians now fight for, or the religious groups to which Christian conservatives belong that are the creations of radicals who split off from the traditional Church.

Liberalism does not deny man's need for belonging, it just denies that Deneen and Hertz know which collectives we should belong to. Liberalism is not about finding all life's meaning in a shopping list, it just says that we need more meaning than can be found in a ballot paper. And that those who seek the meaning of life in collective projects that they try to enforce on everybody have less of a sense of the beautiful richness and diversity of human nature than the alleged cold and robotic market liberals. Do we need something more than our lonely, individual lives? Of course we do, but *what*? Can we even find a single collective project that would make Patrick Deneen, Noreena Hertz, Joel Halldorf and Nina Björk cuddle together in communitarian hygge?

Even then we are still only talking about a small homogeneous group of Western intellectuals who demand a collective political project. What does the collective utopia look like that would fill the empty hearts of such diverse people as Stephen Fry, MrBeast, Elon Musk, Billie Eilish, Roger Federer, Mario Vargas Llosa, Danielle Steel, Richard Dawkins, PewDiePie, Robert Downey Jr, Nick Cave, LeBron James, Larry David, Donald Trump, Kylie Jenner, The Rock, Boris Johnson, Quentin Tarantino, Posh Spice, Robert Smith, Chris Rock, Blixa Bargeld, Neal Stephenson, Kim Kardashian, Lionel Messi, Johan Norberg and some 7.9 billion more?[11]

Liberalism is not based on ignoring the meaning of life but on believing that more people have a chance to find that meaning if they have the freedom to search for it. The counter-argument is that we just can't. That there is something in the very freedom of choice that makes us too selfish, afraid of relationships and isolated, that it's precisely this individual search for meaning in life that creates the epidemic of loneliness that is sweeping the Western world.

But is there even such an epidemic?

One hundred years of solitude?

Few conditions are more destructive to people's physical and mental well-being than the feeling of being abandoned. Loneliness is an individual misfortune and a major societal problem. But most articles I read about an epidemic of loneliness are in fact about the growing number of single households. That's not the same thing. Living alone has its downsides, but there is actually no strong association between it and feelings of loneliness or lack of social support. Sweden often tops lists of most single households, but at the same time it is also one of the countries where people say they feel the least loneliness – clearly below the European average and, interestingly, much below the feelings of loneliness in southern Europe, despite their reputation for big families and warmth. Of course, this could be because Swedes are so introverted that they think a visit to the local shop is sufficient to experience community. But Swedes are also in touch with their friends more often than other Europeans.[12]

The problem with assessing our level of loneliness is that we tend to interpret the difficulties we all experience with relationships and relatives as a sign that such connections have fallen into disrepair, and that there must have been a better time or place when we all lived in more harmonious relationships. It may be worth recalling that the most common violent crime in the traditional society of the nineteenth century was violence against parents (at a time when children often had a legal obligation to care for them), suggesting that an enforced relationship is often a cause of conflict rather than concord.[13]

I often hear the claim that poor and more collectivist countries have a different and deeper form of community than people who live in urbanized, individualized materialist ones (from students in rich countries, that is – I have still never heard it said in poor countries). But when the Gallup World Poll asks people around the world: 'If you were in trouble, do you have relatives or friends you can count on to help you whenever you need them?' a very different pattern emerges. In African countries, an average of 25 per cent answer 'no', in South America and Asia about 20 per cent, around 10 per cent in Japan and Taiwan, while it is down to single digits in Europe, the United States, Canada, Australia and New Zealand.[14]

In November 2022, I read an article in the *Financial Times* with the headline 'Are we ready for the approaching loneliness epidemic?' that claimed 'the share of people who report having friends and relatives they can count on has been steadily dropping'. Yet when I checked the source, it stated – quite to the contrary – that the average level of people who have someone to count on 'is almost unchanged' (at more than 90 per cent) and that satisfaction with relationships has actually increased slightly.[15]

After reviewing research in the field, Our World in Data concludes: 'There is an epidemic of headlines that claim we are experiencing a "loneliness epidemic", but there is no empirical support for the fact that loneliness is increasing.'[16] One reason many believe there is an epidemic is that those who say they are most lonely are the young, but this is based on the belief that they grow up and continue to feel just as lonely as then. However, as teens grow up, stop feeling they are misunderstood by society, establish friendships and romantic relationships, form families and have colleagues, their loneliness tends to decrease (until a partner dies late in life, when the feeling of loneliness increases again). Therefore, a more relevant question is whether those who are young today are more lonely than those who were young before (and whether older people today are more lonely than the older were back then), and the answer seems to be no.

Noreena Hertz wrote a whole book claiming that loneliness is increasing and that we now live in 'the lonely century'. But even though she reports depressing data on the number of people who feel alone, she does not make the case that this share has risen over time. Studies following American college students since 1977 show the proportion who state that they lack friends and feel left out has decreased somewhat. When researchers compare today's middle-aged and older people with previous generations at the same stage of life in the United States, England, Sweden, Finland and Germany, they don't find evidence of increased loneliness.

As far as I know, we have no studies looking at whether we as a society have experienced Gabriel García Márquez's one hundred years of solitude, but we have at least seventy-five years of British loneliness studies and they do not show an increase in the proportion who say they feel lonely.[17] We must also take into consideration that it is probably less stigmatized to talk about feelings of loneliness today than in previous generations.

Swedes have answered questions about social relations since the golden age of collectivism, and their responses show that the feeling of loneliness has diminished since then among younger and older people, men and women. In the early 1980s, more than one in four Swedes stated that they lacked a close friend. Now only just over one in ten do so.[18]

In other words, all these separate, autonomous, nonrelational selves seem to be distinctly social. This should not come as a surprise – after all, we are social beings. So collectivist pressures and political programmes are not needed to make us seek and develop contact with other people. Freedom is not about opting out of relationships but about choosing relationships that suit you and match your values.

If you want to feel lonely, you should refrain from fantasizing freely about how opponents destroy all communities and instead, like the political scientist Caspian Rehbinder, compare data on subjective feelings of loneliness in places with different institutions. This actually shows the opposite of what critics see as the Achilles heel of liberalism. Rehbinder notes that loneliness is reported less where freedom is greater. For every point a country gains on the

Fraser Institute's ten-point scale for personal and economic freedom – in effect, a measure of the classical liberalism of a country – loneliness is on average six percentage points lower. Rehbinder also looks at the equality of distribution and degree of religiosity in a society, since they are usually suggested as remedies to the emptiness of liberalism, from the left or the right. There is no connection whatsoever. If we trust the broad simple correlations, it seems we need personal freedom and free markets to remedy the existential isolation that equality and spirituality can't solve; it's not the other way around.[19]

Several indicators of loneliness and isolation worsened sharply during the pandemic, and it will take a long time until we learn whether this is a temporary dip or a new trend. However, this is the predictable result of government-enforced social distancing, when people were commanded to stay at home and kids were not even allowed to meet their classmates. If anything, it is a counter-argument to the hypothesis that too much liberty and mobility make us lonely.

On average, there is also no evidence for the large increase in mental illness that most of us assume exists (again with the caveat that the pandemic probably worsened these problems, at least temporarily). Once again turning to the Our World in Data project, Hannah Ritchie writes: 'Many (myself included) have the perception that mental health issues have been increasing significantly in recent years. The data… that we have does, in general, not support this conclusion.' On the contrary, it suggests that levels of mental illness have been stable since 1990.[20]

In a review of the literature in the field, researchers found forty-two studies between 1990 and 2017 that used the same methodology to study mental illness in the same geographical area over time. Most studies showed no increase in bad health (although such studies receive less media attention than the few that show an increase) and the overall result pointed to a 'minimal' increase that they believe is due to demographic changes (health changes over the years). The researchers conclude: 'we can be rather confident that the overall global prevalence of mental illness has not dramatically increased in recent decades if it has at all.'[21]

In a population of eight billion, there will always be groups of people in certain countries whose physical and mental suffering increase. There are ominous signs of a certain increase in depression and anxiety in teenage girls in many countries, for example, and in the United States there are the widespread deaths of despair that I wrote about in chapter 3. But globally, the suicide rate has fallen by about a third over the last thirty years, despite the fact that the real cause of death is increasingly being reported as secularized and individualized societies. In Sweden, the suicide rate has halved since 1980, although most of the decline took place before the turn of the millennium.[22]

So why are we so convinced that mental health is deteriorating? One reason is that we have borrowed terminology that was created for clinical health problems to talk about common forms of grief and worry. As many traditional, tangible sources of suffering disappear, the expectation that we should feel good all the time increases, and when we don't we suddenly start talking in psychiatric terms, even though stress and sadness are part of a good life. After observing that the proportion who experience reduced mental well-being is fairly constant while diagnoses and sick leave increase, Christian Rück, professor of psychiatry, concludes that we have confused two different forms of suffering. Some mental pain is simply the abrasions of the soul, says Rück, which is just a part of life, but we have begun to confuse it with the fractures of the soul, which we need help and treatment to deal with.[23]

One hopeful reason to believe in an increase in mental illness is that many taboos have been broken in this area. Previous generations spoke freely about physical ailments but the mental ones were hidden away and talked about only in a hushed voice. Today, it is much more common to report mental symptoms and to talk about them and seek help, and society and the healthcare system is more likely to take it seriously. That is a sign of an increasingly healthy society not a sick one.

The generous egoist

Even if there is no evidence that the free market makes us lonely or mentally ill, it can still make us coarsened and ruthless. What if it distorts our personality and poisons our relationships, as Noreena Hertz and Nina Björk claim? What if the economy displaces all other human motives and makes us see each meeting as an opportunity to take advantage of others?

A common mistake is to assume that capitalism introduced a desire for profit that did not exist before and that would disappear if we had another economic system. Disappointed with the greed of man, intellectuals turn on capitalism. But as the sociologist Max Weber wrote in 1905: 'The impulse to acquisition, pursuit of gain, of money, of the greatest possible amount of money, has in itself nothing to do with capitalism. That impulse exists and has existed among waiters, physicians, coachmen, artists, prostitutes, dishonest officials, soldiers, nobles, crusaders, gamblers, and beggars. One may say that it has been common to all sorts and conditions of men at all times and in all countries of the earth.'[24]

Nor does the desire for profit end when market forces are banned. No one studying Soviet party leaders, the Iranian Revolutionary Guards, Chavist 'boligarchs' or the Egyptian army would argue that these groups are less interested in accumulating property or living a life of luxury than the average person in market economies. The difference is that, in order to satisfy that craving, they do not have to produce goods and services that someone else wants. They can just confiscate companies and plunder the population. North Korea is the world's least market-based economy but probably has the leaders who spend the most on Rolex watches, Mercedes limousines and Hennessy Paradis cognac.

The question of whether market incentives coarsen our profit-hunger and squeeze out all other motives than the material ones is an empirical question that is not best decided by quoting Marx and Barthes. Anyone who has seen people who are as tough in economic negotiations as they are generous to friends and strangers (and vice versa) sees that Hertz and Björk have fallen for a one-dimensional caricature of human psychology. Human beings are big enough to accommodate different motivations and complex enough to behave differently in different relationships. Bill Gates' desire to crush competitors did not diminish his interest in saving millions from malaria.

What evidence does Nina Björk have that market incentives sabotage our humanity? What on earth makes her believe that under free market capitalism 'qualities such as solidarity, empathy, responsiveness, sensitivity, the will to satisfy others without regard to one's own gain become almost a sign of weakness'?[25] She mentions the well-known fact that an external reward for something we used to do out of inner motives, such as money for donating blood, can weaken those inner motives. But that is not even relevant for the issue she is discussing – it does not mean that financial rewards for work, entrepreneurship and saving would make us less interested in donating blood without getting any reward for it. Had Björk studied blood donations empirically, she would have had difficulty explaining why they are most common in individualist market economies. (By the way, when payment for blood plasma was introduced in countries such as Canada and the United States, it did not even result in a reduction in unpaid blood donations; there was actually a small increase.)[26]

A group of American psychologists recently measured the prevalence of seven different forms of generosity and helpfulness in 152 countries: the willingness to donate blood, organs and bone marrow, give to charity, volunteer, help strangers and treat animals well. It turned out that one of the strongest correlations was that the citizens of individualist countries were more likely to help. Even when they allowed for the fact that individualist countries also had more prosperity, better health and education, the correlation remained. Again, the assumptions of anti-capitalist pundits are turned on their head; the more you care about your own self-fulfilment, the more you are willing to put in some extra effort for others in a difficult situation.[27]

Researchers speculate that this may have to do with the fact that those who feel good about themselves and are not forced into self-sacrificing relationships may have more energy and will to help others – a kind of 'put on your own oxygen mask first before assisting others' effect. Another explanation they raise is that individualistic attitudes undermine tribal cultures and make us more prepared to help strangers as well.

Experiments in many societies at different levels of development give a completely different picture of our behaviour than that given by Hertz and Björk. They show that there are indeed societies, as envisioned in Hertz's and Björk's nightmares, where people see every meeting as an opportunity for exploitation and to take everything they come across – but they were the societies that were *least* used to market transactions on a daily basis.

This is the experiment that the researchers carried out: one player gets a certain amount of money and is asked to give some of it to an anonymous player. The other player then approves or declines the offer. If the recipient says yes, the bid goes through, but if she says no, neither person gets anything. What would you offer the anonymous player? Both Marxists and the economics textbooks make us believe that you would offer the recipient as little as possible in this ultimatum game, and this person would still always say yes, because almost nothing is always better than nothing at all. Since the game only takes place once, there is also no reason to build a reputation for being a generous player. For the same reason, there is no incentive for the recipient to turn down a stingy offer to pressure you to become more generous in the future. But many years of research around the world, from Missouri to Mongolia, show that we just don't behave that way. In rich market economies, in fact, the most common offer is to split the amount fifty-fifty; the recipient is so offended by bad offers that they usually say no if offered less than 30 per cent.

Such experiments have been carried out in communities that are at different stages of development, from industrialized cities to peasant communities, to groups of hunters and gatherers. It turns out that the way you play has nothing to do with gender, age, education or ethnicity – it has to do with how familiar people are with taking part in markets. The more people engage in trade in their daily lives, the more they are inclined to make generous offers and to punish stingy ones, even if it comes at their own expense. The market attitude is to be generous, while people in societies without markets 'display relatively little concern with fairness or punishing unfairness', the researchers state. On average, players in the most market-integrated societies offered twice as much as the ones in the least market-based societies.[28]

At first, these results seemed so unlikely that the researchers went back to see if they could repeat their results. They added other economic games and also studied the differences within groups. The results were replicated: the more people are used to buying and selling, the less ruthlessly they behaved. When researchers indirectly reminded research participants about markets, these participants became more trusting and invested more money in interacting with strangers. When the game was played in fifty-three groups of Oromo in Ethiopia, even the distance to a marketplace proved important. The closer you live to the market, the more prepared you are to work with strangers. Those who have no more than half an hour of travel to the marketplace almost always collaborate in the experiments; those who are five hours away from the marketplace almost never cooperate.[29]

The habit of thinking in terms of mutual gain apparently develops a feeling for others and their needs. Of course, researchers do not deny that non-market societies also have strong standards of justice, but those standards are mainly limited to traditional rules for how relatives and friends should be treated. Those who are not used to interacting with outsiders often consider them a threat or a chance for short-term gains. Those who regularly trade, on the other hand, have norms that include a certain openness and generosity that makes it easy for them to find common denominators with strangers. Because people want to socialize and trade with those who seem friendly and generous, such norms are encouraged. 'The more friendly, the more advantageous. Such is the humanity of trade,' as Marx's collaborator Friedrich Engels acknowledged in 1844.[30]

When we merely express our values in polls, we get a similar result. An analysis of World Values Survey data over many years shows that richer and more economically free countries express less materialism and greed. The researchers believe that one reason is the declining marginal utility of money: 'the market makes us richer and being richer allows us to focus on alternative, non-material things.'[31]

In the light of the widespread worry about the decline of trust and solidarity in recent decades, it is also worth looking at changes over time. Researchers have found 511 studies on cooperation between strangers in the United States between 1956 and 2017. Encouragingly, they did not find a decline in cooperation in social dilemmas – instead they found there was an *increase* in cooperation of almost 20 per cent over these sixty-one years.[32] Interestingly, they found that not just wealth but also urbanization and the percentage of people living alone were positively linked to cooperative behaviour. One possible explanation is that people in cities and those who live alone depend more on strangers to achieve what they want in their daily life, and so are also more eager to cooperate as this is something they are already used to doing.

Hertz and Björk may be on to something when they say market attitudes seep into our character, but the poison it spreads is openness to cooperation and generosity towards strangers. It is so pervasive and powerful that we express a keen sense of justice even in a game rigged to expose our unscrupulous materialism. It turns us into competitors *and* collaborators, consumers *and* citizens, takers *and* givers.

The person who cannot see another human being without asking the question 'What do I gain from this?'

and considers every meeting a moment to eat or to be eaten does exist – we have all had an unpleasant opportunity to meet them, in business, in politics, in journalism and in our private life – but the greatest risk of running into such people is at a few hours' walk from the marketplace.

Happy capitalism

So now perhaps we can go back to the original question of whether capitalism really makes us happier. Can money buy happiness? The answer is yes.

In the early days of well-being research, data pointed to the opposite conclusion. Economist Richard Easterlin noted in 1974 that we were getting richer but we did not seem to become any happier. We simply got used to the rising prosperity and instead we compared ourselves to the neighbours who became even richer than we did. This 'Easterlin paradox', which has its roots in Rousseau's critique of materialism and modernity, became famous and it is still the only thing many non-experts remember about the connection between money and happiness. But in the barely half-century that has passed since then, many more surveys in far more places have been undertaken, with more sophisticated methods, so we have been able to follow developments over time. And our knowledge has changed.

When I wrote a book about happiness in 2009, I interviewed the Dutch sociologist Ruut Veenhoven, the man behind the famous 'World Database of Happiness'. He told me he had become interested in well-being research because he thought it showed that prosperity did not contribute to happiness and he was quickly met with interest from politicians critical of economic growth. But as he collected statistics from more countries, a different pattern began to emerge. Growth actually proved to be good for well-being: 'The Easterlin paradox does not exist. It is not supported by the data of most countries and the theoretical basis is incorrect.' In any case, the new insight had a clear political result. 'Then the green politicians stopped calling,' states Veenhoven.[33]

Nobel Prize-winning psychologist Daniel Kahneman is another scholar who has made the case for the Easterlin paradox. But after receiving statistics from several countries, he has changed his mind:

'We had thought income effects are small because we were looking within countries. The GDP differences between countries are enormous, and highly predictive of differences in life satisfaction. In a sample of over 130,000 people from 126 countries, the correlation between the life satisfaction of individuals and the GDP of the country in which they live was over .40 – an exceptionally high value in social science. Humans everywhere, from Norway to Sierra Leone, apparently evaluate their life by a common standard of material prosperity, which changes as GDP increases. The implied conclusion, that citizens of different countries do not adapt to their level of prosperity, flies against everything we thought we knew ten years ago. We have been wrong and now we know it.'[34]

In my book on well-being, I observed that you can buy happiness – but only at a very bad exchange rate. Compared to having health, peace of mind and good relationships, money is not much to write home about. Based on the statistics we had then, I stated that if your mental worry and anxiety for some reason increase by a tenth, you need to increase your monthly salary by around $20,000 to get back to the same level of happiness that you had before. But one reason why individual income is less important for one's well-being is revealed by grandpa's grandma's grandpa's grandma's time machine in chapter 4. Most goods, services and technologies that make a real difference to one's well-being spread quickly in market-based societies, so a few hundred bucks here or there does not make much of a difference to one's happiness. The important thing is to live in a rich, free, capitalist society. If you have been lucky enough to be born there, much of your potential for happiness is already fulfilled.

We are not talking about objective indicators here but about what people say regarding their own emotional state. The sources of error are many: both those who are too depressed and those who have too much excitement in life may not respond to surveys; occasional events play a disproportionately large role in our mood (such as the weather on the day you respond, if you missed the bus or if you happened to find a coin in the elevator just now); not everyone is honest even in anonymous surveys (the French believe melancholy is a sign of intelligence and some think Scandinavians have such low expectations of life that they are constantly pleasantly surprised). So one has to treat this data with great care, but it is fascinating that what well-being research suggests now is completely opposite to the notion that free markets and individualism suck the joy out of life.

The data indicates that individuals' average happiness grows with their income and the population's average happiness grows with the country's GDP per capita, and that both of these levels increase on average over time, as people and countries become richer. In Western Europe, North America, Australia and New Zealand, people report the highest level of well-being. In Africa, South Asia and the Middle East the levels are lowest. The correlation is clear, though not perfect. Latin American countries are happier than their level of prosperity would predict and former communist countries are unhappier.[35]

Richer countries are happier[36]

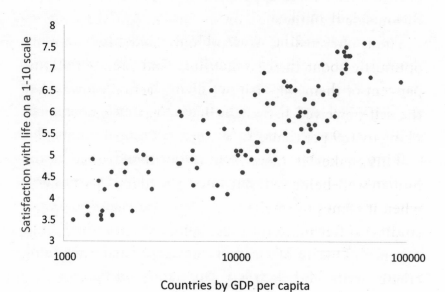

Countries by GDP per capita

Ruut Veenhoven sums up the state of research as '[t]he more individualized society, the happier its citizens are' and the research project World Values Survey documents that the most important factors behind increased well-being are 'global economic growth, widespread democratization, growing tolerance of diversity, and a rising sense of freedom'. After devoting an entire book to talking about a happiness crisis, even the British economist Richard Layard admits that 'we in the West are probably happier than any previous society'.[37]

That people claim to be so satisfied with their lives is in itself a surprise to most people. The British believe that only 47 per cent of Brits perceive themselves as very or fairly happy, while as many as 92 per cent state that they are fairly or very happy themselves. The result is similar in all thirty-two countries where the question has been asked. People apparently look more depressed on the outside than they feel on the inside. And the underestimate is not small. Canadians and Norwegians are most optimistic about their compatriots, and assumed that 60 per cent of them were happy. That is actually lower than the self-perceived happiness in the least happy country, Hungary (69 per cent).[38]

This makes it incredibly risky to speculate about human well-being without relying on data – particularly when it comes to intellectuals, who (according to many studies) suffer more from anxiety and neuroticism than others.[39] This is often what drives them onwards, to create, write and debate in public. Yet it also makes them even more inclined to underestimate the happiness

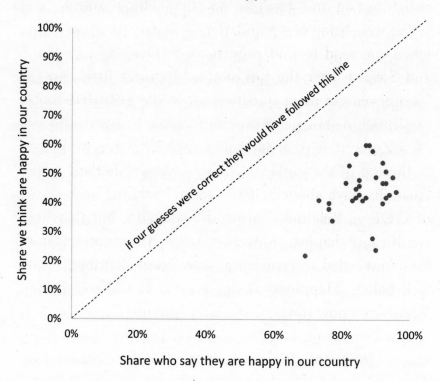

We underestimate the happiness of others[40]

Share we think are happy in our country (y-axis: 0% – 100%)

If our guesses were correct they would have followed this line

Share who say they are happy in our country

of others, especially as they really can't comprehend how someone can be happy with the trivialities of everyday life, unintellectual professions and taco Tuesday. It also makes them inclined to look for causes of these problems in societal structures and in vulgar capitalism. David Hume said of his close friend Rousseau that he just happens to be unhappy but tries to blame it on society instead of his own melancholy disposition.[41]

When seen from the inside, capitalism is not as depressing as most intellectuals assume. Veenhoven, who was active in the Dutch Social Democrats when he began to study happiness, first believed that government redistribution and generous social spending contributed to the well-being of a population. It is easy to assume this when you tend to find countries like Denmark, Finland and Sweden near the top of the happiness lists. But as Veenhoven got more statistics, it became clear that other small, rich democracies such as Iceland, Switzerland and New Zealand, with much smaller welfare states, were also at the top of the rankings. Ireland, the Netherlands and Australia have about half the social spending as a share of GDP as Belgium, Italy and France do, but they are significantly happier. Government redistribution has not even succeeded in creating a more equal distribution of well-being. 'Happiness is not greater in welfare states,' Veenhoven now states, 'I was simply wrong.'[42]

Another conclusion that surprised Veenhoven was that income inequality does not reduce a country's well-being: 'Income inequality is a by-product of capitalist societies and they have such a positive effect on well-being that outbalance the negative effect of being relatively poor.' This is not a popular conclusion in all camps: 'My colleagues are not amused. Inequality is big business here in the sociology department. Entire careers have been built on it.'[43]

There is a strong correlation between economic freedom and subjective well-being, and – contrary to most expectations – it is strongest for low-income earners. The researchers suspect this is due to the fact that free markets introduce autonomy and freedom of choice for those who have a more difficult socio-economic situation: 'For high-income earners, this effect is much less important, as their

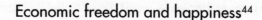

Economic freedom and happiness[44]

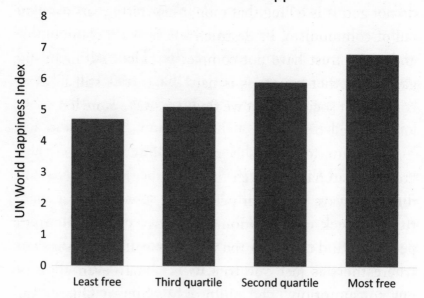

The world's countries by level of economic freedom

income already gives them the access to more choices.'[45] No matter how much critics say we should feel like we are naked and afraid in capitalist societies, people insist on saying that it gives them a sense of control over their lives, at least compared to other systems.

None of this means the problems that critics equate with life in an individualist, capitalist society do not exist. It just means the same problem seems to be even greater in non-capitalist societies. It can be difficult to compete, but competition for resources and positions does not disappear because they are distributed politically instead of according to supply and demand. On the contrary, in capitalism we search for opportunities for mutual gain, while in economies based on distribution from the top we begin to see other groups as threats because what they take is something we do not get. It is telling that more than thirty years after the fall of communism, its destructive effects on communities and social trust have not completely faded. Although the gap with other countries is narrowing, it is still in post-communist societies that we find less trust, more loneliness and less well-being.

The hunt for status is no less brutal because there are fewer arenas in which to compete. If there are many different ways in which people can develop their identity and seek confirmation, there is a chance for more people to find their way than in more collectivist societies where there is just one true way. It may even apply to our consumption. The philosopher Steven Quartz and the political scientist Anette Asp believe that diversity and freedom of choice can be an explanation for the fact that increased inequality has not made us more unhappy – even though they point out that it should: 'As a result, social status, which was once hierarchical and zero-sum, has become more fragmented, pluralistic and subjective. The relationship between relative income and relative status, which used to be straightforward, has gotten much more complex.'[46]

In poorer societies, consumption is often about showing how high one has climbed on the prosperity ladder. That is why, paradoxically, poor societies have such a large share of consumption of pure luxury products that are sought after precisely because they are expensive. That exists in richer and more individualistic societies too, of course, but there consumption increasingly becomes a way of expressing one's personality. People no longer automatically covet the most expensive item but rather what suits their taste and expresses their identity. Someone dreams of a Porsche, but someone else prefers to show his green identity with a Tesla, a third person prefers a cheap and comfortable car because their status is based on not caring about status when choosing a car, while a fourth person talks happily and often about how it is vulgar to have a car when you can get anywhere on a bicycle and public transport. They can all converge in feelings of well-being, even if they diverge in income and taste.

The most important word in economic freedom is not 'economic' but 'freedom'. We are all different with different needs, and our chance of finding relationships, communities, work and consumption that we enjoy increases if we get the freedom to choose. Not everyone wants to constantly work and strive for material rewards, and one of the advantages of an open society is that you do not have to choose that. Even before the pandemic, surveys in the Western world showed that between 20 and 50 per cent of workers in recent years had chosen a less demanding job with less pay, reduced their working hours, declined a promotion or moved to a calmer neighbourhood to focus on their family, make everyday life easier or just to unwind with a less stressful life.[47]

If you do not like the rat race, you can leave it – provided you live in a growing economy with high productivity so that you can do it without catastrophic consequences for the private economy. That is exactly what capitalism makes possible, and that is why the average working time of the average worker has decreased by about half in the last 150 years. In 1870, Britons worked more hours between January and August in an average year than they now do between January and December.[48] In addition, we start working later in life and live for far longer after retirement than previously. That's why you sit here and read and think about the viability of different political and economic systems and their implications for human well-being – a pastime that used to be reserved for a tiny elite with many servants and plenty of free time, or someone who happened to have a generous friend whose family lived off a cotton fortune, as Karl Marx had.

Epilogue

THE EMPEROR'S SINGING CONTEST

'It has been the first to show what man's activity can bring about.'

MARX & ENGELS ON CAPITALISM[1]

To let Karl Marx and Friedrich Engels summarize my case: large-scale, massive progress is something new. Ruling classes were always primarily interested in control and stability, but this inhibited production and innovation instead of promoting it. They had to be burst asunder – and they were, by capitalism.

As early as 1848, the fathers of communism wrote that the then very young market economy had 'created more massive and more colossal productive forces than have all preceding generations together'. In just a few decades, we got industrialism, the chemical industry, electrification, and global transportation and communications: 'what earlier century had even a presentiment that such productive forces slumbered in the lap of social labour?'[2]

What makes the free market unique is that it enabled and presupposed a constant revolution of productive conditions. If everyone is free to try something better, old companies must do the same or fail. When these freedoms spread to more and more people, a wave of creativity and innovation that had been held back by the dams of oppression rushed forward and changed the world for ever.

What Marx and Engels failed to predict was that capitalism would also spread this prosperity within and between nations, as more productive companies offered workers better jobs and reduced the price of goods and services. It was not easy for them to fit changing facts into their models. They quietly replaced the predictions of proletarianization and the iron law of wages with the notion that it is 'very complicated'. In a lecture in 1865, Marx said the wages of British farm workers had increased by 40 per cent in just ten years. In 1892, Engels was forced to supplement his half-century-old description of the plight of the English working class with the words, 'They are undoubtedly better off than before 1848.'[3]

Still, almost all the progress free markets made possible was in the future. Just imagine if Marx and Engels had been alive to see how much more capitalism has produced since then. In the last 200 years, extreme poverty has been reduced from almost nine out of ten people to less than one in ten today. In 1800, only 12 per cent of the Earth's inhabitants could read and write. Today, there are about as few who can't. Global life expectancy has increased from around thirty to more than seventy years, and infant mortality has decreased by about 90 per cent.

Surprisingly, the twenty years since I wrote *In Defence of Global Capitalism* have been the very best. Despite all the wars, injustices and plagues, we have experienced a remarkable era, when indicators of human well-being have, on average, improved faster than ever. The world's newsrooms could have led with the breaking news '138,000 people were lifted out of poverty yesterday' every day during these two decades, despite recessions, wars and pandemics. And it happened the fastest in the countries that did the most to integrate into global capitalism.

In this book I have also shown that this did not come at the cost of good jobs, wage stagnation and unprecedented inequality. I have argued that (on the whole) we did not see a new class of super-rich and monopolies that live and thrive on our expense, but that their innovation and productivity contribute to a distribution of important technologies, goods and services that is more equal than it has ever been before. And I have documented the research that shows that we do not have to sacrifice the environment or our well-being to achieve these results. On the contrary, it is mainly in rich market economies that we have the will and resources to reduce our environmental impact and – even if one should be careful with data on self-reported happiness – it is striking that it is in rich, individualistic and capitalist countries that people consider themselves most satisfied with life.

But everything is not optimist babble (to quote a judgment about me from back in the day). We have serious problems with crony capitalism, which manifests itself in regulations adapted to large companies, occupational licences, building regulations that protect insiders, immigration restrictions that hurt our economy, and a battery of subsidies, tax deductions and tariff protection for companies that are either competitive (so they do not need such help) or not competitive (meaning they are a drag on the economy). Our treatment of financial markets is now reminiscent of our view of mental health: one must be on top all the time and must never, ever be sad, and in that case, central banks must help by prescribing ever-increasing doses of antidepressants. Here we have a source of ugly inequality that also pumps up asset prices in such an absurd way that the fall will be more painful than it would otherwise be.

We also have a welfare system that punishes work and leaves many people on the outside. The death toll from despair in the United States is a cruel wake-up call. We may be able to afford the financial cost of letting an increasing number of people leave the labour market, but we definitely can't afford the human cost. In addition, many forms of environmental degradation are increasing. Climate change has the prerequisites to disturb all our plans in unpleasant ways.

In all these areas, constructive free marketeers – and everyone else too – have an awe-inspiring to-do list. But even if we were to solve all these problems, capitalism is not always beautiful, because we humans aren't and even our utopias are built on trade-offs. The creative destruction that constantly creates wealth and new jobs harms those who lose the old ones. When consumers control production, they will demand a lot of things that are surely illegal, immoral, fattening, addictive, vulgar or impossible. And business owners will not hesitate to satisfy them and become filthy rich and buy a stupid car. Annoyingly, a disproportionately large proportion of those who do this are probably some old classmates of yours who did not understand arithmetic and did not care about ancient literature.

Capitalism does not reward us for merit, despite the fact that it has often been claimed to do so by its defenders. If you are successful it does not necessarily mean that you deserved it; if you fail, it doesn't mean you had it coming. The market is not a meritocracy that enriches the one who is best, smartest or has worked hardest. Someone may have toiled away as best they could but still not succeeded – keep in mind that the market is a minefield and we don't know where the mines are buried – while someone else may have just thoughtlessly turned out a product that happened to become a bestseller. The market does not reward us for our values, talent or effort, but for one thing only: to create as much value for others at as little cost as possible. 'You can be an asshole and still make people's lives much better off,' pointed out the great classical liberal Steven Horwitz, a man who did much of the latter without ever being the former.

In my eyes, it is precisely this insistence on voluntary relations that makes the free market morally superior to all other systems. It is also what lies behind its incredible ability to produce wealth, as it gives everyone a powerful motive to constantly try to find new ways to create value for others. But it also results in a lot of consequences that are hard to stomach. Someone loses their job no matter how hard she works, just because someone else came up with something better. Someone else is in the black just because she happened to be in the right place when demand passed by. Your favourite project or the store you love has to close, while that completely brain-dead retail chain spreads like wildfire. However, if we are to constantly produce smarter processes and new jobs that expand everyone's opportunities, we must also get rid of old outdated ones. We need more filthy rich – and more bankruptcies.

If we are to be able to use the knowledge and creativity of all people, to create the new and unexpected, then we won't know in advance what will succeed and who should be rewarded. We can never predict the outcome. The open society guarantees nothing, in the way centralized systems can at least pretend to. It is not always a joy to live with such openness and unpredictability.

Such problems and shortcomings are enough to make many of us feel reluctant and dream of other systems. Another world just *has* to be possible. It creates that constant temptation to find some kind of shortcut that would give a better result than voluntary interaction and without its downsides. Some want to start experimenting with protectionism, redistribute the resources that could have been invested in the future, or happen to fall in love with the latest populist leader who promises to fix everything.

Sometimes when I present the evidence for the world's unique progress during the era of global capitalism, I get the response: yes, it's good – no one is opposed to it – but why should we be happy with it? Why not make it *even better*? I agree. I'm not saying that's enough. We should be proud but not content. We have begun to see what actually works. And that is a rare thing in human history. We must not take it for granted, we must make sure that it survives and spreads, precisely because we cannot be satisfied with the progress we have seen so far.

What we mustn't do is throw it all away because it is not as perfect as our fantasies. Without the sometimes problematic creative destruction that is constantly transforming our economy and technology, we will stagnate and lose the opportunity to solve the problems we will be surprised by in the future. Without an open world economy and global supply chains, we would be deprived of future development and close the way out of poverty for hundreds of millions of people. The Western world's new ambition to imitate China's industrial policy and repatriated supply chains is a costly and dangerous experiment. Without the awkward and difficult unpredictability of human interaction and creativity, we know exactly what we would be getting, for that is what we have been through for most of the other eras of history.

An old legend is relevant to our situation: to amuse the masses, a Roman emperor agreed to decide which one of two singers was the best. The first one started singing and it was not bad. It was actually quite impressive. The audience got excited – in fact, they had rarely heard something as beautiful. But then the singer hit a note a little wrong. The emperor instantly got up, interrupted the performance and declared that the competition was over. He called the other singer to the stage and gave the prize to him. The first singer had made a little mistake, so the second singer must be the winner. The problem, of course, is that this is not at all obvious. It is not enough to find faults and shortcomings and then fantasize that the alternative could avoid those faults and still be better overall. The first singer made a mistake, but the second singer might make more mistakes. Perhaps he can't carry a tune at all. In the worst case, he might be stark raving mad.

Maybe you think the next singer is perfect, flawless, or that you know how you can get the first singer to avoid all mistakes without creating other problems. It sounds interesting. Please test it. But always listen to both before choosing the victor: do not make the mistake of the Roman emperor. In a complex, unpredictable world, we are not looking for perfection. We're just looking for the best – and the promise of continuous improvement.

And if you are someone who is convinced of the importance of open societies and free markets: do not take them for granted. As I showed in my book *Open*, many historical golden ages of openness and progress have been laid in ruins by authoritarian revolts.[4] Capitalism has meant the greatest social and economic progress humanity has ever experienced, and millions respond by rejecting it in favour of the next singer they have never heard. For the first time, free markets provided broad populations with the resources and leisure to engage in theoretical ideas and political debate, and to a not insignificant extent we have devoted them to rejecting the market economy as unfair and soul-destroying.

Ingenious, hard-working people will continue to strive day in day out to supply us with innovations and growth no matter how much we whine. They will continue to fill your cup with coffee even if they do not know who you are. But the defence of their freedom to do so does not happen by itself. If you appreciate their contribution, you owe it to yourself to protect them. Global capitalism needs friends, advocates and educators.

Liberty and progress can be your project too. We pro-capitalists of the world have nothing to lose but our chains, tariff barriers, building regulations and confiscatory taxes. We have a world to win.

NOTES

Preface: What happened to Reagan and Thatcher?

1. Michka Assayas, *Bono*, Penguin, 2006, and Bono speaking at Georgetown University's 2013 Global Social Enterprise Event.
2. Jimmy Carter, State of the Union Address, 19 January 1978.
3. Gavin Poynter, *The Political Economy of State Intervention: Conserving Capital Over the West's Long Depression*, Routledge, 2020, p.3.
4. Robert Bradley, 'Colliery closures since 1947', www.healeyhero. co.uk/rescue/individual/Bob_Bradley/PM-Closures.html.
5. Deirdre McCloskey, *Why Liberalism Works*, Yale University Press, 2019, p.235.

1. Life under savage capitalism

1. Naomi Klein, *The Shock Doctrine: The Rise of Disaster Capitalism*, Allen Lane, 2007, p.252.
2. These pessimistic World Bank words introduced the prefaces of many of the institution's papers and reports in 1999 and 2000, e.g. its '1999 review of development effectiveness', World Bank 1999. Nader quoted in Gary Wells, Robert Shuey & Ray Kiely, *Globalization*, Novinka Books, 2001, p.23. Archbishop K. G. Hammar interviewed in *Arena*, no.6, 2000.
3. I really recommend these goldmines that have revolutionized access to knowledge.

4. In the first edition, I stated 29 and 23 per cent, respectively, but since then the World Bank has raised its definition of poverty from a consumption level of $1.2 to $2.15 per day, adjusted for inflation and local prices. In this book, I consistently use this new, higher poverty level. The data on global poverty come from the World Bank's PovcalNet, http://iresearch. worldbank.org/PovcalNet/, its Poverty & Inequality Platform, https://pip.worldbank.org/, and World Bank, 'Correcting course: Poverty and shared prosperity 2022', World Bank Group, 2022.

5. Michail Moatsos, 'Global extreme poverty: Present and past since 1820', *How Was Life Part II: New Perspectives on Well-Being and Global Inequality Since 1820*, OECD, 2021.

6. Angus Deaton, 'Thinking about inequality', *Cato's Letter*, vol.15, no.2, 2017.

7. The following numbers are from the World Bank's World Development Indicators, https://databank.worldbank.org/ source/world-development-indicators. For more on such statistics and what they are based on, see Johan Norberg, *Progress: Ten Reasons to Look Forward to the Future*, Oneworld, 2016.

8. https://data.unicef.org/topic/child-survival/under-five-mortality/.

9. International Labor Office and United Nations Children's Fund, 'Child labor: Global estimates 2020, trends and the road forward', ILO & UNICEF 2021.

10. This is an index graph, where the proportion affected in 1990 is set at 100 per cent to track changes. My calculations are based on numbers from the UN Food and Agricultural Organization, the World Bank, UNESCO and the UN respectively.

11. The data on GDP per capita in this chapter are adjusted for purchasing power and inflation. For the period after 1990, I use the World Bank's World Development Indicators, https://databank.worldbank.org/source/world-development-indicators. Before 1990, I use the Maddison Project, a

continuation of the ambitious historical data series produced by the economic historian Angus Maddison. www.rug.nl/ggdc/historicaldevelopment/maddison/.

12. Estimates of historical poverty in countries that are now rich can be found in Martin Ravaillon, *The Economics of Poverty: History, Measurement and Policy*, Oxford University Press, 2016, chap.1.

13. Yes, it's adjusted for inflation, converted to 2011 US dollar values. If you protest that this must be based on heroic estimates and guesswork bordering insanity, you have a point, but even if it contains huge errors every single year, it would not affect the overall appearance of the chart. The sources are Angus Maddison, *The World Economy: A Millennial Perspective*, OECD, 2001, Angus Maddison, *The World Economy: Historical Statistics*, OECD, 2003, and Maddison Project Database 2020.

14. Yes, they also had episodes of import substitution and industrial policy – all poor countries did – but for a shorter period and less extensively than others. For a study of the central importance of openness for these countries, see Arvind Panagariya, *Free Trade and Prosperity: How Openness Helps Developing Countries Grow Richer and Combat Poverty*, Oxford University Press, 2019.

15. Interview with Parth Shah for the documentary *India Awakes*, 2015.

16. Andrea Boltho, Wendy Carlin & Pasquale Scaramozzino, 'Will East Germany become a new Mezzogiorno?', *Journal of Comparative Economics*, vol.24, 1997.

17. Theo S. Eicher & Till Schreiber, 'Structural policies and growth: Time series evidence from a natural experiment', *Journal of Development Economics*, vol.91, 2010, pp.169–79.

18. Christer Gunnarsson & Mauricio Rojas, *Tillväxt, stagnation, kaos*, 2nd edn, SNS, 2004, chap.6.

19. Sara Regine Hassett & Christine Weyd, 'An interview with Fernando Henrique Cardoso', *Journal of International Affairs*, vol.58, no.2, 2005.

20. Max Roser & Esteban Ortiz-Ospina, 'Income Inequality', Our World in Data, October 2016.

21. The seven were Gabon, Guinea, Liberia, Zambia, Nigeria, Congo (Léopoldville, now Congo-Kinshasa) and Rhodesia (now Zimbabwe). Andrew Kamarck, *The Economics of African Development*, Prager, 1967, p.247. William Easterly & Ross Levine, 'Africa's growth tragedy: Policies and ethnic divisions', *The Quarterly Journal of Economics*, vol.112, no.4, November 1997.

22. George Ayittey, *Indigenous African institutions*, Brill, 2nd edn, 2006.

23. Ayittey 2006, p.486.

24. Belinda Archibong, Brahima Coulibaly & Ngozi Okonjo-Iweala, 'Washington Consensus reforms and economic performance in sub-Saharan Africa: Lessons from the past four decades', AGI Working Paper 27, February 2021.

25. World Bank, *Economic Growth in the 1990s: Learning from a Decade of Reform*, 2005, p.271.

26. Scott A Beaulier, 'Explaining Botswana's success: The critical role of post-colonial policy', *Cato Journal*, vol.23, no.2, 2003.

27. James Gwartney, Robert Lawson, Joshua Hall & Ryan Murphy, *Economic Freedom of the World: 2022 Annual Report*, Fraser Institute, 2022.

28. Ibid.

29. Robert Lawson, 'Economic freedom in the literature: What is it good (bad) for?', in James Gwartney, Robert Lawson, Joshua Hall & Ryan Murphy, *Economic Freedom of the World: 2022 Annual Report*, Fraser Institute, 2022. See also Joshua Hall & Robert Lawson. 'Economic Freedom of the World: An accounting of the literature', *Contemporary Economic Policy*, vol.32, no.1, 2014.

30. Esteban Ortiz-Ospina and Max Roser, 'Government Spending', Our World in Data, 2016.

31. William Easterly, 'The lost decades: developing countries' stagnation in spite of policy reform 1980–1998', World Bank,

February 2001. William Easterly, 'In search of reforms for growth: New stylized facts on policy and growth outcomes', working paper 26318, National Bureau of Economic Research, September 2019.

32. Kevin Grier & Robin Grier, 'The Washington Consensus works: Causal effects of reform, 1970–2015', *Journal of Comparative Economics* vol.49, No 1, March 2021. Pasquale Marco Marrazzo & Alessio Terzi, 'Structural reform waves and economic growth', European Central Bank, No.2111, November 2017.

33. Branko Milanović, *Capitalism, Alone: The Future of the System that Rules the World*, Belknap Press, 2019, chap.4.2. Richard Baldwin, *The Great Convergence: Information Technology and the New Globalization*, Belknap Press, 2016.

34. Dev Patel, Justin Sandefur & Arvind Subramanian, 'The new era of unconditional convergence', working paper, Center for Global Development, 2021.

35. Robert Mugabe, 'Statement by Zimbabwe', 2 September 2002.

36. @jeremycorbyn, Twitter, 5 March 2013. 'Venezuela: Latin America's inequality success story', Oxfamblogs.org, 6 August 2010. 'Jesse Jackson, Naomi Klein, Zinn, Kucinich, others express support for Venezuela's Chavez', Venezuelaanalysis, 13 August 2004.

37. Kristian Niemietz, *Socialism: The Failed Idea that Never Dies*, Institute for Economic Affairs, 2019, p.56ff.

38. See, e.g., Johan Fourie, *Our Long Walk to Economic Freedom*, Tafelberg, 2021.

39. Tom G. Palmer & Matt Warner, *Development with Dignity: Self-determination, Localization, and the End of Poverty*, Routledge, 2022, chap. 5.

40. Luis R. Martínez, 'How much should we trust the dictator's GDP growth estimates?', *Journal of Political Economy*, vol.130, no.10, 2022.

41. Samuel Absher, Kevin Grier, Robin Grier, 'The economic consequences of sustainable left-populist regimes in Latin

America', *Journal of Economic Behavior & Organization*, vol.177, September 2020, pp.787–817.

42. Manuel Funke, Moritz Schularick & Christoph Trebesch, 'Populist leaders and the economy', discussion paper 15405, Center for Economic Policy Research, October 2020.

43. Jordan Kyle & Yascha Mounk, 'The populist harm to democracy: An empirical assessment', Tony Blair Institute for Global Change, 26 December 2018.

2. At each other's service

1. 'Globalization and Resistance', an interview with Noam Chomsky by Husayn al-Kurdi, *Kick It Over*, no.35, Summer 1995.

2. I have adjusted for inflation and the growing number of workers. The comparison is inspired by the economist Fredrik N. G. Andersson who used a variant of it in a debate at Café Athen in Lund on 11 April 2019. Göran Greider said this on *Opinion Live*, SVT, 6 October 2019.

3. Lant Pritchett, 'There is only one poverty strategy: (broad based) growth (Part I)', lantpritchett.org, 6 February 2019.

4. David Dollar, Tatjana Kleineberg & Aart Kraay,'Growth still is good for the poor', Working Paper no.596 , Luxembourg Income Study, Cross-National Data Center in Luxembourg, September 2013.

5. Bruce D. Meyer & James X. Sullivan, 'Identifying the disadvantaged: Official poverty, consumption poverty, and the new supplemental poverty measure', *Journal of Economic Perspectives*, vol.26, no.3, 2012.

6. Yes, I know I quoted it in *In Defence of Global Capitalism* as well, but it ought to be repeated at least every twenty years. John Stuart Mill, *Principles of Political Economy*, book V, Liberty Fund, 2006, p.810f.

7. Andreas Bergh & Magnus Henrekson, 'Government size and

growth: A survey and interpretation of the evidence', Working Paper no. 858, Institute for Business Research.

8. James Gwartney, Robert Lawson, Joshua Hall & Ryan Murphy, *Economic Freedom of the World: 2022 Annual Report*, Fraser Institute, 2022, p.17.

9. Ibid.

10. Ibid.

11. A. J. Jacobs, *Thanks a Thousand: A Gratitude Journey from Bean to Cup*, Simon & Schuster, 2018. If you notice a certain resemblance to Leonard Read's beautiful fable 'I, Pencil', you are absolutely right. It is the best depiction of the market's magic collaboration that exists but, thanks to the splendid innovation of the marketplace, no one uses pencils any more.

12. Niclas Berggren & Therese Nilsson, 'Economic freedom as a driver of trust and tolerance', in Gwartney et al 2020. See also Antonio Farfan-Vallespin, Matthew Bonick, 'On the origins and consequences of racism', contribution to the annual meeting of the Association for Social Policy, Deutsche Zentralbibliothek für Wirtschaftswissenschaften, Leibniz-Informationszentrum Wirtschaft, Kiel & Hamburg, 2016.

13. Thomas Sowell, *Preferential Policies: An International Perspective*, William Morrow, 1990, pp.21ff. If you now object that capitalism would not have been possible without cotton, and cotton would not have been possible without slavery, and that capitalism was based on colonialism, then the book you are looking for is Fredrik Segerfeldt, *Den svarte mannens börda*, Timbro, 2018.

14. Swaminathan Anklesaria Aiyar, 'Capitalism's assault on the Indian caste system,' Policy Analysis No.776, Cato Institute, 21 July 2015.

15. You can begin with *The Constitution of Liberty*. If it is deterrently large, start with the essay 'The use of knowledge in society'.

16. Mårten Blix & Henrik Jordahl, *Privatizing Welfare Services:*

Lessons from the Swedish Experiment, Oxford University Press, 2021.

17. Frédéric Bastiat, *Economic Sophisms*, The Foundation for Economic Education, 1964, pp.97f.

18. Jeffrey Clemens, 'Making sense of the minimum wage: A roadmap for navigating recent research', Cato Policy Analysis, 14 May 2019.

19. John Maynard Keynes, *The Economic Consequences of the Peace*, Harcourt, Brace and Howe, 1920, pp.235–48.

20. In addition, it implies that 'state capitalism' is not capitalism. If the state owns companies and controls the economy, we have limited both private ownership and market coordination. State capitalism does not exist, it is just an attempt by Marxists to avoid taking responsibility for state socialism.

21. 'Although to introduce socialism as the punishment for our sins would be to go too far, past injustices might be so great as to make necessary in the short run a more extensive state in order to rectify them.' Anarchy, State and Utopia, Basic Books 1974, p.231. See also Fredrik Segerfeldt, *The New Equality: Global Development from Robin Hood to Botswana*, Timbro, 2014, pp.105ff.

22. Hernando de Soto, *The mystery of capital: Why capitalism triumphs in the west and fails everywhere else*, Bantam Press, 2000.

23. Aristophanes, *Ecclesiazusae*, lines 590, 650.

24. Trotsky did not mind using that principle against his opposition but protested when Stalin used it against Trotskyites. Leon Trotsky, *The Revolution Betrayed: What is the Soviet Union and Where is It Going?*, Pathfinder Press, 1972, p.283.

25. 'Covid-19 exposes EU reliance on drug imports', *Financial Times*, 20 April 2020.

26. Vincent Geloso & Jamie Bologna Pavlik, 'Economic freedom and the consequences of the 1918 pandemic', *Contemporary Economic Policy*, vol.39, no.2, 2021.

27. Christian Bjørnskov, 'Economically free countries have fewer

and less severe economic crises', Timbro briefing paper, no.29, 2020.

28. Keith Bradsher, 'China delays mask and fan exports after quality complaints', *The New York Times*, 11 April 2020. Maria Manner & Paavo Teittinen, 'HS: n haltuun saamat Huoltovarmuuskeskuksen luvut paljastavat, miten vähän Suomen valtiolla oli kasvosuojaimia koronakriisin iskiessä päälle', *Helsingin Sanomat*, 10 April 2020.

29. Johan Norberg, 'Covid-19 and the danger of self-sufficiency: How Europe's pandemic resilience is open economy', ECIPE Policy Brief, no.2, 2021.

30. 'EU should "not aim for self-sufficiency" after coronavirus, trade chief says', *Financial Times*, 23 April 2020. Andrew Edgecliffe-Johnson, 'Manufacturers warn US must do more to maintain fragile PPE production', *Financial Times*, 13 April 2021.

31. Henry David Thoreau, *On Civil Disobedience and Other Essays*, Dover Publications, 2021, p.2.

3. The silence of the factory whistle

1. Robert Z. Lawrence, 'China, like the US, faces challenges in achieving inclusive growth through manufacturing', Policy Brief, Peterson Institute for International Economics, August 2019.

2. Economic Data, 'Industrial Production: Manufacturing', Federal Reserve Bank of St Louis, 2022.

3. Michael Hicks & Srikant Devaraj, 'The myth and reality of manufacturing in America', Center for Business and Economic Research, Ball State University, 2015.

4. 'China's future economic potential hinges on its productivity', *The Economist*, 14 August 2021.

5. Philippe Aghion, Céline Antonin & Simon Bunel, *The Power of Creative Destruction: Economic Upheaval and the Wealth of Nations*, Belknap Press, 2021, p.51f.

6. S. L. Price, *Playing Through the Whistle*, First Grove Atlantic, 2016, chap.11.

7. J. D. Vance, *Hillbilly Elegy: A Memoir of a Family and Culture in Crisis*, William Collins, 2016, p.55.

8. Daniel Clark, 'Detroit autoworkers' elusive post-war boom', The Metropol Blog.

9. Daniel Clark, 'The 1950s were not a golden age for Detroit's autoworkers', *What it Means to be American*, 9 May 2019.

10. US Bureau of Labor Statistics, 'Characteristics of minimum wage workers, 2020', report 1091, February 2021.

11. Michael Strain, *The American Dream is not Dead (But Populism Could Kill It)*, Templeton Press, 2020.

12. Ray Chetty, Nathaniel Hendren, Patrick Kline, Emmanuel Saez & Nicholas Turner, 'Is the United States still a land of opportunity? Recent trends in intergenerational mobility', *The American Economic Review*, vol.104, no.5, 2014.

13. Simeon Alder, David Lagakos & Lee Ohanian, 'Competitive pressure and the decline of the Rust Belt: A macroeconomic analysis', Working Paper no.20538, National Bureau of Economic Research, October 2014.

14. Strain 2020, p.33.

15. Strain 2020, chap.6.

16. Federal Reserve Bank of St Louis, 'Nonfarm Business Sector: Real Hourly Compensation for All Employed Persons', https://fred.stlouisfed.org/series/COMPRNFB.

17. Strain 2020, p.98f.

18. Strain 2020, p.72f.

19. Strain 2020, p.73.

20. 'More than half of British homes don't have a bathroom', *Guardian*, 21 March 1950. And in grandpa's time, construction was not made more expensive by requirements for fire safety, moisture control, child safety, glass safety, accessibility, green space, free space, parking, sound insulation, daylight, solar heating, energy consumption or protection against squeezing, fall, collision or burn, or work environment requirements. See

Mårten Belin, 'Här får vi inte bo', *Sydsvenska Dagbladet*, 25 September 2021.

21. Robert Atkinson & John Wu, 'False alarmism: Technological disruption and the US labor market, 1850–2015', Information Technology & Innovation Foundation, May 2017.

22. United States Census Bureau, 'Table A-1. Annual geographic mobility rates, by type of movement: 1948–2020', www.census. gov/data/tables/time-series/demo/geographic-mobility/ historic.html.

23. Charlie Giattino, Esteban Ortiz-Ospina & Max Roser, 'Working hours', Our World in Data, December 2020.

24. Ibid.

25. Gallup, 'Work and Workplace', https://news.gallup.com/ poll/1720/work-work-place.aspx.

26. David Graeber, *Bullshit Jobs: A Theory*, Simon & Schuster, 2018. Roland Paulsen, *The Working Society: How Work Survived Technology*, Gleerups, 2010. See also Andreas Bergh, 'Tre böcker av Roland Paulsen – en kritisk läsning', *Ekonomisk Debatt*, no.3, 2017.

27. Graeber 2018, pp.xix, xxiv.

28. Magdalena Soffia, Alex Wood, Brendan Burchell, 'Alienation is not "bullshit": An empirical critique of Graeber's theory of BS jobs', *Work, Employment and Society*, June 2021.

29. Sarah Damaske, Matthew Zawadzki, Joshua M. Smyth, 'Stress at work: Differential experiences of high versus low SES workers', *Social Science & Medicine* 156, March 2016.

30. Alan Manning & Graham Mazeine, 'Subjective job insecurity and the rise of the precariat: Evidence from the UK, Germany and the United States', CEP Discussion Paper no.1712, August 2020.

31. See, e.g., Thor Berger, Carl Benedikt Frey, Guy Levin, Santosh Rao Danda, 'Uber happy? Work and well-being in the "gig economy"', *Economic Policy*, vol.34, no.99, 2019.

32. Linda Weidenstedt, Andrea Geissinger & Monia Lougui, 'Why gig as a food courier?', Report no.15, Ratio 2020.

33. Andreas Bergh, 'Låt giggarna gigga', *Arbetsmarknadsnytt*, 2 December 2020.

34. Federal Reserve Bank of St Louis, 'All employees, manu-facturing', https://fred.stlouisfed.org/series/ MANEMP and 'All Employees, total nonfarm', https://fred.stlouisfed.org/series/ PAYEMS. See also Lawrence Edwards & Robert Lawrence, *Rising tide: Is growth in emerging economies good for the United States?*, Peterson Institute for International Economics, 2013, p.15.

35. Adam Posen, 'The price of nostalgia', *Foreign Affairs*, May/June 2021. The data on lost jobs come from the 'Job openings and labor turnover survey' from the US Bureau of Labor Statistics. In 2019, the year before the pandemic, 67.9 million jobs disappeared and 70 million new ones were created.

36. Ildikó Magyari, 'Firm reorganization, Chinese imports, and US manufacturing employment', Job Market Paper, 2017.

37. Nicholas Bloom, Mirko Draca, and John Van Reenen, 'Trade induced technical change? The impact of Chinese imports on innovation, IT and productivity', *Review of Economic Studies*, vol.83, no.1, 2016.

38. Zhi Wang, Shang-Jin Wei, Xinding Yu, Kunfu Zhu, 'Re-examining the effects of trading with China on local labor markets: A supply chain perspective', NBER working paper no.24886, 2018.

39. Jason Dedrick, Greg Linden, Kenneth L. Kraemer, 'We estimate China only makes $8.46 from an iPhone', *The Conversation*, 6 July 2018.

40. Anne Case Deaton & Angus Deaton, *Deaths of Despair: And the Future of Capitalism*, Princeton University Press, 2020.

41. Nicholas Eberstadt, 'Education and men without work', *National Affairs*, no.48, 2021.

42. Deaton & Deaton 2020, p.222.

43. 'The welfare state needs updating', *The Economist*, 12 July 2018.

44. 'Not In My Back Yard', i.e. people protesting against new local construction.

45. Dick Carpenter, Lisa Knepper, Angela Erickson & John K. Ross, 'License to work: A national study of burdens from occupational licensing', Institute for Justice, 2012.
46. Gary Clyde Hufbauer & Kimberly Ann Elliott, *Measuring the Costs of Protection in the United States*, Peterson Institute for International Economics, 1994.
47. Margaret Thatcher, 'Speech opening single market campaign', 18 April 1988, www.margaretthatcher.org/document/107219.
48. Iain Martin, 'Painful as it is, we need to talk about Brexit', *The Times*, 8 June 2022.
49. Pablo D. Fajgelbaum & Amit K. Khandelwal, 'Measuring the unequal gains from trade', *Quarterly Journal of Economics*, vol.131, no.3, 2016.

4. In defence of the 1 per cent

1. Ung Vänster, Facebook, 28 January 2018.
2. Jagdish Bhagwati, *Essays in Development Economics: Wealth and poverty*, MIT Press, 1985, p.18.
3. August Strindberg, *Tjänstekvinnans son II*, Bonnier, 1919, chap.9.
4. Sheryl Gay Stolberg, 'Bernie Sanders, now a millionaire, pledges to release tax returns by Monday', *The New York Times*, 9 April 2019.
5. William D. Nordhaus, 'Schumpeterian profits in the American economy: Theory and measurement', NBER Working Paper no.10433, 2004.
6. Compare with Frédéric Bastiat's reasoning on the invention of the printing press, Bastiat 1964, pp.37f.
7. Donald Boudreaux, *Globalization*, Greenwood Press, 2008, p.32f.
8. Not Gates any more. Jeff Bezos beat him a few years back, then it was Elon Musk and now it is Bernard Arnault. It changes very fast depending on the temporary stock prices of

the companies the super-rich founded, so I'll continue to use Gates as an example for a while.

9. Thomas Piketty, *Capital in the Twenty-First Century*, Belknap Press, 2014, p.444ff.
10. Ibid., p.31.
11. Ibid., pp.435–9.
12. Robert Arnott, William Bernstein & Lillian Wu, 'The myth of dynastic wealth: The rich get poorer', *Cato Journal*, vol.35, no.3, 2015.
13. William McBride, 'Thomas Piketty's false depiction of wealth in America', Tax Foundation Special Report no.223, July 2014. Chris Edwards & Ryan Bourne, 'Exploring Wealth Inequality', Policy Analysis, no.881, Cato Institute, 5 November 2019.
14. Amy Castoro, 'Wealth transition and entitlement: Shedding light on the dark side of a charmed life', *The Journal of Wealth Management*, vol.18, no.2, 2015.
15. Paul Graham, 'How people get rich now', paulgraham.com, April 2021.
16. Milanović 2019, p.63.
17. Matthew Rognlie, 'Deciphering the fall and rise in the net capital share: accumulation or scarcity?', Brookings Papers on Economic Activity, spring 2015.
18. Milanović 2019, pp.26–9.
19. Betsey Stevenson & Justin Wolfers. 'Happiness inequality in the United States', *The Journal of Legal Studies*, vol.37, no.52, 2008. Andrew Clark, Sarah Flèche & Claudia Senik, 'Economic growth evens out happiness: Evidence from six surveys', *Review of Income and Wealth*, 2015.
20. Phil Gramm, Robert Ekelund & John Early, *The Myth of American Inequality: How Government Biases Policy Debate*, Rowman & Littlefield, 2022.
21. Branko Milanović, 'The three eras of global inequality, 1820–2020 with the focus on the past thirty years', Stone Center on Socio-Economic Inequality, working paper 59, November

2022. See also Olle Hammar & Daniel Waldenström, 'Global earnings inequality 1970–2018', *The Economic Journal*, vol.130, November 2020.

22. Milanović 2022.
23. Credit Suisse, *Global wealth report 2021*, Credit Suisse Research Institute, 2021, p.25.
24. Oxfam, 'Time to care', Oxfam Briefing Paper, January 2020.
25. Milanović 2022.
26. Lives on the Line, A Map of Life Expectancy at Birth, https://tubecreature.com/#/livesontheline/current/same/*/940GZZLUKNB/FFTFTF/13/-0.1065/51.5181/
27. Angus Deaton, 'Health, inequality, and economic development', Prepared for Working Group 1 of the WHO Commission on Macroeconomics and Health, May 2001.
28. Deaton & Deaton 2020, p.139f.
29. Fredrik Segerfeldt, 'Sverige är ett klassamhälle. Och?', *Smedjan*, 13 March 2018.
30. Raj Chetty, Michael Stepner, Sarah Abraham, Shelby Lin, Benjamin Scuderi, Nicholas Turner, Augustin Bergeron, David Cutler, 'The association between income and life expectancy in the United States, 2001–2014', *The Journal of the American Medical Association*, vol.315, no.16, 2016.
31. Seth Stephens-Davidowitz, *Everybody Lies: Big Data, New Data, and What the Internet Can Tell Us About Who We Really Are*, Dey Street Books, p.178.
32. P. J. O'Rourke, *Parliament of Whores*, Atlantic Monthly Press, 1991, p.210.
33. Johan Norberg, *Financial Fiasco: How America's Infatuation with Home Ownership and Easy Money Created the Financial Crisis*, Cato Institute, 2012. Johan Norberg, *Eurokrasch: En tragedi i tre akter*, Hydra Förlag, 2012.
34. Ryan Banerjee & Boris Hofmann, 'Corporate zombies: Anatomy and life cycle', BIS Working Paper, no.882, The Bank for International Settlements, September 2020.

5. Capitalism: Monopoly or Minecraft?

1. Council of Economic Advisers, 'Benefits of competition and indicators of market power,' Issue Brief, April 2016.
2. Nicolas Crouzet and Janice Eberly, 'Understanding weak capital investment: The role of market concentration and intangibles'. David Autor et al, 'The fall of the labor share and the rise of superstar firms', NBER Working Paper no.23396, May 2017.
3. US Bureau of Labor Statistics, 'Quarterly census of employment and wages: Employment and wages, annual averages 2019', Table 4, www.bls.gov/cew/publications/employment-and-wages-annual-averages/2019/home.htm.
4. Autor et al 2017.
5. Philippe Aghion, Céline Antonin & Simon Bunel, *The Power of Creative Destruction: Economic Upheaval and the Wealth of Nations*, Belknap Press, 2021, p.66f.
6. Esteban Rossi-Hansberg and Chang-Tai Hsieh, 'The industrial revolution in services', NBER Working Paper no.25968, June 2019. See also Ryan Bourne, 'Does rising industry concentration signify monopoly power?', Economic Policy Brief, no.2, 13 February 2020, Cato Institute.
7. When a student once asked Milton Friedman to sign a Monopoly game, Friedman did so but added the words 'Down with' before the game name.
8. Mark J. Perry, 'Only 51 US companies have been on the Fortune 500 since 1955, thanks to the creative destruction that fuels economic prosperity', Carpe Diem blog, AEI, 26 May 2020.
9. Ludwig von Mises, *Human Action*, Laissez Faire Books, 1966, pp.269f.
10. Hal R. Varian, 'Recent trends in concentration, competition, and entry', *Antitrust Law Journal*, vol.82, no.3, 2019.
11. Mary Amiti & Sebastian Heise, 'US market concentration and import competition', Federal Reserve Bank of New York, 5 April 2021.

12. Tyler Cowen, *Big Business: A Love Letter to an American Anti-Hero*, St Martin's Press, 2019, chap.2.

13. Seth Stephens-Davidowitz, *Everybody Lies: Big Data, New Data, and What the Internet Can Tell Us About Who We Really Are*, HarperCollins, 2017. So remember to never compare your inner self with other people's social media.

14. I suspect that my friend Mattias Svensson knows why this is the case. Don't ask him. Eric Schwitzgebel, 'Do ethicists steal more books?', *Philosophical Psychology*, vol.22, no.6, December 2009.

15. E.g. Nina Björk, 'Klimatet kräver kontroll över ekonomin', *Dagens Nyheter*, 30 August 2021 and Cosima Dannoritzer, *The Light Bulb Conspiracy*, 2010.

16. Dexter Ford, 'As cars are kept longer, 200,000 is the new 100,000', *The New York Times*, 16 March 2012. Bruce Hamilton & Molly Macauley, 'Heredity or environment: Why is the automobile longevity increasing?', *The Journal of Industrial Economics*, vol.47, no.3, 1999.

17. Anna Quindlen, 'Honestly – you should not have', *Newsweek*, 3 December 2001.

18. Robert Wright, *Nonzero: History, Evolution & Human Cooperation*, Abacus, 2001, p.43.

19. For more information about this and its expressions, see Virginia Postrel, *The Substance of Style: How the Rise of Aesthetic Value is Remaking Commerce, Culture and Consciousness*, HarperCollins, 2003.

20. No, actually, the most common question is probably: 'Have you read all these?' Now I'll answer once and for all, so you never have to ask again: no.

21. Erik Brynjolfsson, Felix Eggers & Avinash Gannamaneni, 'Using massive online choice experiments to measure changes in well-being', NBER Working Paper no.24514, 2018.

22. Soave 2021, p.30.

23. Matthew Gentzkov & Jesse M. Shapiro, 'Ideological segregation online and offline', Chicago Booth & National Bureau of Economic Research, 28 March 2011.

24. Levi Boxell, Matthew Gentzkow, Jesse M. Shapiro, 'Is the internet causing political polarization? Evidence from demographics', NBER Working paper no.23258, March 2017.
25. Georgia Wells, Jeff Horwitz & Deepa Seethharaman, 'Facebook knows Instagram is toxic for teen girls, company documents show', *Wall Street Journal*, 14 September 2021.
26. Monica Anderson & Jingjing Jiang, 'Teens social media habits and experiences', Pew Research Center, November 2018.
27. I just replaced 'MySpace' with 'it', otherwise the quote is verbatim from Victor Keegan, 'Will MySpace ever lose its monopoly?', *Guardian*, 8 February 2007.
28. Randall E. Stross, 'How Yahoo! won the search wars', *Fortune*, 2 March 1998.
29. Bruce Upbin, 'The next billion', *Forbes*, 26 October 2007.
30. Robby Soave, *Tech Panic: Why We Shouldn't Fear Facebook and the Future*, Threshold Editions, 2021, p.13.
31. Germán Gutiérrez & Thomas Philippon, 'Declining competition and investment in the US', NBER Working paper no.23583, July 2017.
32. See Tim O'Reilly, 'Data is the new sand', *The Information*, 24 February 2021.
33. Joakim Wernberg, 'Innovation, competition and digital platform paradoxes', Swedish Entrepreneurship Forum, Policy papers on technology, economics and structural change, no.1, 2021.
34. 'The new rules of competition in the technology industry', *The Economist*, 27 February 2021.
35. Ibid.

6. Picking losers

1. Marco Rubio, 'Senator Marco Rubio speaks at National Defense University on the need for a "pro-American industrial policy" to counter China', *The American Mind*, 10 December 2019.

2. Mariana Mazzucato, *Mission Economy: A Moonshot Guide to Changing Capitalism*, Allen Lane, 2021, p.121.
3. Christian Sandström, 'Skapades iPhone av den amerikanska staten', *Ekonomisk Debatt*, vol.41, no.3, 2015. See also Deirdre McCloskey & Alberto Mingardi, *The Myth of the Entrepreneurial State*, American Institute for Economic Research, 2020.
4. Mariana Mazzucato, *The Entrepreneurial State*, Anthem Press 2013.
5. Tim Harford, *The Next Fifty Things That Made the Modern Economy*, Hachette, 2020, chap.24.
6. In an email correspondence documented on NetHistory: www.nethistory.info/Archives/origins.html.
7. Mazzucato 2021, p.123.
8. Oral history interview with R. W. Taylor, William Aspray, Charles Babbage Institute, 28 February 1989. https://conservancy.umn.edu/handle/11299/107666, p.42f.
9. Oral history interview with Paul Baran, Judy O'Neill, Charles Babbage Institute, 5 March 1990, https://conservancy.umn.edu/handle/11299/107101, p.34.
10. Matt Ridley, *How Innovation Works: And Why It Flourishes in Freedom*, HarperCollins, 2020.
11. Jonathan Coopersmith, 'Pornography, technology, and progress', *Icon*, vol.4, 1998.
12. Linda Cohen & Roger Noll, *The Technology Pork Barrel*, Brookings Institution Press, 1991, p.365, chap.12.
13. Sven-Olof Daunfeldt, Patrik Gustavsson Tingvall & Daniel Halvarsson, 'Statliga innovationsstöd till små och medelstora företag – har de någon effekt?', *Ekonomisk Debatt*, vol.44, no.1, 2016.
14. Josh Lerner, *Boulevard of Broken Dreams: Why Public Efforts to Boost Entrepreneurship and Venture Capital Have Failed – And What To Do About It*, Princeton University Press, 2009, p.5.
15. 'Attack of the Eurogoogle', *The Economist*, 11 March 2006. I know what you're thinking – and you are absolutely right.

The Germans wanted a text-based search engine while the French wanted to develop some kind of multimedia search that would appeal to all senses. Everyone got mad at each other.

16. Tim Murphy, 'Your daily newt: A $40 billion entitlement for laptops', *Mother Jones*, 20 December 2011. 'Attack of the Eurogoogle', *The Economist*, 11 March 2006.

17. Mariana Mazzucato, 'Mission-oriented innovation policy', Royal Society for the Encouragement of Arts, Manufactures and Commerce, September 2017. Mazzucato 2021, p.145.

18. Frank Dohmen, Alexander Jung, Stefan Schultz & Gerald Traufetter, 'German failure on the road to a renewable future', *Der Spiegel International*, 13 May 2019.

19. Johan Norberg, *Power to the People*, Sumner Books, 2015.

20. Jan Jörnmark & Christian Sandström, *Den industripolitiska återvändsgränden: En historia om det statliga riskkapitalet*, Skattebetalarnas förening, 2020, p.64f.

21. @Infineon, Twitter, 14 November 2022.

22. Jörnmark & Sandström 2020, p.46f, Anders Gustafsson, Andreas Stephan, Alice Hallman & Nils Karlsson 'The "sugar rush" from innovation subsidies: A robust political economy perspective', *Empirica*, vol.43, 2016.

23. Anders Gustafsson, Patrik Gustavsson Tingvall & Daniel Halvarsson, 'Subsidy entrepreneurs', Ratio working paper, no.303, 2017.

24. Karl Wennberg & Christian Sandström, *Questioning the Entrepreneurial State: Status-Quo, Pitfalls, and the Need for Credible Innovation Policy*, Springer, 2022, p.11.

25. For a systematic examination of the relationship between funding, research and innovation, see Terence Kealey, *The Economic Laws of Scientific Research*, Palgrave Macmillan, 1996.

26. Even if they could probably make a lot of money on such innovations without prize competitions. It should also be noted that many of the most productive prize competitions have been established privately, such as the X Prize Foundation.

27. 'The world's most pointless rocket has been launched at last', *The Economist*, 16 November 2022.

7. China, paper tiger

1. Ronald Coase & Ning Wang, *How China Became Capitalist*, Palgrave MacMillan, 2013.
2. Kate Xiao Zhou, *How the Farmers Changed China: Power of the People*, Westview Press, 1996, p.56.
3. Coase & Wang 2013, p.63.
4. Barry Naughton, *The Rise of China's Industrial Policy 1978 to 2020*, Enero 2021, p.41.
5. Bradley M. Gardner, *China's Great Migration: How the Poor Built a Prosperous Nation*, The Independent Institute, 2017.
6. 'World Development Indicators', World Bank, 2022.
7. Doron Ben-Atar, *Trade Secrets: Intellectual Piracy and the Origins of American Industrial Power*, Yale University Press, 2004.
8. US–China Business Council, 'Member survey', 2019 and 2020.
9. Scott Lincicome, 'Testing the "China shock"', Policy Analysis no.895, Cato Institute, 8 July 2020. Jeffrey J. Scott & Eujin Jung, 'In US–China trade disputes, the WTO usually sides with the United States', Peterson Institute for International Economics, 12 March 2019. James Bacchus, Simon Lester & Huan Zhu, 'Disciplining China's trade practices at the WTO: How WTO complaints can help make China more market-oriented', Cato Institute, 15 November 2018.
10. Paul R. Gregory & Kate Zhou, 'How China won and Russia lost', *Policy Review*, Hoover Institution, 1 December 2009.
11. Weiying Zhang, *The Logic of the Market: An Insider's View of Chinese Economic Reform*, Cato Institute, 2015, p.xx.
12. Naughton 2021, p.47.
13. Nicholas Lardy, *Markets over Mao: The Rise of Private Business in China*, Peterson Institute for International Economics, 2014.

14. World Bank, PovcalNet, 2022.
15. David Shambaugh, *China's Leaders: From Mao to Now*, Polity, 2021, chaps 4 and 5.
16. Shambaugh 2021, p.246.
17. For a summary, see Daniel H. Rosen, 'China's economic reckoning', *Foreign Affairs*, July/August 2021.
18. Naughton 2021, p.14.
19. Listen to, e.g., Jeffrey Bader in the *US–China Dialogue Podcast*, 19 August 2019, https://uschinadialogue.georgetown.edu/podcasts/jeffrey-bader-part-one.
20. See, e.g., Minxin Pei, 'China's coming upheaval', *Foreign Affairs*, 5 April 2020, and John Mueller, 'China: Rise or Demise?', Policy Analysis no.917, Cato Institute, 18 May 2021.
21. Stephen Roach, 'Xi's costly obsession with security', *Foreign Affairs*, 28 November 2022.
22. Greg Ip, 'China's state-driven growth model is running out of gas', *The Wall Street Journal*, 17 July 2019.

8. But what about the planet?

1. Intergovernmental Panel on Climate Change, 'IPCC second assessment climate change', 1995.
2. At the UN Climate Action Summit in New York, 23 September 2019.
3. Daniel Gerszon Mahler, Nishant Yonzan, Christoph Lakner, R. Andres Castedana Aguiilar & Haoyu Wu, 'Updated estimates of the impact of COVID-19 on global poverty', World Bank Blog, 24 June 2021. FAO, IFAD, UNICEF, WFP & WHO, *The state of food security and nutrition in the world 2021*, FAO 2021.
4. Norberg 2015.
5. Hannah Ritchie, Pablo Rosado & Max Roser, 'Natural disasters', Our World in Data, 2022.

6. Zeke Hausfather, 'Covid-19 could result in much larger CO_2 drop in 2020', *Breakthrough Institute*, 30 April 2020.

7. Andrew McAfee, *More From Less*, 2019, p.67. See also Marian L. Tupy & Gale L. Pooley, 'Superabundance: The story of population growth, innovation and human flourishing on an infinitely bountiful planet', Cato Institute, 2022.

8. 'Air pollutant emissions data viewer (Gothenburg Protocol, LRTAP Convention) 1990–2019', European Environmental Agency, 11 August 2021.

9. Z. A. Wendling, J. W. Emerson, A. de Sherbinin, D. C. Esty, *The Environmental Performance Index 2020*, Yale Center for Environmental Law & Policy, 2020, p.69.

10. Ibid.

11. 'Household air pollution from solid fuels – level 4 risk', Institute for Health Metrics and Evaluation. www.healthdata.org/results/gbd_summaries/2019household-air-pollution-from-solid-fuels-level-4-risk.

12. Claude Martin, *On the Edge: The State and Fate of the World's Tropical Rainforests*, Greystone Books, 2015, p.141.

13. United Nations Environment Program, *Protected Planet Report 2020*, updated May 2021, chap.3.

14. FAO, *Global forests resources assessment 2020: Main report*, Rome 2020.

15. Jesse Ausubel, 'Peak farmland', Lecture for the Symposium in Honor of Paul Demeny, 16 December 2012.

16. Joseph Poore, 'Call for conservation: Abandoned pasture', *Science*, vol.351, 8 January 2016.

17. Jonas Grafström & Christian Sandström, *Mer för mindre? Tillväxt och hållbarhet i Sverige*, Ratio, 2020.

18. Nikolai Shmelev & Vladimir Popov, *The Turning Point: Revitalizing the Soviet Economy*, Tauris, 1990, p.128f.

19. Apparently, Jevon's son complained to Keynes that the children still had failed to use up their father's paper reserves. Milanović 2019, p.256.

20. Karl Marx, *Capital*, Chicago: Charles H. Kerr and Co., 1909,

vol.III, pt I, chap.5. See also Pierre Desrochers, 'Did the invisible hand need a regulatory glove to develop a green thumb? Some historical perspective on market incentives, win-win innovations and the Porter hypothesis', *Environmental and Resource Economics*, vol.41, February 2008.

21. For a discussion of how free market liberalism can and should be combined with environmental regulations, see Mattias Svensson, *Miljöpolitik för moderater*, Fores, 2015.

22. 'Indira Gandhi's Address', *The Times of India*, 15 June 1972.

23. Andrew McAfee, *More from Less*, 2019, p.67. The State Secretary was Kjell-Olof Feldt, who said this at a seminar at Chalmers.

24. Hannah Ritchie, 'Where does the plastic in our oceans come from?', Our World in Data, 1 May 2021.

25. Wendling et al 2020, p.39.

26. Ibid.

27. Bishwa S. Koirala, Hui Li, Robert P. Berrens, 'Further investigation of Environmental Kuznets Curve studies using meta-analysis', *International Journal of Ecological Economics and Statistics*, no.S11, vol.22, 2011.

28. Thomas van Goethem & Jan Luiten van Zanden, 'Biodiversity trends in a historical perspective' *How Was Life? Volume II: New Perspectives on Well-Being and Global Inequality Since 1820*, OECD, 2021.

29. Hannah Ritchie, 'You want to reduce the carbon footprint of your food? Focus on what you eat, not whether your food is local', Our World in Data, 24 January 2020.

30. Vilma Sandström, Hugo Valin, Tamás Krisztin, Petr Havlík, Mario Herrero, Thomas Kastner, 'The role of trade in the greenhouse gas footprints of EU diets', *Global Food Security*, vol.19, 2018. Desrochers & Shimizu 2012, p.154.

31. 'Airfreight transport of fresh fruits and vegetables: A review of the environmental impact and policy options', International Trade Center, 2007. Martina Alig & Rolf Frischknecht, 'Life cycle assessment cut roses', *Treeze*, July 2018.

32. Hannah Ritchie & Max Roser, 'Air pollution', Our World in Data, January 2021.
33. Wendling et al 2020, p.47. See also Amaryllis Mavragani, Ioannis Nikolaou & Konstantinos Tsagarakis 'Open economy, institutional quality, and environmental performance: A macroeconomic approach', *Sustainability*, vol.8, 2016.
34. IEA, Energy Efficiency Indicators Statistics report, December 2020.
35. Max Roser, 'Why did renewables become so cheap so fast?', Our World in Data, 1 December 2020.
36. John Burn-Murdoch, 'Economics may take us to net zero all on its own', *Financial Times*, 23 September 2022.
37. Wendling et al 2020, p.129.
38. 'Economic growth no longer means higher carbon emissions', *The Economist*, 8 November 2022.
39. Jonas Grafström, 'Public policy failures related to China's wind power development', Ratio working paper, no.320, 2019.
40. Now you may be wondering if I want the EU to abolish its tariffs and quotas regardless of the policy in other countries. Yes, good point. But that is my ideal solution. Another of my ideal solutions is for all countries to introduce carbon taxes. This is not about my ideals but about what is politically possible in an imperfect world. For a more elaborate version of this argument, see Svensson 2015, p.101ff and Fredrik Segerfeldt and Mattias Svensson, *Frihandel för nybörjare*, Timbro, 2019, chap.7.
41. IEA, 'Fossil Fuel Subsidies Database', www.iea.org/data-and-statistics/data-product/fossil-fuel-subsidies-database.

9. The meaning of life

1. Noreena Hertz, *The Lonely Century: A Call to Reconnect*, Sceptre, 2021, p.228.

2. Patrick Deneen, *Why Liberalism Failed*, Yale University Press, 2019, p.16f.

3. George Monbiot, 'Neoliberalism – the ideology at the root of all our problems', *Guardian*, 15 April 2016.

4. Joel Halldorf, 'DN:s liberalism dog i Immanuelskyrkan', *Dagen*, 23 September 2019.

5. Hertz 2021, p.14.

6. Nina Björk, *Lyckliga i alla sina dagar*, Wahlström & Widstrand, 2012, pp.176f and 173.

7. Deneen 2019, pp.32ff.

8. John Locke, *Two Treatises of Government*, Part II, Cambridge University Press, 1988, §77.

9. Adam Smith, *The Theory of Moral Sentiments*, Liberty Fund, 1976, p.116.

10. Deneen 2019, p.185.

11. See Nozick 1974, p.310, for a developed version of this argument.

12. Henrik Höjer, 'Svensken är inte så ensam som vi tror', *Svenska Dagbladet*, 20 October 2019.

13. Birgitta Odén, 'Våld mot föräldrar i det gamla svenska samhället', i Ida Hydle, *Overgrep mot eldre*. Nordiska minister-rådet, 1994.

14. Gallup World Poll 2021, data quoted by Max Roser on Twitter, 25 May 2021. https://twitter.com/MaxCRoser/status/1397213506802442243.

15. Federica Cocco, 'Are we ready for the approaching loneliness epidemic?', *Financial Times*, 24 November 2022. *How's Life? 2020: Measuring Well-being*, OECD, 2020.

16. Esteban Ortiz-Ospina, 'Is there a loneliness epidemic?', Our World in Data, 11 December 2019.

17. Ortiz-Ospina 2019. Christina Victor, Sasha Scambler, Sunil Shah, Derek Cook, Tess Harris, Elizabeth Rink & Stephen De Wilde, 'Has loneliness amongst older people increased? An investigation into variations between cohorts', *Aging & Society*, vol.22, no.5, September 2002

18. Henrik Höjer, 'Ensamheten minskar i Sverige', *Forskning & framsteg*, 13 April 2018.

19. Caspian Rehbinder, 'Ensamheten är mindre där friheten är större', *Smedjan*, 18 February 2020.

20. Hannah Ritchie, 'Global mental health: Five key insights which emerge from the data', Our World in Data, 16 May 2018.

21. Dirk Richter, Abbie Wall, Ashley Bruen & Richard Whittington, 'Is the global prevalence rate of adult mental illness increasing? Systematic review and meta-analysis', *Acta Psychiatrica Scandinavica*, vol.140, August 2019.

22. Mohsen Naghavi, 'Global, regional, and national burden of suicide mortality 1990 to 2016: Systematic analysis for the Global Burden of Disease Study 2016', *BMJ*, 2019.

23. Christian Rück, *Olyckliga i paradiset: Varför mår vi så dåligt när allt är så bra?*, Natur & Kultur, 2020.

24. Max Weber, *The Protestant Ethic and the Spirit of Capitalism*, Routledge, 2005, p.xxxi.

25. Björk 2012, p.99.

26. William English & Peter Jaworski, 'The introduction of paid plasma in Canada and the US has not decreased unpaid blood donations', SSRN, July 2020.

27. Shawn Rhoads, Devon Gunter, Rebecca M. Ryan, & Abigail Marsh, 'Global variation in subjective well-being predicts seven forms of altruism', *Psychological Science*, vol.32, no.8, 2021.

28. Joseph Henrich et al. '"Economic man" in cross-cultural perspective: Behavioral experiments in 15 small-scale societies', *Behavioral and Brain Sciences*, vol.28, no.6, 2005. Joseph Henrich et al, 'Markets, religion, community size, and the evolution of fairness and punishment', *Science*, vol.5972, no.327, 2010.

29. Joseph Henrich, *The Weirdest People in the World*, Allen Lane, 2020, chap.9.

30. Friedrich Engels, *Outlines of a Critique of Political Economy*, Deutsch-Französische Jahrbücher, 1844.

31. Megan V. Teague, Virgil Henry Storr & Rosemarie Fike, 'Economic freedom and materialism: an empirical analysis', *Constitutional Political Economy*, vol.31, 2020.

32. Mingliang Yuan, Giuliana Spadaro, Shuxian Jin, Junhui Wu, Yu Kou, Paul A. M. Van Lange, and Daniel Balliet, 'Did cooperation among strangers decline in the United States? A cross-temporal meta-analysis of social dilemmas (1956–2017)', *Psychological Bulletin*, vol.148, no.3–4, 2022.

33. Interview with Ruut Venhoven, 23 April 2007.

34. Daniel Kahneman, 'The sad tale of the aspiration treadmill', *Edge*, 2008.

35. Johan Norberg, *Den eviga matchen om lyckan*, Natur och Kultur, 2009. Esteban Ortiz-Ospina & Max Roser, *Happiness and life satisfaction*, Our World in Data, May 2017. An important paper pioneering this reassessment was Betsey Stevenson & Justin Wolfers, 'Economic growth and subjective well-being: Reassessing the Easterlin Paradox', *Brookings Papers on Economic Activity*, no.1, 2008. See also Ruut Veenhoven & Floris Vergunst, 'The Easterlin illusion: Economic growth does go with greater happiness', EHERO working paper, no.1, 2013. Ed Diener, Louis Tay & Shigehiro Oishi, 'Rising income and the subjective well-being of nations', *Journal of Personality and Social Psychology*, vol.104, no.2, 2013.

36. Ortiz-Ospina & Roser 2017.

37. Ruut Veenhoven, 'Quality of life in individualistic society: A comparison of 43 nations in the early 1990s', in M. J. deJong & A. C. Zijderveld (eds), *The Gift of Society*, Enzo Press, 1997. Roland Inglehart et al, 'Development, freedom and rising happiness: A global perspective (1981–2007)', *Perspectives on Psychological Science*, vol.3, no.4, 2008. Richard Layard, *Happiness: Lessons From a New Science*, Allen Lane, 2005, p.235.

38. Bobby Duffy, *The Perils of Perception: Why We're Wrong About Nearly Everything*, Atlantic Books, 2018, chap.1. How is this consistent with what we saw in chapter 5? That we present

a happy facade on social media and google our anxieties in secret? Good question. Maybe we disbelieve people's unbelievable social media updates *too much?*

39. Ortiz-Ospina & Roser 2017.
40. Daniel Nettle, *Happiness: The Science Behind Your Smile*, Oxford University Press, 2005, p.101.
41. David Edmonds & John Eidinow, *Rousseau's Dog: Two Great Thinkers at War in the Age of Enlightenment*, Harper Perennial 2007, p.131. Shortly afterwards, Hume and Rousseau became enemies for life.
42. Interview with Ruut Veenhoven, 23 April 2007.
43. Ibid. Eric Weiner, *The Geography of Bliss: One Grump's Search for the Happiest Places in the World*, Twelve, 2008, p.16.
44. James Gwartney, Robert Lawson, Joshua Hall & Ryan Murphy, *Economic Freedom of the World: 2022 annual report*, Fraser Institute, 2022.
45. Hans Pitlik & Martin Rode, 'Free to choose? Economic freedom, relative income, and life control perceptions', *International Journal of Wellbeing*, vol.6, no.1, 2016. Kai Gehring, 'Who benefits from economic freedom? Unravelling the effect of economic freedom on subjective well-being', *World Development*, vol.50, 2013. Boris Nikolaev & Daniel L. Bennett, 'Economic freedom and emotional well-being', *Journal of Regional Analysis and Policy*, vol.47, no.1, September 2017.
46. Steven Quartz and Anette Asp, 'Unequal, Yet Happy,' *The New York Times*, 11 April 2015.
47. I saw the first study about this in Robert William Fogel, *The Escape From Hunger and Premature Death, 1700-2100: Europe, America, and the Third World*, Cambridge University Press, 2004, where 48 per cent had calmed down in the past five years.
48. Charlie Giattino, Esteban Ortiz-Ospina & Max Roser, 'Working hours', Our World in Data, December 2020. See also Andreas Bergh, 'Tre böcker av Roland Paulsen – en kritisk läsning', *Ekonomisk Debatt*, no.3, 2017.

Epilogue: The Emperor's singing contest

1. Karl Marx & Friedrich Engels, *The Communist Manifesto*, Progress Publishers, 1948, chap.1.
2. Ibid.
3. Karl Marx, 'Salary, price and profit', 1865. Friedrich Engels, 'Preface to the English edition', in *The Working Class Situation in England*, Progress Publishers, 1977.
4. Johan Norberg, *Open: The Story of Human Progress*, Atlantic Books, 2020.

INDEX

NB Page numbers in *italics* indicate illustrations

About the Author

Johan Norberg is a historian, lecturer and commentator. His books, which have been translated into thirty languages, include the international bestseller *Progress*, and *Open*, which was a Book of the Year in *The Economist*. Norberg is a senior fellow at the Cato Institute in Washington DC and regularly writes for publications such as the *Wall Street Journal*, *Reason* and the *Spectator*.